Running to Stand Still

Running to Stand Still

Bearnárd O'Riain

First published in 2005 by
Jacana Media (Pty) Ltd.
5 St Peter Road
Bellevue, 2198
Johannesburg
South Africa

© Bearnárd O'Riain, 2005
www.bearnardoriain.co.za

ISBN 1-77009-078-9

Cover design by Disturbance
Printed by CTP Book Printers

See a complete list of Jacana titles at www.jacana.co.za

For Verne
The truth has set us free.
From the moment you surprised me by asking me to write this book,
you have never lost faith in it or in its ultimate goals.
You have been my strength when my own had drained away.
Thank you, my friend, my travelling companion, my lover.

For Mama and Dada
You did your best

I have written this book for
our five children and to their mothers

Author's notes and acknowledgments

Some names have been changed for reasons of privacy.
The title of the book was inspired by a track from U2's 'Joshua Tree' album.
I was christened Bernard. My family pronounces it 'Bernid'.
At age fourteen I changed my name to the Irish form, Bearnárd, pronounced 'Bernaard'.
And Ryan became O'Riain.

I thank our children, (in order of age); Natasha, Roger, Angela, Justin and Graeme whose forgiveness I've had to earn.
The late Éamonn MacThomáis and his wife, Rosaleen, Bill Egan and Tony Hayde, who read the IRA chapters – comrades-in-arms who encouraged me all the way.
Robin Binckes, a good, staunch and perceptive friend, and Gail Iris Neke, who both read the manuscript and whose incisive comments I took to heart. Louis Gishen, who was – and is – there for us with his wisdom and wit; the late Miles Myers who said, "Buy a PC and write!"; Marion Scher who taught me about writing and who pointed the way to Maggie Davey of Jacana, saying, "Do not take this book anywhere else!"
Maggie Davey, Publishing Director of Jacana, who championed the work and encouraged me all along the rocky road.
Denis Beckett, who read the first fifty pages and said, "Go for it."
Bob Quinn, who, when I was losing my way, said, "We write to find out what is going on with our lives."
Jill Skowno and Nick Christodoulou, our counsellors, who

listened for many hours and had faith in the power of healing.
Amanda Patterson, Anne Schuster, Laurence Cramer, Susan
Landau and Michelle Jacobs, each of whom added to my
knowledge of writing; Nicholas Tee, who told me to tell this story,
warts and all.

And my editor. Lynda Gilfillan, thank you. You stood your ground
and said, "Take that out" when I was being 'self-indulgent', and
you performed the balancing act of correcting my English but
allowing the Irish idiom its freedom. You empathised with the
women in the book and it is the better work for that.

Chris Cocks at Jacana Media, who pulled the whole work together
with patience, encouragement and attention to detail and his
colleague Brett Rogers at Jacana whose dedication was vital.

My brothers, who jogged my defective memory.

Antony Farrell, who at a critical moment, said, "I like this."

Stephen Connolly who suggested how to improve the IRA scenes
for non-Irish readers.

Thank you to all those who read the advance story on the book,
and who wrote to us in support, and to Adam Cooke of *Men's
Health* who published the story.

Bearnárd O'Riain
Johannesburg, June 2005

Bernard Ryan, later to become Bearnárd O'Riain

Contents

Foreword

When Verne first came to see me I already knew who she was. She was a member of the Black Sash and among other things she was the organiser of one of the stalls for the annual morning market, the 'Nearly New' a sort of upmarket jumble stall. I remember her described in one of the newsletters as having great flair. Flair she certainly has. She was at the same time a fierce opponent of the old South African regime. I also knew who Bearnárd was. He was known in the northern suburbs of Johannesburg as a successful real estate businessman. Bearnárd and Verne were (and still are) a handsome and articulate couple.

As always when stories of abuse emerge in my consulting rooms I listen with a mixture of sadness and a sinking heart. Abuse is a rigid and recursive pattern of behaviour, which many would say, has only a small chance of significant change. As I began to explore their story I saw no reason to think this would unfold any differently from many others. I had a lot to learn.

Abuse is very easy to oversimplify. We have all heard people say, "Why doesn't she just leave?", "I wouldn't stand for it." We have said these words ourselves. This takes no account of the complex weave of love, dependence, familiarity, fear and shame, which sustains such relationships. The discourses, which support both the giving and receiving of abuse, are powerful. Finding and amplifying alternative discourses is daunting. This is what this book is about.

As South Africans we know the healing power of story telling. We listened with horror as the stories of abuse emerged at the Truth and Reconciliation Commission, following on our first democratic elections in 1994. And we were collectively amazed at the reservoir of forgiveness, which emerged. Bearnárd has told his story, and change and forgiveness has followed. One story generates a thousand others and his account has opened up the space for others to tell theirs.

It has been a privilege to be a witness to this story.

Jill Skowno
M.A.Couns. Psych. S.A.

Preface

I wish to pay tribute to my husband, Bearnárd, for his courage in writing this book and revealing himself with such honesty.

I am indebted to our children for their constant love and eventual forgiveness. And in particular to our daughter Angie, who had to bear the burden of far too much, too soon. Thirdly, my gratitude goes to Ursula, my friend and cousin, and her family, for always being there for me, for providing a safe haven when I needed one, and for never judging me.

It is my hope that our story will help others in similar situations to speak out, and in doing so, to end the violence that infects so many homes and causes such damage and destruction.

I do not dwell in the past but live every day with a belief in tomorrow.

Verne O'Riain
June 2005

PART ONE

Prologue

Breakfast up

I'm sixteen years old and I've just upended the breakfast table all over him and my brothers. Him is my father.

My short fuse has blown. That's what my mother calls it. But this is the worst yet.

It starts like this always. Mama asked me questions about what I'd been doing last night. I didn't answer her and concentrated on getting my boiled egg out of the shell without spilling the yolk. She is trying to impress him that she's checking up on me. Doing her duty.

Then he says, You can't let him out to the pictures this weekend because he's still going out with that Protestant girl.

Before Mama can answer I shout at him, You don't know anything! I wasn't with the Protestant girl last night. It's over.

How can you speak to your father like that? Mama's almost crying now.

Dermot, my next brother, and the two younger ones' eyes are huge.

It's bad enough having to go to school, without this shit. The room is crowded with our nerves.

Dada's staring at Mama now and he's very angry. Are you going to allow him to get away with this?

I can't believe it. He still won't speak to me, he's speaking to her, even after I've insulted him.

There's a sort of triangle at mealtimes. Him, her and me. I have to listen while they argue. Usually about me. So I answer her back and then I feel sorry for her because she doesn't know what to say.

He's muttering now. He says that we all know why I'm not going to Holy Communion, it's because of the Protestant girl and being in a state of mortal sin.

Why don't I just laugh at him? I always take myself so seriously. But by now the whole bloody room is serious.

Dermot asks me to stop all this. Please, he says then to Dada. Dada is pouring his tea into his saucer, and that sets Mama off at him. Don't be doing that in front of the children, she says. You know it's not nice.

Dermot's face is sort of dark. Turned in on itself.

My throat is tight. What is Dada saying now? That I am to stay in? Stay in? In this place? Stay in? While all my friends are out there? Going to the pictures, going with their girls?

His hand is shaking as he lifts the saucer of tea. Some of it spills. I want to shake the table so he'll spill the lot.

I look at my father. He's standing up to leave. Got his napkin in his hand.

You're not going anywhere, I yell at him.

And then I do it. I stand up, grab cups, plates, saucers and hurl them on the floor.

Please, Bernard, Mama cries, these are wedding presents.

Then I hoist that whole table high at my end. All the breakfast stuff starts to slide. Eggs, bread, precious food, scalding tea all on their laps. Knives and forks slide, hitting the floor first. Then the plates and the rest follow with a crash. My brothers' faces are terrified. I can feel the power as I stand up to my full height.

The teapot slides past me last. I hate it. His tea. I pound the pot twice – hard – with my right fist, holding the table up with my left. It shatters. Bits of it fly around, brown tea spreading out over the tablecloth. I am shouting at them, at this breakfast, at all the breakfasts that have gone before this one. And at my own guilty conscience.

I can see the tea all over his trousers, there at the end of the table. He's looking at me now, trying to say something. He's coming out from behind the table. He's stammering with anger. I put the table down and face him. I see the fear come into his eyes then.

It's as if I'm taller than he is. For the first time in my life. Is he going to hit me? He'd better not try. I know that I could hit him, and it frightens me. But I hate him.

I've got to get out now. I push past the back of Dermot's chair and burst out the door. Straight into my room across the hall. I slam the door and collapse in the chair, crying. I notice the blood dripping onto the carpet from my right fist. There are bits of the teapot sticking out of it. I pick the bits of Delft out one by one and put them in a little heap on the lino next to the carpet. The blood keeps dripping. I think, we'll never get the stains out. My tears are joining the blood on my hands and I'm finished. The anger has run out of me like water down a drain. I am choking with tears now, with the sorrow on my mother's face.

Yet that rebellion has given me power. I can't explain it, but it's like things will never be the same again. It's not the first bad row, though it's the worst one yet. And they won't carry on like that any more at the breakfast table. What'll they do? Probably talk to the priests about it. Fat lot of good that'll do. I won't talk to a priest. I'll have to tell it in confession, but I'll just give the bare minimum.

He has a kind of respect for me now that he didn't have before. I hate him for that.

He's stopped muttering about me when I'm around. Mama is nearly driven mental because he does it now when I'm not there. We can hear them at night when we're in bed. There's a sort of droning from the dining room.

Who are they talking about tonight? one of us will ask. If his voice rises and he stammers, he's criticising her, and it's usually about me. If Mama talks a lot, it's about the price of things, and how are they going to manage? I feel sorry for him. He works all hours and they never seem to have enough money. And yet we have clothes and food. Well, most of the time.

1

Dada holds my hand

DON'T LET HIM FALL in the stream, my Ma calls. Dada and me are
out the gate now. I look up at him and he smiles. I look back and
she has gone inside. So I pull off my woolly glove and put my hand
in his. I can feel his warm skin. He closes his hand around mine. I
love that. He smiles at me again. He is my father.

We get to the field where the houses stop. There is a path in the
long grass. I want to pick flowers but he says we'll do that on the
way back. We go off the path into the grass and the seeds stick to
my socks.

Are you tired? he asks.

I look up at him and say no.

We'll walk as far as the stream then, he says.

He watches me when I bend down to look at the pinkeens
swimming in the water. In case I fall in. I put my hand in the water
and it's cold.

Careful, he says. The little fish are so fast.

Can we catch some, Dada? I ask.

They will die if we do that, he says. Come and pick your flowers
for Our Lady's altar.

We pick buttercups and cowslips for the altar in my bedroom and

Dada and Mama, Llandudno, Wales 1935

some for Mama's as well. Cowslips are like little yellow bells and hide in the grass.

The cowslips are shy, aren't they, Dada?

Yes, he says, and his eyes smile.

He has a black moustache, so I can't see his mouth. But I know he's smiling.

I wait every day for him to come home from work. He rides his bike up from Booterstown station. If it's raining, I wait at the front

Bernard and Dada

window. I kneel on the armchair to see out past the raindrops. But
when it's not wet or windy, I wait at the gate. Even when I'm
playing with my friends, I stop and watch him when he comes
around the corner on his bike. He rides slowly because he's tired.
When I see him I run down the road shouting, Dada, Dada. Mama
tries to stop me doing that. She says it's not nice to shout on the
road.

When he sees me, he smiles. He doesn't mind me yelling. It's for
him.

He wheels his big black bike around the back and puts it in the
shed. If it's raining, he takes off his galoshes on the back doorstep. I

put them in the shed for him. Mama doesn't allow them inside. Then he stands in the kitchen and says hello to Mama. I kneel down on the floor and pull off his bicycle clips from his trousers and hang them on a hook on the dresser. He hangs up his coat and hat in the hall. I bring him his slippers and he comes back into the kitchen.

The tea is in the pot, Mama says, and smiles at him.

I'm tired, he says, and I could e-e-eat a horse. I always laugh at him eating a huge big horse. Mama fusses and makes more tea. She lets me eat with him if he's early. He cuts everything up real small on his plate and pushes it around before he eats it. I love to watch him.

<hr />

Yodel-ay-ee-tee! Yodel-ay-ee-tee! It's Sunday afternoon. That's what he does. He calls me and the other children in from the fields in the summer by yodelling. No other father can do that. All the kids are told that when they hear my father's voice they are to come in for their tea, too.

Your father can't yodel, I say to the other boys.

My father doesn't stutter, one yells back.

Mama says that Dada learned to yodel in Switzerland. He went there for six months to get better because he was sick in his chest. He wasn't very strong after that, she says. That's why he is slow riding up the hill. Other fathers are quicker. I can tell she wants to sort of protect him. So do I.

Where did he learn to stutter, Mama?

That was when he was a little boy. He's much better now, she says. Dada is not as tall as the other fathers. He has black hair and brown eyes. He speaks slowly, so as not to stutter too much. He never shouts. Mama says it'd be hard to shout and stutter at the same time. He is a nice man and is my friend. When we go for walks he holds my hand. That's how I know that he likes me.

This day Mama is angry with me. Me and my friend Brian Graham from next door are chased by a man from the new houses that they are building. The man shouts at Mama that we are stealing his wood.

What did you do, you bold boy? she asks.

We just wanted some bits of wood, Mama, to make a boat. That man is so mean.

When she comes back from the shops she shows me a little yellow cane.

This is for Dada to smack you with, she says, when you are very bold like this morning.

She hangs it on the picture rail in the dining room. And goes back in the kitchen. I pull a chair over to the wall and climb up on it and take down the cane. I bend it, but I can't break it. Little bits of it stick out of the bend, like hairs, but it won't break. It looks ruined. Mama comes in.

What are you doing?

I don't want Dada to hit me with that cane.

I'll have to tell him what you've done when he comes in, she says.
I wait for him down the road. When he comes round the corner, I run to meet him.

Dada, Dada, I say. I was bold, and Mama wants you to hit me with a cane.

Let me talk to Mama, he says.

He looks tired. She tells him about the wood and the man, and I watch his eyes.

Just tell him not to do it again. I'm tired now.

He doesn't want to hit me. But he doesn't speak to me about the wood. And they don't buy another cane. He never hits me. Neither does Mama.

Bernard and Mama

Mama is right. I want to go off on my own all the time. One day
we get on the train at Booterstown station where the Quink Ink
signs on the wall are huge, with big blue and white splotches.

Where are we going today, Dada?

Arklow. To see the boats in the harbour, he says.

And to have lunch, Mama says. She says 'lunch' and he says
'dinner' in the middle of the day. Mama has more rules than Dada.
Don't shout on the street, wear your gloves, put on your coat,
take off your muddy shoes. It's a lot of things to remember.

Why do you say 'lunch' and Dada says 'dinner', Mama?
My father looks out the window of the train and starts to smile.
Mama doesn't want to answer, I can see that. I like it when this
happens. So I ask Dada.
He smiles at her and says, you tell him then.

It's just that I was brought up to say 'lunch' in the middle of the
day, and 'dinner' at night.
I look at Dada, but he's staring out at the seagulls flying over the
beach. He doesn't want to talk about this, so I go and look at the
waves and the birds with him.

⸺⸺

We get off at Arklow harbour. They say we can go to see the boats
in a minute. Mama goes into the shops for something. Lots of
people are walking around in the sunshine. Dada picks up a
newspaper outside a shop. Nobody is looking, so I get lost on
purpose. I walk down to the boats and keep looking back to make
sure they can't see me. It's like hide-and-seek at school.
There are blue and white boats with strings and ropes hanging all
over the place. The wind makes rattling noises in the boats. There
are no clouds, just sun. It's lovely.
I smell seaweed and fish. The wet paint is hot and smells nice on
the upside-down boats. Crowds of people are walking about,
talking and laughing.
Then a big man beside me says, don't go near the edge or you'll
fall in. He has red hair on his head and in his nose. He asks me if
I'm lost.

I'm with my Mama and Dada but they are somewhere else. I'm
not lost, I tell him. I'm here.
He laughs, and rubs my hair and walks away. And I still don't
know where Mama and Dada are. It's great.
I look back. Women walk in blowy, flowery dresses. Then I see my

mother, running and crying and laughing all at the same time. My father is behind her. I try to run away, but the man with red hair catches me.

My mother shakes my arm till it hurts, and says thank you to the man. She is crying, sort of. Then she smiles. Dada is smiling too. He doesn't worry like Mama does.

I'm not glad to see her. Being lost is over.

Mama buys a baby

I don't want a little sister or brother, Mama, I say. I just want you and Dada.

Mama's tummy is huge. Her apron hangs way out from it. When she carries a pot from the stove she says a funny thing. I walk like a duck, she says. Mind out of my way. Quack, quack.

I laugh so much. Say it again, Mama, I yell.

Quack, quack, quack, she says, and I die laughing.

She is laughing too. Then she says she's going into the hospital for a few days next month to get the baby and will I please be good when I'm with Aunt Tracy during the day.

But why don't you take the baby out here, Mama?

Only a doctor can do it, she says.

I don't want this baby. How can they have two of us in the same house? That's all she talks about these days. Clothes for the baby, my cot for the baby, food for the baby. There's no time for Dada and me.

Then Dermot comes home from the hospital with Mama and he's very small and there's great excitement. I think he is lovely until he cries.

Can you take him back to the doctor, Mama, and change him?

No, Bernard, I can't.

How did you get him out of your tummy then?

She smiles at me like I've said a funny thing.

He was a present from God, she says. All babies cry. Now I want you to help me with him, there's a good boy.

So I helped her then, and when I came home from school.

Mama is not as tall as Dada and she can walk quickly again. Dada is slower. She's got ginger hair, sort of wavy. When she laughs I always want to laugh too. She has her worried face on a lot when Dermot cries. He annoys me. And now she gets tired quickly, with Dermot and all.

2

The tricycle

MAMA AND DADA GIVE me a big surprise. They call me out to the
shed one Saturday morning when my brother is asleep.

Look inside, says Mama.

It's all shiny black and silver and it's got a bell. I'm shaky all over,
I'm so excited.

It's a tricycle, I shout.

Mama says they got it from another family. The three wheels have
spokes and mudguards, just like Dada's big bicycle. The handlebars
and the saddle are all the same, only they are smaller.

Can I take it out? I look up at Mama, and she's all red with
smiling too. I have to climb up on it, and Dada helps me. He says
he'll fix the saddle for me so I can reach the pedals. I am so
excited that I have no patience.

You hold that, he says, pointing at the saddle, and I'll loosen the
nut. He never stutters when he's talking to me about things. At
last it's ready and he asks me to get on, and I ride around and
around. He smiles and says, Good boy! Is it high enough?

Then he gets his hat and takes me out on the road and helps me steer.
We go down to the shops. I wave to the other boys. They just stare.
He takes his hat off to the ladies that we meet. Everybody likes Dada.

Good morning, Mr Ryan, Mr Arigo the shop man says.

May I have a p-p-penny wafer for Bernard here, Dada says, and a packet of S-s-sweet Aftons?

That's a grand bike, says Mr Arigo.

And I am so happy that I forget to say thank you for the ice-cream.

Next day Mama says that she can't walk with me to school every day because she has to look after the new baby. So I can ride my tricycle there if I'm very careful. She walks with me for the first two days and shows me where to cross the road. Mrs Graham next door minds Dermot. Then Mama lets me go on my own all the way to Sion Hill convent in Blackrock from our house in Trimbleston Gardens. Only one other boy at my school has a tricycle.

Bye-bye now. Mind crossing the road, Mama calls from the gate. I peddle down the road, looking back, and giving her a wave. This is my first day on my own. My schoolbag is on my back and I'm only four and a half.

Tring, tring, says my bell and the dogs get up all stiff legs to get out of my way. The other children are walking. It's only me that has a trike. That's what Dada calls it, a trike. It feels like there's nobody else but me and the trees and the lamp posts and the dogs lying on the path. Down at the bottom of the road I stop and look into Arigo's ice-cream shop. They sell other things too, but mostly ice-cream. I only have a ha'penny, and a wafer is a penny, and anyway I'm not to stop, Mama says.

I turn right on to the main road and stand up on the pedals and ride to the tram stop. A tram stops for some people. It's an open-air tram. I stop and look at the boys hanging out over the railings on top. They shout down at me and I don't know what they are saying, and I shout back that I'm going to school and goodbye. I love the trams. Nnnnngggggggg it goes off into town, all green

The tricycle

and clangy and a Bovril sign on its side. Other children have to
walk. I am the only one with a trike.

Now it's nearly Booterstown. At the shops I stop. This is where
Mama says I must cross the road. I look right, then left, then right
again. I'm a little bit afraid. There's only the Kennedy's bread van
outside the shops, and a horse and cart. I go over quick, though.
The horse is plopping and I don't look. Mama says the horse
doesn't like people to look when it's doing a number two.

Mama shops here and I want to say hello to Mrs Connolly. She
might give me a honeybee. I park my new tricycle outside

against the mud scraper to stop it rolling away down across the road and over the railway tracks and into the sea and across to Holyhead in Wales. Because that might happen if I don't park it properly.

Mrs Connolly says, good morning, Bernard, and how are you? So I tell her that this is my first time going to school on my own on my new tricycle, and can I have two honeybees. I take the halfpenny out of my pocket and put it up on the counter.

Ah, sure isn't he a dote, says one woman, and the others all laugh. Mama's friends all say 'dote'. I think that's for babies. I don't really like it.

These are for free, says Mrs Connolly, for your first day on your own, and she gives me four sweets. That's a whole penny.

I say thank you and put three in my pocket down deep and take the paper off the last one and put it in my mouth. I look around at the smiling faces. I feel like I'm a grown up.

Say hello to your mother, says Mrs Connolly. Be careful now. One woman says, He's young to be out on his own. I frown at her like Dada does.

I stand on the pedals again for the long hill up Booterstown Avenue. I pretend I'm a tram on the two mend lines running along in the concrete where the men put down pipes. I keep my back wheels on those lines all the way to the top. Only one car goes past. Dada says the war is a great time for the horses. I ride in at the gates of my school. Sister Catherine is standing on the top step.

Did you come all on your own today? she asks.

Yes, I say. My Mama says that I know how to do it myself.

Oh, I'm sure she's right, she says.

Yes, I think, she's right. Of course she's right.

But Mama worries too much. One day I fell into a builder's trench in the field up the road. A man had to pull me out all wet. Mama got a big fright.

Next day, Mama's two sisters are having tea with her and I hear what they are saying about me. Aunt Tracy is the nice one and Auntie Gertie is the one that tells people what they must do. Mama is saying that I am always going off into the fields around our house on my own and she's worried I'll get lost or killed or drowned or something.

He'll get into mischief if he can, she says.

But he's not bold, is he? Aunt Tracy asks.

Well, he is sometimes.

You must punish him then, Lily, when he's bold, says Gertie. Tom insists I smack Brendan if he disobeys. They understand that, you see. She talks just like Miss Lawlor at school that we all hate. And Mama never smacks me – well, only a little bit, but not hard.

But I do worry, Mama says then. I don't want to lose another child.

I don't know what she means by that. Me and Dermot are the only ones.

One Saturday morning Mama calls me in from the road. I pull my trike in onto the grass behind the hedge because I don't want the other boys getting on it. I go in, and say, What?

Pardon, not 'what', I've told you before, she says all cranky.

But I want to go out to play Mama. She's always calling me in for silly things.

Come into the kitchen, she says.

There's a sandwich on a plate and a glass of milk on the table. It's a bit early for them, I think.

Sit down, she says, and pushes the plate over to me. The last time she did this was when she was telling me about going away to the hospital to get the baby. So I get nervous and look at her face. It's all worried.

I'm afraid that you can't ride your tricycle to school any more, Bernard, she says. But she's not looking at me, and she's chewing her lip. She always does that when she wants to say something terrible. What, Mama?

You have to walk to school now, like all the other children. You can play on your trike when you come home. Our road is safe. She's looking at me now.

No, Mama, I cry. That's not fair, that's not fair! I love riding my tricycle to school and back, I'm always careful, and I've never had an accident!

No, Bernard, she says, there are more cars these days. And people say it's too dangerous, you see.

What people? What do they say? Who, Mama, who? I shout at her.

This is stupid. She's always worried about what other people will say. If my shoes are dirty she says I must clean them or what will people think. She listens to her sisters, too. That's it, I think. Aunt Gertie, she's always interfering.

Did Gertie say something then?

Aunt Gertie, Bernard. And she looks away, and then I know.

It was Aunt Gertie, Mama. What does she know about me? I'm really shouting now. I know all the lines on the paths on the road to school and I play tram drivers on them and my trams never crash. No other boys have tricycles on our road. And now my mother wants to stop me. I jump up and say I'm going out to ride the trike and she mustn't think she's going to stop me on Monday. I see tears in her eyes and I get tears too, and run out. Dada's gone to Mass because it's some special day. When he comes in I'm waiting for him. But Mama comes out on the step. The other children are standing there because I've told them all about it.

Dada, Dada, Mama says I can't go to school on my trike any more – please, it's not true is it?

He turns around and looks at all the children standing there and says to me to go inside. Mama calls out for us to come in, that we don't want the whole neighbourhood to know our business. I run inside and wait for Dada. As soon as the hall door is closed I start to cry. Their faces say it is true. Dada won't look at me. Mama's face is all red.

Come into the kitchen at once, she says to me. Now she's getting angry. She does that when I don't listen the first time. She pours a cup of tea for Dada and he stands there, looking out the window.

Gertie can't tell Mama what to do, Dada, can she? I say to him. Mama is older than she is, isn't she?

It's none of her business, he says, and I think he's taking my side. But your mother is rearing you, and not me.

As soon as he says that, rearing me, I know he's not on my side at all. I start to yell then.

You are stupid, Mama, to listen to Gertie. She's not my mother. She's horrible, she's ugly. Aunt Tracy would never do that. She's nice.

Go up to your room, Mama cries, with tears in her eyes again. I'm doing this for your own good and you are an ungrateful boy. Go straight to your room.

Dada is looking at her. He won't look at me. I run out and slam the door. Halfway up he stairs I stop and listen. They are arguing. But Mama will win. She always does. She is rearing me.

Dada locks my trike in the shed on Sunday evening and I walk to school next day. I do not say goodbye to either of them.

I don't like Dermot, I say to my Ma one day.

Oh, you mustn't say that, she says.

Are you going to give him my trike? I ask.

Of course not, she says. Go out and play.

I'm five and a half now. Dermot is starting to walk. He runs up to Dada like I used to when Dada comes home. Dermot is quiet and sits on his lap smiling up at him. He is no trouble at all, and I am bold.

One day they have a row over me. Rows happen a lot now.

Why don't you come in when you are called? Mama asks. You worry me to death when you stay out in the dark.

I was playing with Gerry Reilly. His mother lets him stay out, I say back to her.

I can see Dada frowning.

What am I going to do with this boy? my Ma says, all worried.

Well, you are bringing him up, not me, he says. You've always spoiled him.

No she doesn't, I say to him. She took away my tricycle.

Now don't contradict your father, she says.

Then he picks up Dermot, who just sits in his lap like a fat smiley lump.

Can I have some more butter on my cabbage, please, I say.

He's had enough, says Dada.

I look at Mama.

Well, just a little bit, she says. He frowns.

You've no time for anything else except spoiling him, he says with his cross face.

Dada doesn't like me now because he thinks I am Mama's pet. Even though I have to share her with Dermot.

He is spoiling Dermot now. Like he wants to get his own back on her. Dada and me stop being friends then.

Willies

I walk to school, now. One day I'm streeling home up the road
and I see all my friends already playing outside our house. Brian
Graham lives with his parents next door and he comes running
out. They are Protestants from Glasgow in Scotland. My parents
like them.

Let's see your mickey, one boy says. He has his pants down and
we can see it.

One of the girls pulls her knickers down and we all try to look.
We giggle like mad. I can't see anything. Brian pulls his pants
down and shouts at me, so I do it too. I feel I'm going all red. One
boy says that Mary Brown hasn't got a willy, and all the boys
laugh. I turn around to look at our house. Mama is not there.
Now Brian giggles and pulls his pants down again. We all look and
laugh at the girls. Another girl says, Look at mine, look at mine. I
didn't see any girl's willy because they didn't have any, just their
funny knickers and pink skin where we have our things. The girls
are pointing at the boys and laughing their heads off.

Then someone shouts and I turn around. My mother is out on the
front doorstep. She looks angry and calls me in her worried
voice. All the girls run away screaming and laughing. She calls me
inside. Her voice is funny. I don't want to go inside. But she says
she'll smack me if I don't. I know something is bad.

That's very rude what you were all doing, she says. Go to your
room.

She doesn't talk to me at teatime. I know something is wrong, but
I don't know what . That night I hear them talking and arguing in
the dining room. I go downstairs and listen at the door. Mama says
something to Dada about Protestants being different in the way
they look at things. But I remember that we all looked at each
other the same. And I remember that Brian has a long piece of
skin on the end of his willy. But so do most of the boys. It's my

37

willy that's different because me and Gerry Reilly are bare at the top like a sort of knob.

I don't know what this is about. I don't know which of my friends is a Protestant. Except Brian and Derek. Then Mama says to Dada that we must move. I don't know what she means by that. I can't hear what he says. I hear her chair scrape on the floor. I run back upstairs and jump into bed. A few weeks later, Mama says we'll be moving to Blackrock.

No, Mama, we can't! First you took my tricycle and now we're leaving this house and the stream and my friends and all.

Go upstairs to your bedroom if you're going to be a baby, she says.

I look out my bedroom window at our garden and Brian's next door. I start crying and rush downstairs and shout at Mama.

Why, Mama? Why? Why are we leaving here, Mama? Why? All my friends are here and Brian and everything.

She doesn't tell me why.

But please, Mama, is there something wrong with the house?

No, I can't tell you. Go and play in the back garden.

I remember the night that they talked.

Is it because our willies are different, then? Or the way we looked at them?

Her face doesn't look at me.

Some of your friends are Protestants, you see, Bernard, and they're different, not like us.

Yes they are, Mama, I saw them, I say. They are only a bit different from me. They have a bit of skin hanging off and me and Gerry Reilly don't.

She looks really worried then, but she says nothing. But I'm worried too, because Brian has that bit of skin and he's a Protestant.

I ask Dada when he comes home. He just looks at me and picks up Dermot.

I th-th-thought I asked you to explain this to him, he says to Mama.

Why don't you, she says, I'm making the tea.

Please, Dada, I say.

Are you going to cause another r-r-row, he says to me. I've only just come in, and there's trouble already.

But, Dada, Brian's parents are your friends too, they are Protestants too, so why did Mama say that, Dada?

He just looks at Mama coming in with his soup, like he doesn't know what to say. Something bad has happened and they won't tell me. I want to cry because he won't talk to me. I run out of the house and stay out till after it's very dark. They're so upset when I come in the door.

Don't ever do that again, they say. No supper for you.

Next day after school I tell Brian what my parents said.

Will we run away? I ask him,

Why? he asks. Because I hate my mother, I tell him.

Move to Blackrock

We go to live in number 8 Mount Merrion Avenue in Blackrock. It's a big old house with scary dark stairs. We have the ground floor and the basement. Not nearly as nice as the last house. My parents don't own it, just renting for a while, they say. It's on the same road as Sion Hill, my school. My trike is in the cupboard under the stairs. On the first day of school I think that they'll let me ride it again.

My school is much nearer now, Mama. It's just up the road. Can I have my trike back now?

No, it's a busy road for a tricycle to cross, so no. She says it in that voice that means don't argue.

The only good thing about our new house is Blackrock Park.

There's a lovely park where you can play with your friends, Bernard, says my Ma.

My friends are all at our old house, Mama.

You'll make new ones. Take your marbles down to the park now and play while I go out to the shops.

Can I ride my trike in the park then?

No. Only if we are with you at weekends, maybe.

But I can't forget my trike. Now it's locked in the glory hole with the big black spiders under the stairs that go down to the old kitchen. The key is in Mama's purse. I mustn't look there, though. That's where she keeps the food money and the pennies for the gas and the shillings for the light. The big old range in the kitchen doesn't need money in the meter, just wood and some coal if there's money enough to buy some. The wood is kept under the stairs, too, where it's dry. Mama gives me the key.

Run upstairs like a good boy and bring me down some wood for the range, Bernard.

It's afternoon, and she's going to cook the tea. She'll be busy for ages down there.

I rattle the wood around a bit to frighten the spiders. My trike doesn't shine any more. It looks sad.

I give Mama a big armful of wood and ask her does she want any more.

She looks at me funny. Well, I don't always ask her that.

No thanks, she says, now you play in the garden, will you?

She doesn't ask for the key, so I sneak back up the stairs, and wangle the trike out slowly so's not to make a noise.

The hall door squeaks, so I open it very slowly. It goes eek, eek, eek, but not loud. I push the little button up on the lock so it can't click shut. I'll leave it open. I won't be long.

Down the stone steps I go, half-carrying my lovely tricycle. Dust all over it. Dada hasn't looked after it.

Out the gate and I look back. No sign of Mama. She'll think that I'm down at the park. I stand up on the pedals and off I go like the

At Blackrock (with Dermot in the background)

wind up the road and round the corner into Frascati Park. Frascati is where Aunt Gertie is, so I turn around and go on up Mount Merrion Avenue. The pavement is real wide, and ladies with dogs and children smile at me. They don't think it's dangerous. Every few minutes a car goes up or down it, so it is quite busy, I suppose.

Near my school at Sion Hill, a big guard is helping some older children to cross the road. He sees me and waves. I wave back.

Better go home now or she'll start looking for me because
Dermot is asleep by this time.
She doesn't notice a thing. I lock the trike in under the stairs and
say goodnight to it.

See you tomorrow, I whisper.
I stop asking them to ride my trike after that. I sneak out with it
when Mama's cooking or washing or cleaning the kitchen.

It's my job to chop up orange boxes and logs for the black range.
One day I chop up some old furniture lying in the weeds in the
back garden. When the landlord notices this he goes mad.

Those things belonged to my mother, he says.

Well, why did you leave them out in the rain? my Ma asks,
standing up to the old scarecrow. That's what Dada calls him. The
scarecrow says he'll add it to the rent. After he's gone, I say I'll
pay out of my sixpence-a- week pocket money. Dada smiles at me
when he hears that.

Just watch your mother when that scarecrow comes next time,
he says.
My mother is nervous when the landlord comes. I can see this
because she twists her little white hanky into knots.

Here is a list of all the things that we want repaired in this
house, she says to the landlord. He stares at the list.

These are hard times, Mrs Ryan. There's a war on, you know. I
can't afford any of this.

Well, at least you must stop the rain coming under the back
door here. And seal the windows. They'll rot away, and that'll cost
you more.
He looks at her. Dada was right. I'm watching her. She's tough
with this fella, like she is with me and my tricycle. But now I'm
proud of her.

He sniffs, takes the rent money, and looks at the door and the windows.

All right, then. I'll send a man round, and he leaves. With bad grace.

She says, half to herself, that's the way to do it. I love her for that.

The policeman makes a mistake

Mama and me go to the shops together one day. Aunt Tracy is minding Dermot. We wait for a tram to pass, and then cross the street to Haffners. Mama buys all our rashers and sausages and black and white pudding there.

Mr Haffner is a German, she says, and they are the best pork butchers.

This is our Saturday and Sunday breakfast that she's buying now. We go back outside and the big guard from outside my school is helping people cross the street. He sees us and touches his cap to my mother and gives her a big smile.

Good morning, ma'am, he says with his big red face.

Good morning, Guard, she says. It's a fine day, isn't it?

'Tis a grand day, ma'am, he says. And how's the young fella? He puts his hand on my shoulder and I grin up at him. I love they way the country people talk. Everything they say is 'grand' and 'tis' and 'bejay' and 'dis', 'dat', 'dese' and 'dose'.

He's well, thank you, says my Ma, smiling down at me.

Then the guard says, 'Tis grand to see him managing his tricycle so well. I do wish that the motorcar drivers would be that careful now.

And he pats me on the head. I look at Mama. She doesn't know what to say.

Well, I'll be off now, says the guard. God bless ye.

What does he mean, Bernard? Have you been out with your trike without telling me?

The day is ruined. She's so upset.

Even the guard says I'm careful, Mama. What are you worried about?

But you disobeyed us. When you're six you'll have to confess that. You could have been killed, she says. You are such a worry to me. I argue and argue. It's no good. She locks my trike in the spare room upstairs.

<hr />

I don't know what to do with him, Mama tells Dada in her worried voice when he comes in, telling him about the tricycle. And Dada frowns.

He's your responsibility, he says. You're rearing him.
Maybe fathers don't know how to talk to their children. Boy dogs don't do anything for their puppies, and neither do tomcats. Dada is the same. He brings home money for food, like the blackbird in the garden. Maybe the birds and the animals argue, too. I'm sure they do. The cats screech at night and dogs fight in the street and the birds chase each other round and round the garden, chirping their heads off. Fathers are the same.

But will you speak to the child, Dada? she asks him.
He just frowns and reads the paper. Dermot smiles up at Dada. He's nearly two now. His clothes always look neat. I hate him for that, too.

Stealing for the nuns

I learn to steal when I'm six and a bit. Every day I walk up Merrion Avenue to school because my trike is still in the spare room. Some of those big houses have lovely flowers. Behind the railings.

Who would like to bring flowers for the altar? asks Sister Margaret one day.

The nuns love flowers. They put them in front of all the statues on all the altars. I put up my hand, and a few of the girls do as well. I look around. I am the only boy with his hand up. I take it down again, but I'm not quick enough.

The nun says thank you and smiles straight at me.

We look forward to your flowers tomorrow, Bernard, she says. Baby Jesus loves flowers, doesn't he?

She is all wrinkles when she smiles. I like her. She doesn't shout at us or slap us like the others.

Yes, Sister, I say.

A real sissy I am. But I'll do it for her.

Our garden doesn't have altar flowers, those long ones, red and white and yellow. Mama says our nasturtiums are no good in vases. Then she forgets about it because she's washing Dermot's nappies.

The sun is shining again in the morning. I stop outside the best garden. Clumpy pink and purple flowers grow next to the railings. Baby Jesus will like them. I can just reach. I pick a bunch. I do that the next day as well.

The third day I hear a screech. An old woman sort of hobbles down the path.

What are you doing, you bold boy? she shouts. I am afraid, and squeeze the flowers.

Give them to me, she says, very angry.

Then another lady stops on the pavement.

What's going on here? she asks, sort of cross.

This boy is stealing flowers.

What's your name? the new lady asks me.

I tell her.

I'm giving them to Sister Margaret for the altar, I whisper.

Ah now, isn't that lovely, says the lady. He's only got a few snapdragons. That won't hurt your garden.

And she smiles at me.

Run along now, and don't be late for school.

I see her glaring at the woman in the garden.

I give the flowers to the nun. She says, tell your mother thank you very much.

But I tell my mother the whole thing, about the women too.

Were the flowers snapdragons? she asks.

Yes.

So is that old woman. And she laughs to herself.

It's years before I understand what she meant by that.

3

I can't move God, he's stuck

WRITE DOWN YOUR SINS on a piece of paper, boys, for your first confession. You don't want to be forgetting any, says Sister Margaret.

After a bit, she looks over my shoulder and I see her smiling.

I thought all those flowers were from your own garden, Bernard? she says.

I'm so ashamed. Now she knows that I stole the flowers. She puts her hand over her mouth and I can see she is laughing.

The priest said we must never leave anything out. Not even a venial sin, which is smaller then a mortal one. You go to hell forever if you die with a mortal sin on your soul.

And you committed a sin with your tricycle, too, she says, still reading my piece of paper.

I cross out the seventh commandment bit about stealing then. I put it under the fourth. Honour thy father and mother. I don't want to try and fool God. You can't.

She goes on to the next boy with a smile on her face. It's very quiet in class and everyone has their hand bent around their piece of paper so no one else will see.

The priest who came to see us yesterday walked quickly up and down and made a swishing noise with his black soutane. He said that sins make our souls go black and make baby Jesus cry. And Sister Margaret is laughing at mine. She is the best nun, and isn't cranky like the others.

On Friday we queue up in the church outside the confessional box. The first boy out trips and we all giggle. I am frightened I'll forget something. I take out my piece of paper and it's all wrinkled up. It's dark in the church, so I can't read it properly. Raphael Byrne next to me is crying. I look around for Sister Margaret and she comes over, kneels down beside him, and starts whispering to him. Sister Margaret stands up and says shhh and smiles at us.

Don't be nervous, she says. God will be very glad to hear you. I'm frightened it'll be the same priest who said our sins make baby Jesus cry. He'll be bawling his head off when he hears mine. Lies, stealing, getting lost, and upsetting my mother and hating my little brother.

Raphael Byrne comes out and he looks all right. I go in and kneel down in the dark. It smells of wood and old clothes. I can hear the squeaky voice of one of the other boys and then the priest's voice. But I can't hear what it is they're saying. Then a little door slides back. He leans over to the wire mesh separating us, and I can see his face.

Bless me, father, for I have sinned. This is my first confession.

Go ahead, my child.

He's not the one who said our souls would go black. I tell him everything that I remember from my list. It's screwed up in a ball in my fist.

He says, Is there anything else, my child?

No, Father.

Why do you not like your little brother, my child?

Because my Dada likes him better than me and he's good and I get into trouble all the time, Father.

Now, son, I want you to have a little talk with your mother about this. Will you tell her I said that?

Yes, Father, I say.

Now I'm mortified because I've been in here so long.

Say a prayer for me, my child. Say three Hail Marys for your penance, and now a sincere Act of Contrition. Then he starts saying all the Latin words. Talking to God.

The lads look up at me when I come out, like I've got two heads. Sister Margaret winks. She's bold. A nun that winks in church. I say my penance and wait outside in the sunshine. It's freezing inside the church.

Sister Margaret gathers all the boys around her and says we mustn't worry about staying in a state of grace until our First Communion in two days.

Sure, you are not sinners at all. Just do what your parents say, and you'll be fine.

———

Why do you hate Dermot? my Ma asks me when I get home and tell her what the priest said. We sit at the kitchen table with bread and butter, and I have a glass of milk.

Because Dada likes him more than me. Don't say he doesn't, Mama.

He loves you both, Bernard. He just shows it differently, that's all.

Well, why is he always complaining about me to you and he doesn't talk to me and he never does that about Dermot, even after Dermot ruined the carpet upstairs?

It's partly my fault, she says. You see, I make too much of a fuss of you. She looks sort of sad now. You are my first child, and I'm always worried that you'll have an accident or get lost or get sick, you see.

You don't spoil me. You took my tricycle away.

That's for your own good, Bernard. You might easily be hit by a car or something.

I get up to go out to the garden. I am angry when I think of my tricycle locked up. I know they are going to give it to Dermot. I am already a bit too big for it.

No, I haven't finished yet, she says, and pours me more milk. I have to stay for that.

You are our eldest, she says, and they are always special to a mother. To both parents. I'm going to tell you something now that you don't know. I had a baby boy before you, she says. He was born dead. We called him John. I was very frightened that I would lose you too. That something would happen to you.

Her eyes have tears in them now. There was another boy older than me? I don't understand.

Then you came along, she says, and I didn't pay enough attention to Dada. He felt a bit left out.

She stops and looks at the kettle boiling on the range. She gets up and wets the teapot.

And I spoiled you too, she says.

No you didn't, I say. You took my tricycle away.

She looks like she is going to cry. She calls me back in and says, Please don't hate your brother before your First Communion, will you promise me, Bernard?

I promise, Mama, I say. I'm feeling a bit sad for making her cry.

—◆—

First Communion is next day because they don't want to give us time to spoil everything by going and committing whoppers again. The church is filled up with all the boys and girls and relations and things. They're singing hymns upstairs next to the organ and there are three priests saying Mass. My pals' faces are serious, and their mothers are trying to flatten the hair that sticks up on their heads. My hair lies down by itself. But the girls are all smiling and loving their white dresses and veils and shoes. They whisper like mad, and their mothers just smile. But when one of us boys opens our mouth we get a dig in the ribs.

It's the same priest that heard my confession that is giving out the communion to the boys. The young one. I try to remember what they told us. Just let the wafer lie on your tongue. It will melt by itself. Then go back to your seat with your head down for the Body of Christ that is inside your mouth, and pray for ten minutes.

Out of the corner of my eye I see the boy next to me getting God. Then I stick out my tongue and close my eyes. *Corpus Domine Nostrum*, says the priest. The Body of Our Lord.

Where is He? Then I feel Him on my tongue. I wait. The priest nudges under my chin to shut my mouth because I'm still kneeling there like an eejit with my mouth open.

I open my eyes and he's gone on to the next boy. I get up and turn around. My mouth is dry. Where is God? He's stuck to the roof of my mouth. He's not supposed to be up there. He's supposed to be on my tongue. They didn't tell us about this. I curl my tongue up and try to get Him down, but He's stuck.

When I get to our pew, I look up and I see Dada has tears in his eyes. If only he knew that I've got Him in the wrong place. I kneel down and feel God again with my tongue. My face is scarlet. Can anybody see what's going on?

My tongue pushes Him further back in my throat and I think I'm going to choke.

I try to swallow again and this time He peels off and is back on my tongue. Then He just melts. I feel dizzy.

I stay with my head down until Mama nudges me.

Are you all right? she asks.

Yes, thank you, I say. He was very dry and He got stuck.

Shhh, she says, and looks around to see if anyone is listening. We walk back home, and the kitchen is full of aunts and uncles and neighbours and friends of Mama and Dada. Nearly all of them give me little holy pictures to put in my prayer book. Only some of them give me money.

Now it's not about money, my Ma whispers in my ear. It's the greatest day in your life.

Dada calls us all out in the garden and takes snaps of me on my own against the hedge, and then with all the others.

Dada says to me, Are you all right? Yes, I'm fine, I say. He smiles at me, and I think that Mama is right. He does love me a bit.

Another move

After a year, we move again. And this time it's to Dún Laoghaire. It's a little house on a quiet road called Tivoli Terrace North. There's an East and a South, and York Road is where the West should be. In the middle are the two big fields where the Kingstown Grammar School boys play hockey and cricket.

Are they Protestant games, Dada? I ask him.

English, yes – cricket is – but I played hockey myself.

And he was very good too, says Mama. He played for Ireland once. He raises one eyebrow and goes on stirring his tea. I ask him more about that, but he doesn't say much.

Dada calls our new house a bungalow because it's got no upstairs and no other house is joined on to it. It's the first place with its own name. Maryville.

What's that mean, Mama?

Well, the house of Mary I suppose. Ville is a house or a town in French.

She knows lots of things like that.

It's a little house with only two bedrooms and our own garden in front for Mama to plant her flowers.

The back garden is for vegetables, Mama says, would you like me to teach you how to plant seeds?

Yes please, Mama, I say.

I like doing things with her. So I dig up the earth and shake out the sods and weeds. Then I break up the lumps with my hands and make seed beds like she shows me. We plant lettuces, radishes, carrots and scallions.

My mother, Nana, taught me, she says.

My grandmother Nana comes to visit. I show her the little seeds coming up.

Oh, you've got the green fingers, she says, like your mother and myself.

I love tea and biscuits with Nana. Mama always uses the best china that was a wedding present, she says. Not a piece broken.

And the way they talk. Nana tells all the funny stories about her sons and daughters. And about Papa, my grandfather. Me and my cousins are a bit frightened of him.

Well, you know he was a captain in the British Army. He had to be strict with his men.

He must be a brave man, I think. I want to be a soldier like him.

Then I ask Nana, How did you have fourteen children?

Shhh, says Mama.

No, he can ask me that, says Nana. She turns to me. Yes, I did. Fourteen lovely babies. You see, whenever Papa looked at me I had another baby, and she laughs a sort of deep laugh that makes her cough. She takes her cigarette out of its black holder and Mama pushes Dada's ashtray closer.

He just looked at you, Nana? Then Dada mustn't look at you, Mama. We only have two bedrooms, I say.

Did you have enough money to feed them all, Nana? I ask.
Her face looks a bit sad then and she looks at my Ma in a funny
way.

Not always, Bernard, she says. Sometimes it was a struggle, a big
struggle.
And she stands up and pats her mouth with the little lace napkins
that Mama only brings out for her and special friends.

Are you going now, Nana? I ask. Can I walk down to the tram
stop with you, please?

Yes, of course, love. I want a young gentleman at my side.
I am so proud. She is taller than my Ma and she walks up straight.
She has the fur of a fox around her neck that has a head with
brown glass eyes and teeth that she clips onto its tail so that it
doesn't fall off. And a little black hat on her head, and a veil half
over her face. I hope all the neighbours are watching when we
walk down Tivoli Terrace together.
When we get to the poor houses in Cross Avenue with all the
little hooligans, they never shout at me when I'm with Nana. They
look at her and their mothers nod and some of the fathers touch
their caps. I think my granny is a queen.

Now that we are living in Dún Laoghaire, I have to go to the
Christian Brothers. On my first day when Mama and the other
mothers have gone, the Brothers say, Go and play in the yard. One
boy asks me my name. I tell him Bernard Ryan.

Is that like a rasher rind? And he laughs.

No, I say. It's Ryan.

Look at him, the boy says, You are like a skinny streaky rasher.
Rasher Ryan.
That is my name now. It's better than Snots Sullivan. He had a
green boogie in his nose the first day, and somebody saw it.

Look at that snot, they shouted. Snots Sullivan.

I tell my parents about all this.

The Brothers are very strict, Dada, I say.

Oh, they take no nonsense, he says.

There's one Brother called O'Kane, and he gave Toby Farrell six wallops with the leather today for laughing, I say.

Mama looks a bit upset, but Dada says that the brother is living up to his name.

But you don't hit us. Even when you're angry with us, I say.

Ah well, m-m-maybe we should, he grumbles and picks up his paper. We can see he doesn't mean it, though.

On the way to school, I pass Woolies in George's Street. There are loudspeakers outside the shop that play music. Every day we hear 'Lily Marlene', the German song. It's a sad song, but lovely as well. Some people stop and listen. Others shake their heads and mutter. That's because there's a war on, my Ma says.

The war is in our school as well. At recreation time we split into the RAF and the Luftwaffe. Most of us want to be German fighter planes. The British always lose these battles. The Brothers and the teachers smile at this.

Being Irish

When I'm eight and a bit, our teachers go on strike. They stop coming to work. It's great. Dada says it's for more money. But not the Christian Brothers, because they aren't allowed to get any money. Just the ordinary teachers. So my school closes. They send me to Marlborough Street National School in Dublin, which is free. The best is that I go in and out on the trams. I love the open air ones and sit up in the front, even if it's raining a bit.

We do all our subjects in Irish. My parents want me to learn Irish, because no matter if you get a hundred per cent in all subjects and fail the Irish language, you fail the whole exam.

Good jobs are hard to get, Mama says. You must get your exams. I even think in Irish now. Irish history makes more sense in the Irish language. The English changed all our names. Our name Ryan used to be O'Riain, but Dada says they couldn't pronounce Irish or Scottish names so they just changed them.

My mother feels proud of being Irish. She used to live in Cambridge over in England and went to school there. She tells us about the English girls asking if everybody in Ireland lived in thatched cottages. She tells it like it's something funny. She isn't annoyed by it. But I think it makes her more Irish. Not like her father, who is pro-British. There is a bit of rebellion in her. I run home one day to tell her what happened on the tram. An old lady with a posh accent asked the conductor for a ticket to Kingstown, the old English name for Dún Laoghaire.

He said, You're on the wrong tram for Kingstown, ma'am. The last tram for Kingstown left twenty-one years ago.

She glared at him. Then she saw that he was wearing a German Swastika badge.

You are a traitor for wearing that badge, young man. You should be ashamed. Irishmen are dying for their country.

Not *my* country ma'am, he says.

Most of the other people are smiling now. She's a silly old lady. But then another lady starts.

Yous are both entitled to your opinions, she says, but we are a neutral country now, so yous are not allowed to fight, anyway. So shut up, both of yous.

My Ma loves that story. She stops making the big bed in her room and smiles at it all.

What's 'neutral', Ma? I ask.

That's when a country refuses to take sides, to fight in a war. Mr de Valera is keeping us out of this war.

Why do you always say *Mister* de Valera and Dada never does?

She thinks a bit.

Dada doesn't like Mr de Valera, she says. He says that he is not a friend of the working man.

Do you like the working man, Mama?

Sure, aren't I married to the hardest-working man of them all? And she smiles at me like she hopes that I agree. I do.

And why do some people say 'yous', Mama?

Well that's because there's no word in English for saying 'you' when there is more than one person that we are talking about. So the Irish down the country say 'ye' and some Dubliners say 'yous'. So that they can still speak as they would if they were speaking in Irish.

She stops and looks at me to see if I understand. I don't yet.

So why do we not say 'yous' or 'ye'?

Well, and she smiles, in this part of Dublin we like to think we speak the best English. More like the educated English.

But we're not really English, Mama, are we?

No, not at all, she says. But we like to speak properly.

So why don't we all just speak Irish as well, and get our exams and all?

She goes over to the window and wipes away some dust from a windowpane.

Can you stand on the chair, Bernard, and wipe the top panes for me, please?

So what about Irish then? I ask.

Someday I'd like to learn it. Will you work hard at it now? Maybe you can teach me when you are fluent?

I will, Mama, I say.

A few days later, she tells me that I am to go to elocution lessons with Miss Fawcett after school two days a week.

Your accent is getting very Dún Laoghaire, Bernard, she says. It's not like we speak.

Miss Fawcett is good looking, and I get a warm feeling when I'm with her on my own. 'Dis', 'dat', 'dese' and 'dose' are out now, and I must never say 'yous'.

Bandit country

There is a big problem with going to my new school in town. When I get off the tram, on the way home I have to walk through the poor people's houses at the bottom of York Road.

Here's your stop, sonny, says the conductor to me.

Thank you, I say back to him. I know it too well.

Anybody else for bandit country? he shouts, and the people laugh.

I don't laugh, because I'm frightened. This road is a sort of mongrel. The bottom is poor and the top of it rich. Our house is in a small terrace off the posh part.

At the top of it is the Kingstown Presbyterian Church, all shiny white granite, a Protestant orphanage covered in Virginia creeper, the Kingstown Grammar School for Boys, and four-storeyed houses for the rich people. The houses stand behind tall trees and neat little gardens.

But below the tramline is the old, poor part of York Road leading down to the harbour. Rows of dark red brick council houses with dozens of kids in raggedy clothes live there. Workers in black suits from the coal boats and fishing trawlers hang around the pubs. Then the Dún Laoghaire County Council built more houses for the poor people on the 'good' side, above the tramlines. They stopped only eight hundred yards from all the Protestant Kingstown places. It was a real shock for these rich people. My father tells us at dinner time about their letters to the editor of *The Irish Times*.

They say that this is what independence in Ireland means, says Dada. Falling standards. Humph, he says.

Mama looks warningly at him. Like he might say 'bloody' any minute. I love it when he talks like this. When he talks at all.

They objected, held meetings, wrote letters, but the houses went up, he says. Their protests failed. He shakes out his paper. But I wish that those rich people had succeeded. For me, these houses are a nightmare. I call it 'bandit country' now too. I know why it's called that.

In the morning, going to school, I walk down York Road and through it all. It's fine then, as the poor kids are at school too. But coming home in the afternoon, my tram stops in the middle of it. At the best of times I am a bit of an eejit. I love staring at strange people and things, and it gets me into trouble.

Hordes of snotty-nosed, screaming boys play cowboys and Indians with bows and arrows and sticks for guns. Girls play hopscotch on their magical chalk squares on the concrete pavement or jump over skipping ropes real fast without falling. This is the cause of my first fright. I gape at the girls' knickers flashing white on and off and on again as they jump the ropes.

Hey, you. Would ya ever feck off? the girls yell at me.

One calls her brother, and I run. My heart is thumping. They chase me, yelling their heads off. I run, with my school bag bouncing on my back and my chest paining in the lungs.

They stop where the council houses come to an end. I look back, out of breath. The next few days I walk through, pretending to be the invisible man, but still panicky. Nobody notices me.

One day I feel my leather satchel being grabbed from behind. My heart jumps. My schoolbag's a target. These kids use a belt or string to hold their schoolbooks together. They can't afford leather satchels. They empty out my school bag with little careful shakes onto the pavement. Exercise books, four or five lesson books, all in Irish, a ruler, two pencils, a rubber, a pencil sharpener.

Can you talk Irish? demands the leader, the biggest fellow. He's got a book open.

The others jeer. *Póg mo thón!* they yell. Kiss my arse.

I want to cry. I am very frightened. The shouting is all around me. My things are being passed around in their dirty hands. Mama'll kill me if I lose all this. She can't afford to buy them again.

Say something in Irish then, they shout.

Cad is ainm duit? I say.

Is that all you can say? 'What is your name?' They jeer.

Tabhair mo rudaí ar ais dom le do thoil, I say.

What's that mean, are you being cheeky now?

Please can I have my things back? That's what I said.

'Pleez can I have my tings back,' the leader imitates me.

Let me burn the little bollix at the stake, Larry, pleads an Indian.

Yeh, we'll burn him, then we won't have to give him back his stuff, says the leader. They scream with delight, and bring sticks and newspaper from behind a hedge in a front garden. I start to snivel. I am not brave.

Who's got matches? The jeers are terrible when they see the tears. I never see these kids crying, even when their parents beat them on the street with a belt or a stick. One or two adults are in the distance down at the shops. I think my only hope is to cry and to beg, so I do. I feel ashamed.

I've only got one pair of shoes, I whine. If you burn them I'll get into terrible trouble.

Larry, the leader, is looking at me, a sneer on his face. You better promise us that you'll go home another way. We don't want you here on our street, do we?

He turns to his gang. Go home another way, they all yell together. They untie me, throw the bag at me, and tell me to feck off and not to come back.

I run. At the top of the road, where the posh houses begin, I sit down on the kerb. I feel terrible, like my heart is going to burst. But everything is in my bag except the pencil sharpener.

My Ma stops peeling the potatoes and listens to my story. Then she says I could borrow a sharpener at school until next month when she'd buy a new one. That one of yours will sharpen every pencil on York Road, she says with that little smile she uses when she thinks something is funny but doesn't want to show it.

And I can't get off the tram at York Road any more, I say. I really want a bit of sympathy.

Well, why don't you get off the tram at George's Street and come up through Cross Avenue?

That's three stops further on, and it's a halfpenny more. That's…em, I work it out in my head, twopence halfpenny a week.

Well that'll be cheaper than losing all your books, my Ma says. Then she smiles again.

Did they light the newspapers? she asks. I swear she was smiling, and I am hurt because she thinks it was funny, I can tell.

No, I tell her. They had no matches.

She laughs and touches my hair then.

Dermot is listening with big eyes to all this. Then he says, I wish they had lit the fire. I slap him on the side of the head.

Mama says, Now stop it, or you'll both go to bed with no supper.

Dermot starts to cry and says to Mama, Will you tell Dada when he comes in, Mama, that Bernard hit me?

Go to your room, Bernard, and you go out in the garden, she says to Dermot. I go out and slam the door, and run away down the road. I have a penny saved up, so I buy four honey bees.

Patrick arrives and Dada makes holy show of me

I want to write to Mama in hospital please, Dada.

Use a piece of your exercise book, he says. And hurry up now. I'm going to see her in a minute and I don't want to miss visiting hours. It's four years since Dermot came along, and I'm almost nine years old. We need a girl. I'm very excited. Maybe it'll be a girl, and then Dada will prefer her and not Dermot. He's always saying he wants a girl. I think boys are a bit disappointing, maybe.

The day after Mama is gone he makes a holy show of me.

Get the cart out, Bernard, he says. I can hear a horse.

Now I know he's going to make a show of me. I pull the little wooden box on its four old pram wheels out of the coal shed and down the side entrance to the front gate. I can hear the horse neighing down the road.

I look at the road. No droppings. I hate what comes next. Dada comes out of the house, waving the coal scuttle shovel. We don't have any coal, but that's what we call it. We only have turf, because of the war. When I ask Dada if we'll get coal again from England, he asks me if I know that the man Swift who wrote *Gulliver's Travels* said: 'Burn everything English, except its coal.'

But why, Dada?

Because he wanted the English to get out of Ireland, you see.

I think of all the English things in our house. The cups and saucers, my shoebrush, my toothbrush – all with 'Made in England' on them. If we burn all that we'll have nothing left. Except the turf that's cut out of our bogs for burning.

C'mon now, says Dada, and we go out the gate and follow the sound of the horse. He talks like he's going to enjoy himself.

I look around to see who's gawking at us. Down at the bottom of the road, there's the horse and cart and the man pulling sacks of turf off to deliver to somebody. I can see the trail of brown droppings from here on the black tar.

C'mon, calls my father again, and I pull the cart behind me.
He's scraping the balls of manure together into little piles. He
scoops them up with his shovel and plonks the stuff in my cart. It's
got steam coming out still, and smells sweet like grass.

Just then, Mary O'Brien comes along and says, Nice day to be
doing that. She's my friend Davey's older sister, and she'll tell him
and all the neighbours. He's made a real show of me, so he has.
A horse doesn't do it like a cow – all in one place. He walks along
the road dropping his number two. So I have to walk all the way
to the bottom of the road after him. It's terrible.

Back in the front garden, Dada picks up his big gardening spade.
This is all free, he says. And it's the best manure for spuds.

He smiles sideways at me. He talks like this when he's with me on
his own. He doesn't stutter, either. When Mama is there he just
keeps quiet.

He throws a spadeful into the first drill. He's delighted with
himself, I can tell.

I help him spread the horse's stuff all along the drills he has dug
where we used to have a lawn. He's already planted two rows. He
puts the seed potatoes carefully along the bottom of an empty
drill. I help him throw earth on top.

Will the potatoes we grow here taste of horse, Dada? I ask.

No, they won't, he says. These spuds will be the sweetest you
ever tasted.

I love helping him when he lets me, but not when he makes a holy
show of me.

So I write a note to Mama that night.

'My dear Mama. How are you Mama, are you very well? And
I'm going to call the baby Bernadette, would you like to call it
that? But Mama Dada is making a show of me. Please God you
will be home soon again. Love from Bernard. x x x x x x x x x x '
When we visit Mama I give her my letter and tell her what

happened, while Dada is talking and smiling with the nuns. She starts to laugh. I go red.

It's not funny, Mama, I say, but then I start laughing as well. The new baby is not a girl, and he's called Patrick.

In case we die

Mr Kelly is a big fat insurance man who comes at the same time every week. During the school holidays I like to listen to what he says to Mama.

Why does Mr Kelly always say that death is just around the corner, Mama?

Well, I suppose it's his way of saying that we have to be ready for it.

What do you give him a penny a week for?

That's in case any of you children die. If you do, the insurance will pay for your funeral.

Next week, I ask big fat Mr Kelly which corner death is around.

Oh, it can be any corner or every corner, he says. Consumption, diphtheria, scarlatina, typhoid, cholera, polio. They're all out there waiting. That's why your mammy is very wise to buy the insurance in case you die. The cost of dying is very high, y'know.

How much is it to die?

Before he can tell me, Mama arrives from the kitchen and says, Now don't be asking all these questions. Mr Kelly is very busy. After he's gone, I ask Mama. Might I die?

Remember I told you about the first baby that was born dead? she says. Lots of children die in Ireland because there are so many diseases. And we had to pay a lot of money to the priest and the funeral people for his burial.

What was his name, Mama?

John, she says, and looks away.

I don't like my name. Can I be called John?

Your second name is John, she says. And she smiles like she's done something good.

Why did you call me Bernard, then?

Because we had a relation on Papa's side in France, Bernard Mullett, who was a Cistercian monk. He was a very good and holy man. The people there want to have him canonised a saint.

Do you want me to be a saint, Mama?

Well, that would be lovely, Bernard, but it's very difficult. She looks sort of sideways at me. No, I wouldn't want you to be. But I do want you to be good and not to get into trouble or get into bad company.

She pulls her green cardigan across her chest and carefully picks a long rusty hair off.

Will you promise me those things? she asks. My poor brothers were lovely boys, just like you. And they got into bad company and ended up very unhappy.

Was it whiskey that made them unhappy? I ask. Uncle Gerald had come to visit us a few weeks before. He put down a big bottle on the table and laughed and winked at me. Mama came in from the kitchen with her worried face, wiping her hands on her apron and said, Don't be joking about that stuff, Gerald, and he said, Let him have a drop, and Mama said, Are you mad? He's only a child.

It was whiskey, she says. And other things.

The Rosary doesn't work, so no more babies

It's three years later, I'm eleven and Mama is back in hospital. This time we kneel down at night and offer up the Rosary for a girl. Every night.

But it's another boy, and they say he's called Thomas. His hair is black this time, and his eyes are brown like Dada's. He's the only one of us like Dada. So the Rosary is not for girls.

Will you ever have a girl? Dermot and I ask Mama.

She says no, because Baby Jesus is not going to send any more babies.

I'm glad, Mama, I say, because where are you going to put us all?

4

Dada and his mailboat

WE'RE GOING ON the mailboat! We're going on the mailboat! shouts Patrick, and Dada smiles like he is happy too. Patrick is big enough to shout now. Dermot carries the egg sandwiches that Mama has made for us. Thomas is too young to come.

Dada never has his cross face on when he takes us somewhere. I think he gets excited quietly inside. I know that he likes it when he has us to himself. Without Mama. Now he's in charge. I watch him quietly. When he looks at me he smiles, and I know it's going to be a good day.

He gets free passes on the mailboat to Holyhead over in Wales. We arrive at the boat pier at half past eight in the morning. The porters tip their caps to Dada and I feel proud of him. He's an important man down here. They all know him because he works for the London, Midland and Scottish Railways, and they own the mailboat. He raises his hat and smiles back.

The *Hibernia* sails with a lot of fuss, because she has to go out backwards. We wave to the people at the end of the east pier. She blows her siren three times to say goodbye to Dún Laoghaire.

We can run all over the boat, except to first class. We go down below to the engine room with Dada. The noise and steam and brass things are great. He is very careful, and holds Patrick's hand all the time. Dermot follows them.

Don't go wandering off, he says to me.

Can I go into the engine room, Dada? I shout over the clanking.

No, it's too dangerous, he says. You could be killed. And he frowns at me. I don't want to upset him because he's in a good mood and he's talking to all of us.

We sit out on deck and Patrick is on one side of him and Dermot on the other. I don't mind little Patrick, but I wish Dermot would go for a walk and get lost.

Have you been up at the front yet? I ask him.

Dada shakes his head at us and Dermot doesn't budge.

You call it the 'bow', says Dada, and the back is the 'stern'. He looks at me like he has more to tell, so I stand in front of him and ask him if he's ever worked on a big boat like this.

Then Dermot says he can't see the sea because I'm standing in the way. Dada doesn't hear his whinging, so I kick him on the foot.

I used to go on the B&I boats from the North Wall to Liverpool, says Dada.

Dermot pulls his sleeve and says, Dada, he kicked me.

Did not, I say without thinking. But I think he had seen.

S-s-sit over here, he says to me, pointing to the space next to Patrick. When he thinks there is going to be trouble, he stutters. I hate Dermot, the little troublemaker. Dada is quiet now and doesn't say anything else. We go for a walk around the deck. Dada is a nervous sort of man and doesn't like us to wander off, so I stay with him.

In Holyhead he takes us to a fish and chip shop with mugs of tea and all. We walk to the engine sheds, and there are huge engines – much bigger than the Irish ones.

They have to pull the Irish Mail to London, says Dada.

When can we go on that train? we ask him.

When you're bigger.

Noise and steam and coal dust are all around us. A shunting engine clangs past, and the driver waves. Dada looks at his watch and says we must listen for the siren of the Cambria. It's taking us back home at three o'clock.

We love the mailboat and the trains and the different places Dada takes us. He is happy doing those things. He likes a bit of adventure, we can tell.

Stealing a tram

Davey O'Brien, my best friend, has red hair and is nearly a dwarf he's so small. But he can run and escape the bigger boys when we're in a fight and I get caught. He's clever, too.

Both of us love the trams. One day after school we decide to steal one. I feel the thrill swirling around in my stomach and I'm afraid too. But it's a great feeling. We watch the trams come in to the stop at the top of Marine Road. We wait till a conductor gets off the platform and strolls into the sweet shop to buy fags and chat to Dolores Doyle.

We look at each other and Davey says, Go! We jump onto the platform and I bash the dinger. Ding! One for 'go'. We stare at the driver's back but he doesn't look over his shoulder. He pulls the big handle and stamps on the bell on the floor to get people on the street out of the way.

Uwwwwwwnnnnn. We're off.

Watch the driver, I whisper to Davey, and I'll let the people on and off.

Davey sits just inside, where he can see the driver. When we see the conductor running out of the shop, arms waving and his mouth wide open shouting after his tram, we burst out laughing. But I feel panicky as well, and nearly jump off at York Road. Maybe some bandits will get on. Please God, no. They'll know.

But only one old lady climbs on and says, Me feet are killin' me. I smile, and she goes inside.

Almost all the way to Blackrock we get away with it. People get on and off, some still with their pennies in their hands, wondering where the conductor is.

A free ride, eh, lads? says one smart Alec. Have yous kidnapped yer man? and he grins like he knows.

When I get home, I tell my Ma. Sometimes she enjoys these things and I think that she was a rapscallion too when she was young.

That's very bold, Bernard, she says with her funny smile. Her mouth goes like the equilateral triangle that we learned about in geometry last week.

Euclid would like your mouth, Mama, I say.

Why?

Because you make your mouth like a triangle when you don't want us to see you laughing.

Who's Euclid? asks Dermot.

Feck off, I whisper in his ear.

Oh, Mama! Bernard said the F word.

No, I didn't. I said 'feck'. I give Dermot a dig in the ribs.

Now you are being bold, she says. But she is still thinking of the fella on the tram who said we'd kidnapped your man. Mama's great gas when she's not worrying about something. I really like her when she's smiling.

She doesn't tell Dada the tram story. I hoped she would, because he might laugh too. He isn't very well.

He's got a duodenal ulcer, Mama says.

That night, Dermot and I ask him how he's feeling.

He smiles and says, It's my 'Ulster' and you know that's trouble. Then he puts on his headphones and says no more.

What'll happen to him, Mama? Will he die?

Oh please God no, she says. Don't say such things.

She has her worried face on now most of the time.

A few months later, Davey and I and Dada and Patrick are raging. They are stopping the last of the trams and bringing in the buses. My father calls the authorities 'bloody eejits'. It's a crying shame, he says. Mama frowns at him for saying 'bloody' but we can see that she's upset too.

Our trams were made here in Inchicore, you know, Dada says to the teapot. Hundreds of Irish jobs gone now. Those blackguards have kow-towed to the English again. Leyland howareyou. They'll regret this.

He's really angry. Dada gets a seat off the last tram from a friend of his when the hooligans pulled it to pieces after its last journey. He puts it in the hall where we see it every day after that. It makes me sad every time I look at it.

So, it's the boring green Leyland buses after that, and tar in the tram tracks so the old fellas on their way to Mass on their bikes won't get stuck, some eejit says.

Sure, if they got stuck before this they went straight to heaven when they got hit, says Davey's father.

Cold, hungry and tired

The winter is very cold and wet. It even snows. It's mostly dark and raining when my father comes home from work. He cycles up the Dublin quays from the North Wall to Tara Street station every night. In the rain, wind and darkness. He reads his paper on the train to Dún Laoghaire, and then unlocks his other black Raleigh bicycle in the dark station shed and rides two miles uphill home. He says we are a two-bike family. One night his galoshes are filled with rain and his raincoat has let in the water too – he can't afford a better one. I feel sorry for him and remember that I used to take off his bicycle clips when I was little, in our first house.

I can see that he's cold and hungry and tired. He pulls off his galoshes at the hall door and bangs them on the wall to get all the water out.

Mama comes into the hall and says, Won't you close the door, it's freezing. I can see that annoys him. How can he close it until he has finished with the galoshes?

Can I take off your clips, Dada, I say before I realise what I am saying.

He looks around surprised. What d-did you say? he asks.

The wind and rain are making a lot of noise. I point down at his wet trousers and say, Don't you remember I used to take your clips off? But I'm nervous now to just do it. It's been years since I was little. I can see that he's embarrassed.

If y-you l-like, he says, and hangs his hat on the hallstand.

I go down on one knee and reach for his ankle. He moves his foot, and I'm afraid he really doesn't want me to do it. But now he's taking off his raincoat and I see the shine of the clip. I pull it off with a snap and look up. He's heard the snap and is smiling at me. So I search his other ankle and pull off the other one and stand up and hang them in their place.

I'm f-famished, he says and gives me little grin.

At that moment, I love him. I love my father who is so grumpy always with his 'Ulster' and his stutter and not being able to hear properly. I just know he's a good man. I hope Mama doesn't tick him off any more tonight.

But my mother has to tell him anything that I have done right *and* wrong during the day. I think that she is just trying to involve him, but he doesn't want to be.

I remember one day when I'd heard Mama complaining to Aunt Tracy that Papa ignored his sons and look what happened to them.

Ah now, said Aunt Tracy, Gerry doesn't ignore Bernard, does he? All my aunts and uncles call him Gerry when we're not there.

That's his real name. Gerard Mary Ryan.

Yes, he does ignore him, and he never praises the child, Mama said. Even when he makes lovely Meccano models and draws trains, you'd imagine he'd show an interest.

They don't talk for a bit. Then Mama says, You know that he was brought up by his sister, Aunty Kitty. She never married. Should have been a nun. She was much older, and not a person to bring up a-nine-year-old boy. So he never learned what it is like to be part of a family, you see.

I think that maybe Mama is afraid to punish me herself, and wants him to do it instead.

One night he says to her, Why are you t-t-telling me all this? Do you want me to b-b-be the ogre? Do you want me to smack him? Why don't y-y-you do it yourself?

But tonight we all go quiet at the table and watch her. I feel nervous because this is about me. He's right for once, I think. She gets up and goes back into the kitchen. I can see that Patrick and Thomas are just waiting for the row to begin tonight. It's coming. I can feel it too. Dermot looks like he's enjoying it.

Then Mama does it. She tells him that I'd thrown stones at the cat next door.

I didn't throw stones, Mama. Only *one* stone at that cat. I hate it that she says 'stones' and there was only one. It was going to catch the baby chickens, Dada, she could see that.

Don't call your mother 'she', he says.

Then Dermot says, He threw sticks as well, Dada, I saw him. I grind my teeth and turn on him.

Telltale! He's a telltale tattler, I shout.

Mama says not to fight. I don't know who I want to hit. But someone. I often want to hit someone these days when the rows start. She begins to make more excuses, without telling my brother to shut up. She'd encouraged him by starting it. She doesn't mean to, but she does. And my clever little brother knows how to make things worse.

I want to eat my supper in peace. I look at Dada. It seems ages since I took off his bicycle clips in the hall. I feel like a right fool to be fighting again. I need to ask Dada about my homework. The sums are hard, and I don't want to go to school tomorrow if they're wrong. Brother Lynch will lynch me.

Dermot starts to say something else in that voice of his, all goody-goody. Something breaks inside me and I can't see properly. I turn around on my chair and punch him hard on the arm. He yells, and starts to cry straight away – too soon, like he wants to. To make me look even worse.

You are a feckin' telltale. You are a little shite. I'll kill you if you tell tales again on me.

Dada is staring at me with his knife and fork in the air. He starts to stutter something.

You can go to hell too, I shout at him.

I don't know how this is happening, and I don't want it to, but it happens.

I glare at him, livid. You don't mind him telling tales. Davey O'Brien's father won't allow telling tales in their house. He says it's cowardly. Cowardly! I shout at him. He looks shocked.

Dermot is snivelling.

Please stop shouting, Mama says to me. She's crying now too.

Will you stop telling Dada things that I did? You started it. What kind of a mother are you?

She is so stupid.

Mama's heart, soul and head

I'm thirteen and a bit now. I hate my Ma's worried face, but I love it when she smiles, makes a joke or just listens to my blather. When she won't listen I want to smash something or somebody. I

74

hate and love my mother at the same time.

It's great when I can get something from my Ma without a row, something ordinary. And it's not so hard.

You're annoying the heart and soul out of me, she says when we pester her for something. When she says that, we know that she is going to give in. Like money for the pictures. One morning during the summer holliers she has her red hands in the kitchen sink up to the elbows washing clothes. I sit on the orange box with its new home-made cushion, waiting to put the wet clothes through the wringer for her. I pester her and she says it: You're annoying the heart and soul out of me.

Silence. I must wait a few minutes. Then, It's a shilling I need. When do you think I can have it Mama?

When you finish the drying up *and* make your bed *and* tidy your room *and* wring the clothes out *and* hang them on the line, she says.

What happens if you lose your heart and soul, Mama?

She turns and looks at me. Well, I suppose you only have your head then.

When do you say somebody has lost their head, then? I ask.

She plunges her hands in the suds. You lose your head when you're in love, she says.

Are you in love with Dada?

She stops in the middle of squeezing, and I see her give her triangular smile to a soapy shirt. Oh yes.

It's true, I can see that. I almost forget the shilling.

Open my purse, there are two sixpenny bits there. What picture are you going to see?

'The Durango Kid' and another one with James Cagney, I tell her.

I know Cagney's Irish, but he's very rough, she says, and looks at me sort of doubtful.

But it's OK today. We are getting on well.

He is tough, Mama. That's why we like him.

I say goodbye and fly down the garden path before anything can go wrong.

Dada loves the way Dubliners talk. Jems, he calls them. One nice evening he comes in early.

I heard these two Jems talking in a shop, Lily, he says to Mama. They were very serious. Then one Jem said to the other, 'an the next 'ting happened was... I said nuthin'!

Dada's shoulders shake with laughing, his eyes water. Then he says, wouldn't Jimmy Joyce have loved that?

It's great to see them like this.

The library versus Mass

At the beginning of the school holidays, Mama says that she wants me to go to Mass every day.

But why, Mama? We don't have to.

She bends over the sink. She often tells me things that I don't like when she is looking into the kitchen sink. Father Martin was saying that if we really love God we'll go whenever we can.

My stomach gets tight. But I want to go to the library, Mama. Please. Not Mass.

She turns around and looks at me with my angry face. Does my Ma really believe this? I'm already thinking of the lies I'll have to tell her. I slam the hall door shut and don't say goodbye to her.

Next morning, I cut to the left at Cross Avenue and down Library Road. I love the granite steps leading up to the big wooden doors with their big shiny brass knobs at the Carnegie Library. It smells of books, like a dry sort of perfume.

First I go into the Newspaper Reading Room. Old men go in

there and it's got a lovely smell of ink. One day at home, my
father had put down his paper and said to Mama, If you want to
read about love, go to the murder columns. Shhh, said my
mother, the child is listening.

I wasn't interested in love, but the rest sounded exciting. And
what did she mean 'child'? I am nearly fourteen.

All the papers are clipped in behind wooden sticks on big stands.
All you hear is coughing and the clearing of throats and rustling
paper. Some of the old men ignore me, and some of the ones I see
every day smile at me. I turn to the murder and accidents pages.

Murder makes the world go round, said one old fella one day in
a loud voice.

Ah, don't talk shite, Tommy, answered another.

One murder and you're a villain, said the first man, and kill a
million and you're a hero.

I cross the hall and go into the book part of the Library. The lady
there says it's for children who are interested in reading, and you
are very welcome young man, indeed you are.

When I get home, Mama is dusting in the drawing room. I say
hello and go into my room. But Mama calls out. Who said Mass,
Bernard? she asks, and what was the sermon?

All about John the Baptist and the River Jordan, Mama.

She asks no more questions. But I hate telling lies to my Ma. It
spoils the library, and it's worse if I get caught. I hate the priests
who tell my mother these things.

5

Boy Scouts banned

MAMA, MAMA, I'M going to join the Boy Scouts, I yell.

What do you mean? she says. Won't you bring the biscuits in to the drawing room please, Bernard.

But she's got her worried face on. I run out to the kitchen. Fig rolls, my favourites.

Mama is sitting on the settee, staring out the window. She pulls a cover over the hole worn in its arm. I hold out the plate to her. She says thank you.

No, Bernard, I don't want you joining the Scouts, she says.

Ah, Mama, you don't mean it, I say. I must join the Scouts. David and Colm are joining. They're joining this week, and they're getting their uniforms and all. What do you mean I can't join? What's wrong with them?

You can't join because … She pauses before she continues. I don't like some of the boys who belong to the Scouts. They are not a very nice type of boy.

Who, Mama?

My voice is rising. I can tell when she's got a bee in her bonnet and is not going to give in. I'm panicking now. I'm afraid and angry at the same time.

What boys, Mama? You know David and Colm. You like them.

It's some of the other ones, she says, like Gerry Hannigan and Tommy something. They are corner boys.

No they are not, Mama. What's wrong with them?

They are not respectable boys, she says. Their families are poor, I know, but I've seen Mr Hannigan coming out of public houses and going into the billiard saloon down near the park. Only riff-raff go into those places, Bernard.

I'm getting desperate now. When she gets going like this she's very stubborn. She's stupid about what other people are like. And I hate that voice that says she's going to half-cry.

We can't afford the uniform anyway, Bernard, she says, frowning now. Please don't argue with me. I don't want you mixing in bad company and meeting the wrong people. You never know where you'll end up.

You just worry I'll turn out like your brothers, I shout back at her.

I can see her face going hurt and sad. That's not a nice thing to say, she says.

Well its true that's all you worry about, I shout at her. You've said that before. I don't drink whiskey or go out with Protestant girls or marry them like your brothers did, and anyway, if I did I'd stay with them and not run away to England.

Now I'm angry and saying things that hurt her. I hate these daft reasons and I'm frightened that she really will stop me.

I'm going to join. Whether you like it or not, I say. And I'm going to ask Dada this evening when he comes home.

I'm shouting loud now. I pick up a rubber ball that's lying on the floor and smash it into the fireplace. Bits of wood and sticks and ashes fly out onto the rug. She can tell him if she likes. I hope Dada is not working overtime, because we can't talk to him when he's tired and hungry. But maybe he was in the Scouts when he was young. Maybe he'll know about the campfires and the cooking, the tents, the knots and the hiking and all, those things that I have heard about. It's adventure, said Colm, you must join.

Will you lay the table please, Bernard, Mama calls out. She hasn't told him about the ball in the fireplace. She's feeling guilty. I want to say, Lay it yourself. But I'm not that stupid. I can hear her telling Dada about the Scouts. I lay the table, and then Dermot and Patrick come in and sit down. Thomas is asleep. My brothers are looking nervous because they can tell when there's trouble coming.

Mama brings in the tea. Smoke from the frying pan fills the room like a blue fog. There's a stack of fried bread on a dish, and another one of mixed fruit jam for afterwards. Dada comes into the room and sits down. He doesn't look at me. He never does. Mama puts down his plate of tripe and onions.

Then she brings in a fresh teapot for him and shows him her worried face. Nobody says anything. I can feel the room getting tight. Nobody talks until Patrick says he'd like a puppy dog. He's seen one today down the road and can he have one, please?

Dada likes dogs and he likes Patrick. Everybody likes him because he's got glasses and he's very young for them. And he's got a nice nature and never causes trouble like me.

Dada says, Yes if your mother agrees.

I wait.

She looks sort of confused and says, If we can afford it.

Dermot says that the Gregans are giving the puppies away and Patrick says he wants to call it Lassie.

I take another piece of fried bread from the pile.

And can I ask a question, Mama? She doesn't look at me, and I turn to Dada.

Is it all right for me to join the Catholic Boy Scouts of Ireland – David and Colm are in it already and the uniforms are not expensive and please I'll be good and help Mama around the house and you with the garden. All in a rush.

There is silence. All I can hear is my brothers munching their fried bread. Patrick slurps his milk. Mama's face is red, and she looks like she's going to cry.

I look at Dada. Will he say yes or will he say well it's your mother's decision.

Well, it's your mother's decision, he says. She's bringing you up.

I hate him I hate him. I turn to her.

You know what I said, Bernard.

I'm not your brothers, I'm just an ordinary boy. There's nothing wrong with the Scouts for God's sake! I shout.

Don't use the Lord's name, says my father.

I'm standing up now and shouting. I'm so angry, I think I'll do something terrible.

I'm nearly fourteen and you won't tell me why. You won't listen. You just say no to everything I want to do!

Dada looks across me to Mama at her end of the table.

You had better deal with this, he says to her.

He won't take my side, he won't talk about it, he won't talk to *me* about it, he just says to Mama, You deal with it.

I jump up from the table and knock my glass of milk over.

He can leave the t-t-table if he is going to shout at his father like this, he says.

You are not a father, I say. The other boys talk to their fathers all the time. You are just a lodger!

Mama says, Oh Bernard, don't say things like that.

Well you said it once yourself to him, I say. We heard you. Didn't she? I look at Dermot.

I don't remember that, he says in his holy voice.

I thump him on the arm. He yells and starts to cry. I sweep his fried bread into his lap.

There! You little telltale, I shout at him.

I kick the empty glass. I grab the door and open it and bang it against the wall.

I'm not doing my homework. I don't care about school. I'm leaving this house and it's all your fault! I yell.

I slam the door and run down the hall and slam the front door as well. I'm sobbing now with anger.

I go down the road and knock on Colm's front door.

How are you, Bernard, Mrs Brennan says. Colm is doing his homework, and what about you at this hour of the night?

I want to say, can I come and live with you, because both Colm's parents are calm and don't worry all the time about daft things. I just say, Please tell Colm that I'll see him tomorrow, and goodnight, Mrs Brennan.

She looks at me funny and says, Safe home, now.

I climb in the bedroom window when I get home and go to bed without seeing anybody. Then the dining room door opens and I hear Mama's footsteps. I know she's looking in at our door and I pretend to be asleep.

Next day, I get slapped six times by three different masters because I haven't done any work. I go with David and Colm to the Scout Hall after school and they can't believe what my mother says. I feel ashamed of having a mother like that. Colm, who is our leader, tells the Scoutmaster.

Will it help, the Scoutmaster asks me, if I give you a second-hand uniform that is near enough the right size and will cost your parents the price of a scout belt for a shilling and the badge that is threepence?

Colm grins and and I say thank you very much. Maybe it's the money after all, and I can't wait to get home to tell Mama.

I rush in all excited, and tell her.

Her face sort of crumples up.

What's wrong, Mama?

I don't know what to do, she says. I'm trying my best to bring you children up properly and now I just don't know what to do. I look at her there with her red hands in the sink, and the steam, and a big basin of wet clothes on the floor. I feel suddenly sorry for her and my insides are all empty. Like I've gone through the wringer, too.

Will I help you to wring them out, Mama?

Yes, please. Will you do that for me?

I pull a sheet out of the basin and feed it in between the wooden rollers of the wringer.

Mind your fingers, she says.

But isn't it good news? Mama, I say. I can get it all for one and three.

She doesn't smile or say anything. Her face looks terrible.

What's wrong, Mama?

I can't let you join the Scouts because of bad company, she says. You know it's my God-given duty to protect you all from it. I look at her face and try to talk. But I can't, and I run out of the house. Next day I tell the Scoutmaster a lie and say, My mother says thank you very much.

I dress up in the uniform, it's all pressed with creases, and the belt is two colours, black and yellow, and a snake like an S to fasten it with. I come home at teatime, wearing it all. Dada's in early for once. My brothers are playing in the front garden, and when they see me they rush in all excited and say, Look, Mama, Bernard has got his new uniform.

She can't say no this time. She can't.

But she cries. My father won't even look at me. He says, You are not going to disobey your mother.

Next day, Mama takes me to the Scout Hall and makes me give it all back.

I'm nearly fourteen, and I don't know what to say in front of the boys that are there and the Head Scout. He is very sorry and says, Maybe next year, and pats me on the head. I can't say anything, because if I open my mouth I think I'll cry in front of all of them. I am so ashamed.

Christmas Day

It's Christmas Day and we are all back from Mass and communion. Dermot is in the grey corduroy armchair under the Christmas tree in the drawing room. He has that little smile on his face.

I heard the Boy Scouts are going camping tomorrow up to the Dargle Valley, he says.

I know that, I say.

And you're not going, he says.

I feel hot, and my eyes feel stingy. I don't care, I say.

It's because Mama doesn't trust you, he says. And he sniggers. I feel the hotness coming up through my body. I can't see properly. Next thing, I have my hands around his neck and I'm squeezing hard. Hard.

I'm grinding my teeth and he's gargling and Patrick shouts, Mama come quickly! Then Mama is pulling my arm and crying. I jab one elbow back and feel it hitting her chest, all soft. Dermot screams. I strangle him again. Dada is there now with his arm around my neck, pulling. I can smell the cigarettes off his jacket. I've never been this close to him since I was small.

He is stronger than I am and pulls me off. Dermot runs choking out of the room.

I hate Dermot, I say. One day I'll really kill him when you're not here!

I go out in the garden. I don't want their stupid presents.

Lent

When Lent comes round we all see how long we can keep the ashes on our foreheads without washing them off. Mama says it's just an excuse not to wash. I tell her no, Brother Clancy says, Keep them there as a sign of your faith, boys.

Lent is the worst time for everybody. That's when the Redemptorists come out of their monasteries to scare us. It's coming up to Easter and it's a very holy time. My father says the Redemptorists are a holy terror. He's funny like this. He criticises even the Church sometimes. He just loves criticising. But even the Brothers at school seem a bit scared of the Redemptorists. Brother Kennedy says the missioners go out to Africa and foreign places, teaching the heathen about God.

And you lot are as bad as the heathen, you little kaffirs.

Is that a Latin word, sir? asks Raphael Byrne.

No it is not, he says all cross. Stand out to the line.

Raphael has to stand next to the wall for the rest of our Latin class.

Why do they bring these priests to shout at us during Lent, Mama? we ask.

They don't shout, she says. They emphasise things.

But I can see in her face she knows they shout to scare us. Then she says, We get used to our priests during the year, and the missioners are specially trained to tell us what we must and must not do.

In what, I ask, shouting?

Now don't be cheeky, she says, and carries on ironing.

Well, I like going to hear them raising their voices, I say, because they make a change from boring old Father Martin and them.

And the others. Not 'and them', she says.

You see, even you say that our priests are boring.

No, I didn't. I was correcting your grammar.

So we survive the cold and the wet and the missioners, and summer tries to get into Ireland by the back door. The wireless says that there is sunshine on the Irish Riviera.

That's the part around Glengariff, says Dada, finishing his dinner. That's where the Gulf Stream hits the coast. He adjusts his headphones and the last thing he says is, They have palm trees down there, just like Spain. Then he is gone. Into the world of the BBC. While he listens, he runs a crust of bread around his plate, mopping up the gravy as usual.

I check my geography book and he's right. I saw all the places with Mediterranean climates in my atlas. California, South Africa, Australia, Chile. It'd be great if he talked more.

Strange relations

Mama gets a letter from England, from one of her brothers. Her face goes all serious because her brothers lose children and wives and jobs all the time.

Then she smiles and says, There's good news from Harry, he's got a new job and he's stopped drinking. Her eyes water a bit. I want to get her off those brothers.

Besides all your brothers, where else have you got relations, Mama?

In Wexford. Would you like some tea?

Yes, please.

Tea means that she wants to talk. Dermot is away playing down the road.

She brings the tea in and puts it on the dining-room table. There's a plate of fig rolls. This is a treat.

You're a bit young to be hearing about these things, she says almost to herself.

James Mullett, Chairman, The Invincibles, 1882

I'm nearly fifteen, I say.

My grandmother was a Protestant called Brownrigg, she says. They had a farm near Enniscorthy. When she married Papa's father, her family never spoke to her again.

Why?

Because he was a Catholic, she says. The other part was that he was a merchant. He owned a public house.

Is that the same as a pub? Yes. She pours more tea.

Can I have another biscuit, please? I love talking to her like this.

Then he was arrested for being a member of *The Invincibles*, part of the Fenian Brotherhood.

What's that?

They were men who were fighting for Ireland, but they were very violent, she says, and stares out the window. They murdered two English officials in the Phoenix Park. Your great-grandfather was lucky not to be executed. He went to jail for ten years in Kilmainham.

Hey, that's great Mama, I say – and I mean it. I've got a famous great-grandfather. Mr O'Malley, our history teacher, will love this. He's always telling us about the English. Tell me more about him, Mama, please.

It's not great at all, she says, and I don't know much more. All I know is it broke my grandmother's heart. She died without her family, and her husband was broken when he came out of jail.
I think about this. She gets up and comes back with a big brown photograph of a nice-looking man wearing an old-fashioned suit and bow-tie.

There he is, James Mullett, she says. Then she puts a little leather case on the table and opens it. And that's his tie-pin.
I open the tiny case and look at it carefully. It is a piece of gold with a pearl in it at the top of a long brass pin.

Hey. Is this yours, Mama?

It will be yours one day, she says.

But Mama. His son must be Papa, your father. How did he become a captain in the English army, then?

Well that's how things are in Ireland. They say that rebellion skips a generation.

So is my great-grandfather a hero then? I ask.

I'm sure he was a brave man.
I think about what she has said.

So you should go to jail for Ireland, Mama, and I should join the British Army then?
She laughs and says, God forbid, and we hear Dermot coming in with his friend.

I don't want you to have a life of trouble and unhappiness like my family has had, she says. I pray every day to protect you from that.

She never says that about Dermot. He's not going to do those
things, I suppose. But me? I just think James Mullett is a hero.

O'Malley and Irish history

Mr O'Malley is our history teacher, and he's mad about Ireland.
We don't understand everything he says, but we don't interrupt
him. He's a storyteller.

Cúchulainn was the champion and defender of Ulster, he says.
Cú means 'hound'. The Hound of Ulster. He pauses for a moment.
It wasn't the little British puppet state that we have today. Oh, no.
Ulster was the whole nine counties and the strongest province
long ago because Cúchulainn defended it against Queen Maeve of
Connaught. Cúchulainn and his men beat her back. But he was
wounded. He knew he was dying. And what did he do?
He looks around the class. Silence.

There's forty of you here, and none of ye know. Ye are a right lot
of eejits. Who has seen the statue in the General Post Office?
There is silence, but a few of us put up our hands.

What do you see there? he asks.
Declan Finn says, A bird sir, a bird on his shoulder.

OK Finn, at least you still have a tongue in your head, he says.
When Cúchulainn knew he was dying he tied himself to a pillar.
Maeve's soldiers were afraid to advance because they thought he
was waiting for them. Then after three days, a raven landed on his
shoulder. That's how they knew the hero was dead.
He paused to let this sink in.

And why is the statue in the GPO?

Because of the 1916 Rebellion, sir, says Davey O'Brien.

Good, O'Malley says. Why? I'll tell you. Because the greatest
heroes that Ireland has produced since those ancient times gave their
lives there in defiance of the Sasanach. He lowers his voice and
walks to the middle of the classroom. The British Empire, he says.

My backbone tingles and I feel myself blush. I watch the other boys out of the corner of my eye. We all stare at O'Malley. We love him when he does this. One day, the September sun streaming through the windows and chalk dust floating in the afternoon sunbeams, he tells us about the Nine Years War: The English just couldn't conquer Ulster, but because of an error by our Spanish allies, we were eventually beaten, and the English took the Spaniards prisoners and killed the Cork and Kerrymen who'd gone to help their friends at Kinsale.

Why did they do that, boys? he asks us. I'll tell you. Because England wanted to destroy Ireland and everything Irish.

Then they drove the northern armies back to Ulster. Elizabeth sent thousands of Scottish Protestants and Presbyterians over to take the northern lands, and drove our leaders out to France and Spain.

There is an awful silence in the classroom. Two of the lads giggle, and we fear for their lives. But O'Malley does nothing.

He is close to tears, we can see.

After that, he says, the old Gaelic way of life was destroyed. The old laws, even the language, were in terrible danger. The land was taken. The land. The land is the most important thing of all, boys. Remember that. And our language. *Gan Teanga gan Tír*, Pearse said. Without a language, without a country.

He writes some of our names out in Irish on the blackboard.

You can change your names, boys, he says. If you want to. We have two official languages, you know.

Write mine in Irish too, please, sir, I say.

That night after supper, Dermot goes to do his homework in the drawing room and Patrick and Thomas are in bed. I've got my parents to myself.

I'm changing my name, I say.

What do you mean? asks Mama.

1951 school report

I'm changing it to Irish, I say. Look, Mama. Mr O'Malley showed me how to spell it. Bearnárd Ó Riain. I write it on my history exercise book.

She looks at me. I can tell she's interested. She doesn't say no you can't.

I suppose that's all right, she says, and looks at Dada.

Irish is the other official language, so anybody can change their names, he says. Ryans used to be O'Riains before the Famine. But I don't know what good it will do.

I listen to Dada because I've never heard him talk like this before.

Dada, if you could hear Mr O'Malley, you'd want to change your names as well, I say.

Ah, says Dada. But he stares out the window. I know he's thinking about it all.

What did he tell you then? Mama asks.

I tell her about O'Malley's history lesson. Dada has gone back to the wireless and his headphones. Mama looks a bit worried as I get hotter and hotter under the collar about the war and the last lost battle.

The English are such a bad people, Mama. I look at Dada. I want to hear what he says because I think that he knows this.

Now, not all of them, Mama says. But English rule in Ireland is bad. Remember that, Bernard. And she looks at me in that way she does when something is important.

Dada takes the headphone off his good ear.

Ordinary English people are all right, I work with them every day in the office, he says. It's the ruling class that are blackguards. I can see he is angry just thinking about it. I've never heard him say anything like this before. My parents are surprising me tonight.

What's your name in Irish, Mama?

Oh, I don't know, it's so long ago, and she gets a faraway look in her eye. Yes, we did Irish at school, but Papa never approved. I've forgotten.

Why did Papa not approve?

He says that Ireland is backward, and that England is the most advanced country in the world. So we should try to be like them. I see Dada's disapproving face.

But is Papa a Catholic? I ask her.

Of course he is, says Mama.

But the English are not, Mama, I say.

Dada smiles now and looks across at me. He heard that. I feel thrilled that I said something that he likes. Mama sometimes says she thinks he can lip read.

You've got him there, Dada says. Will you tell Papa what B-B-Bernard said? he asks Mama.

Oh no, I will not, she says.

Now it's her turn to have the disapproving face.

Will we all change our names then? I look at Dada again. He is smiling to himself. But he's back listening to the BBC.

Oh, I don't know, she says. We're a bit old for that now.

That night I change my name on all my schoolbooks and practise writing it. Next morning at breakfast I have a brainwave.

Let's change the name of our house, I say.

What will it be? She doesn't say no, so I find out at school that it's *Teach Mhuire*. House of Mary. A week later I sit on the wall opposite our house and look at the new sign on the gate that Mama has ordered. She's great at getting things done if she thinks it's right.

I will do something for Ireland, I say to myself. I will be part of the next Rising. Then all the names in Ireland will be in Irish again and they can send their Black and Tans to burn them down and I will be there to throw them back out again, out of this country forever.

Dada, you just look away

Your disapproving face, Dada. My heart sinks when I see it. Especially in the summertime when it is warm enough to go to the strand. And it isn't raining.

I watch you one day out of the corner of my eye sitting on the sand in your bathing costume, straps over your shoulders holding the top half up. Covering your chest for modesty. Mama is fussing over the sandwiches and plates.

My dam building is coming on. The water is glinting, speckled with sand behind the dam wall. My eyes dart backwards and forwards, watching for the sand slipping slowly away from the muddy walls. I scoop up a handful and put it carefully where the wall seems to be breaking. I am going to be an engineer when I'm big, I tell anybody who asks. I tell you, Dada, but you just look away. You are not interested. You are watching the other two, Dermot and Patrick, who are splashing around in the sea, and you wave at them.

He should be leaning to swim at his age, he says. 'He' is me. My mother tries to make up for this. She asks if my back is getting burnt.

Your critical face, Dada. It makes me so sad. I never want to see it again. What must I do to make it go away forever? Be like Dermot? But I'm not like him. He's good, and doesn't get into trouble.

I don't try to annoy you. I don't. Sometimes when I'm angry with you or Mama, I say things that I don't really mean, like I hate you or I won't go to bed or I'm going out and I don't know when I'll be back.

But I would like you to know what I'm doing and to talk to you about things. I know you have a lot to worry about because Mama tells us about it. What can I do to help? Well, I know one thing, work hard at school and get good marks, that's a big one, isn't it? So I want to do that, and I want to do so many other things too. I want to breed prize budgies and have them win rosettes at the big exhibition where all those rich people go, and I want you to come with me and smell the birdseed and hear the squawking and see the fantastic opalines and lutinos and rare albinos and all the other sorts of budgie. Will you, Dada?

Kingstown

One evening Davey and me are sitting on the railway station wall watching the trains.

Look at that feckin' thing, I say to him.

There is the word 'Kingstown' in brackets under 'DÚN
LAOGHAIRE' on the station signboard over platform one.

We could paint that out, he says.

His father is Station Master, so what we are going to do is brave
for Davey. We climb over the wall and down onto the tracks at a
quarter to ten one night. I carry a small pot of black paint and a
brush. The next train is due in half an hour. I carry a station
stepladder out, and Davey climbs up while I hold it steady and
keep nix. I open the pot and hand it up to him. It doesn't take him
long to paint out this leftover from the English.

We treat ourselves to fish and chips and wonder who will notice it
first. But nobody notices the missing 'Kingstown'. Not even
Davey's father and all his porters.

Maybe I'll hit him...

When we're wide-awake in our beds at night my brothers and I
talk. This is forbidden. Mama hears us and looks in the door.

Turn your heads to the wall, no talking, and go to sleep, she says
nearly every night.

They're talking about you, says Dermot to me one night.

We can hear my parents' voices in the dining room. It's after ten
o'clock and we're supposed to be asleep. It's a hot summer night
and the sky is still light. We have to be up early for Mass
tomorrow, it's the Feast of the Assumption.

What are they saying? I ask him.

Go and listen, he says.

I get out of bed carefully because it squeaks, give Dermot a thump
– but not too hard, in case he yells – and tiptoe across the hall.

Why don't you take him out for a walk and tell him yourself,
Dada? says my mother.

What's this about, I wonder.

He-he-he's your responsibility, he says. And how do you know he's ready?

The stains are on his sheet every morning when I make his bed, she says.

I go red with shame. I can't hear the next bit because he's stuttering.

Well, it's now that a father talks to a son, you know, she tells him.

He should be doing his schoolwork, Dada says. Look at the school f-f-fees we're paying, and he's not even interested in athletics. If Dermot can win r-r-races why can't he?

He plays rugby, and if you don't talk to him about sex, then I'll have to – and that's not right, she says.

He's not interested in school. And goes overboard with everything else. Look at the fees. He's a bloody idler. I can hear Dada's getting angry now.

Oh, he's not an idler, Mama is saying.

I want to rush in there and shout my head off at him. But I'm frightened of what will happen, what I'll do. Maybe I'll hit him. I don't think Dada knows how to talk to Mama either. Maybe he's angry because she expects him to work all day and do overtime, and then talk to us as well. Parents don't agree about much, except what you mustn't do and what you can't have.

I jump back into bed and the springs make a bad noise.

Shhh, says Patick, who's only eight but wide-awake. What are they saying?

Just the usual, I say.

6

Are you a Protestant or a Catholic?

WHY DO YOU WANT to hitchhike to Belfast? My mother has her worried look on.

To talk to Protestants, I say.

For months now, we have been hearing from Mr O'Malley and Brother Gibson all about the North. There was some disturbance between Catholics and Protestants in Derry.

Is Davey going with you?

No, I say. He's busy with his father.

Davey is working his head off to get honours in his Leaving Certificate because he wants to be a Jesuit and they only take the best. But I don't mention this.

You mustn't go on your own, she says.

Well, nobody else is interested and I want to hitch, I say. Everybody does, if they haven't got the money. I don't tell her that I'm nervous and excited all at the same time. She makes me sandwiches, still telling me that I shouldn't be doing this, but all mixed up with please be careful. I am surprised that she doesn't put up more of a fight. I nearly say that the company I'll keep in Belfast will be more dangerous than in the Boy Scouts. But I don't.

I take the bus from Dublin out towards the airport to get onto the main Belfast road.

I'm nearly sixteen, and for months now, I have been reading everything I can get my hands on about Irish history. The second-hand bookshops in Nassau Street and Dawson Street know me well. There is stuff in there that is like family secrets. Apart from Mr O'Malley at school, nobody talks about what happened in the North and how Ireland came to be divided. Even O'Malley keeps off the recent stuff, as it is frowned on by the government and the school. The headmaster, Brother Gibson, has started taking us for religious doctrine. He talks about the Catholic struggle for emancipation from the Protestant English government and their bigoted Irish allies in the North. What has got me going is that as far as I can see, the British have fooled the Protestants of the North into thinking that they are better off staying part of England.

I stand on the side of the Belfast road. It is springtime and there is a rich smell of fresh earth from the ploughing. Seagulls fight over the worms. Birds sing, and the sky is a pale blue with not a sign of rain for a change. I start walking. Five minutes goes by, and only two cars pass and one lorry. Am I mad to be here? What if nobody stops? What if the Prods tell me to go to hell? A lorry pulls over. I climb up on the step and open the door.

Where are you going? the driver asks in a Dublin accent.

Belfast, I say.

Hop in, he says. I'm goin' to Dundalk.

It's just before the border.

That's great, thank you.

Have you got family up there? he asks.

No, I'm going up to talk to Protestants.

He looks at me strangely.

What about?

Well, about why they prefer to stay part of England.

He stares ahead, and I can see that he's thinking about this.

Will you be seeing people that you know like, that you've met before? And he looks hard at me.

No. I've never been there. But that's all right. I come from Dún Laoghaire and I have Protestant friends. They don't mind me asking questions.

He says nothing while we pass through Drogheda.

The Northerners know which side their bread is buttered on, he says. The price of butter is half what it is here, and their dole is twice as much.

Why is that, then? I ask him. Isn't it because the British partitioned us in the first place?

As I climb out of his cab he wishes me luck.

Hey, he says, remember that the Prods in Belfast won't be like your friends in Dún Laoghaire. Be careful up there, and don't get yourself beaten up.

I can't understand that at all. Sure it's 1952, and there hasn't been trouble since the early forties.

The next driver is another Southerner, from Dundalk. So I tell him too.

I'll drop you in the middle of the Shankill, he says. Do you know where that is?

Oh, that'll be great, thanks, I smile back at him. Here's a man that understands. The Shankill, I know from my reading, is the heart of the extreme Protestant part of Belfast. Like the Falls Road is the Catholic one.

He looks at me funny and says nothing for a while. Then he grins over at me. Lowering his voice so that I can barely hear him over the engine, he says, You can buy frenchies in Belfast, and the priests forbid them here. I've got six children and I'd like to drown the half of them.

I'm at bit shocked because he sounds like he means it. We go into the customs at the border post and I show my passport. A customs man asks me why I'm going up there. I tell him. I'm real proud of this.

Mind they don't lock you up, boy, says a giant guard with a Cork accent. If I had my way, we'd resurrect Michael Collins and drive the Orange hoors into the sea.

I am shocked. What a way for a Catholic to speak. And about his fellow Irishmen, too. But I decide it's better not to argue with him.

Then he says, Off with you. Will we ever see you again, do you think?

By now I'm feeling a bit of an eejit. The drivers and the cop are pretty sarcastic. My stomach in a knot, I decide to tell the Ulster cops, the Royal Ulster Constabulary, straight out. I have a little speech prepared about coming in peace, and so on. But the RUC aren't bothered at all. Just wave me through the barrier before I can open my mouth.

My driver says he will not be dropping me off in the Shankill. I was only joking. I don't want them boys seeing where my truck comes from, he says.

I don't know whether to be glad or not. He drops me in the middle of a busy wide street in the city centre. I'm standing next to a bus queue. I think to myself, here goes.

Excuse me. Do you mind my asking you if you are a Protestant or a Catholic? I ask a lady about my mother's age.

I'm a Protestant, she says, and smiles. Why?

Do you mind if I ask you some questions, please?

Not at all, she says, but here's my bus. And on she gets with a friendly little wave.

She probably thinks I want to sell her a raffle ticket.

The queue moves up. They're looking at me as I think they've heard my Dublin accent. So I try another lady with shopping bags.

Do you mind…?

She interrupts me with a grin. Not at all, and I'm a Presbyterian, she says.

Just like that. The others are smiling too and I think, what a friendly lot. You see, just give people a chance.

Do you know what a Presbyterian is? she asks.

Oh yes, I say. Henry Joy McCracken was one, wasn't he? And I say the name of a Republican leader who was executed by the English in 1798. They're staring at me.

And he died for Ireland, didn't he? I say.

She turns around and says to the others, The wee fella knows his history then, and she turns to me. But sure he's long daid, she says.

She said, 'daid'. I love the Belfast accent. At that moment their bus arrives and all of them get on, and the lady waves goodbye.

I stand next to a man who is still waiting at the bus stop.

What kind of a young fool are you to be asking questions like that in this town? His voice is low and aggressive.

Are you a Catholic? I ask him, a bit nervous.

Aye, from Derry, he says.

But all those people were friendly, I say.

Don't meddle where you don't belong. And he jumps on his bus.

I go to look for a room for the night.

'Clean Lodgings' says the sign in the window in a Protestant street. I know it's Protestant because a few Union Jacks are flying. A man wearing braces opens the door.

How much is a room for the night? He tells me, and I hesitate.

Come right in. Are you from down South?

I am, I say.

Well, you're welcome anyway. Do ye want your tea?

It is half past six in the evening so I sit down with three men already there.

What are ye doin' up here then? one asks in a friendly way. Silence. One of them rattles off something in such a strong accent that I have to ask him to say that again, please.

Ye'd be better off down South getting that Church of Rome off your backs, the owner of the house says. But he has a kind voice, and he smiles while he's talking.

One dark-haired, silent type pushes his chair back suddenly and disappears.

Don't mind wee Billy, he doesn't take kindly to Fenians. That's what we call Roman Catholics.

Why doesn't he? I ask.

His father was killed in the riots in the thirties, he says.

What happened?

I'll tell ye, interrupts a man opposite me. Because the priests told the Taigs to go out and burn Protestant houses, that's why.

Now hold on, says my host. This young fella is tryin' to find out what's wrong wi' us up here, why we fight, and so on.

He laughs while he talks and they all like him, I can see.

I'll tell you son, he says. I might get a smack from yon Orangeman there, but if the English were gone we'd all get along fine. We're as Irish as you are, except that you kick with the other foot.

What does that mean? I ask him.

We say that Catholics kick with their left feet and us Prods with our right, y'see?

So when we play rugby we all kick with both feet? I ask them. They burst out laughing. Maybe we do, maybe that's why we're good. Sure we won the Triple Crown in 1948 with three Macs in the back row, two Prods and one Catholic.

Everybody nods and grins.

Why can't we join our two Irish soccer teams together as well then? I ask.

They all look like they're thinking hard.

Then one says, because there are priests and ministers and politicians on both sides who don't want change.

The woman of the house comes in then and the talk changes.

The landlord goes out of his way the next day to direct me to the main road south. Maybe for my own good.

Did you find your Protestants? asks my father.

They're the same as we are, I say. But they can't stand the Catholic Church.

He looks down at a log burning in the fireplace. You'll find very f-f-few Christians in Catholic countries. Some of our Irish Catholics are the worst.

He says this with a little smile. He knows that Mama won't like that. Sure enough, she gets a frown on her face and it goes a bit red.

And Belfast is my favourite city in Ireland, he says.

Why is that, Dada? I ask him.

I love the accent, he says.

Mary Delaney

Girls make me nervous, but I'm looking at them every day now. Secretly. The feeling in my willy these days and the throbbing in bed, is great. There is some connection between the two. But I don't know what it is.

Will you get me the *Catholic Herald*, please? my Ma asks me as she hands me tuppence.

We're coming out of Mass on Sunday from the shilling door on to Marine Road. We used to go to the sixpenny door, but now Mama says we can afford to go in where we should be.

What she means is that the shilling door is for the respectable people with fur coats and hats and perfume that kills me, and who don't sing the hymns like they do in other parts of the Church. Old Mr Flannery sings his head off in the sixpennys and you can't hear yourself pray. And the ladies in the shilling seats always look round at him with little frowns and cross faces.

Mary Delaney from the Legion of Mary is standing there this Sunday selling the Catholic papers. Now I have to buy the paper from her. She is one of those holy types who are always doing good works and going to Holy Communion every day, if they can. But she's beautiful. In a bold kind of way. Her eyes crinkle up when she smiles. She's my age, I think. And while Mama is talking about all the good works the Legion does, Mary Delaney gives me one of her crinkly smiles and says, Why don't you join us? I nearly die. I'm shaking my head but I don't know what to say.

That's a great idea, Bernard, Mama says. Mary here can show you what the Legion does.

I'm looking at Mary Delaney's chest and having bad thoughts. Next thing she gives me the Legion's little blue, white and red leaflet.

It's like the Army, Mary says, the Roman Army.

Are you here every Sunday? I ask her.

I am, she says, and gives me another of the crinkly smiles. I don't know where to look.

Mama has to say something else, of course, but I'm halfway up the road by now.

So I join the Legion of Mary. I want to be in something, to be doing something. But as far as I'm concerned, she's the only Mary in it. Most of them are real sissies and goody-goodies. They sell Catholic papers door to door as well as outside the churches. My Ma is delighted and says things like, This is far more suitable than the Scouts. I say nothing to that.

Bernard is doing well in the Legion, Dada, she says.

Oh I hope he does as well with his schoolwork, he says.

Oh stop grousing, she says, can't you say anything nice?

He hides behind his paper. I feel brave now with Mama speaking up for me.

I'm sitting here, Dada. Why don't you ask me if I am doing well? Ask me, I say.

Ah now, please don't row over this, says my Ma.

Is he never satisfied? Feck him. When the lads see me on Sundays next to Mary Delaney selling the papers outside the church, they laugh and ask me what indulgences I'm getting.

How many days off of purgatory are you gettin', Rasher? asks one.

Ah, no matter how many, it won't be enough for him. He's goin' to hell, says another.

Would you ever feck off? I whisper in his ear.

The Legion wants us to go in pairs to sell the papers door to door at night. I go out with Mary Delaney. It's a cloudy wet night and people keep asking us in for a cup of tea. She always says, No, we have to finish our rounds. We've ticked off almost everyone in the little book and collected money from all the others, and I'm in a state. Will I ask her to come to the Roman Café for a coffee?

Mary, I think that the Legion is great, The Roman Army and stuff. Would you like a cup of coffee in a real Roman place?

She looks at me like I'm making a joke and says, What?

The Roman Café on George's Street. Mrs Quinn owns it. We're all wet and cold.

What time is it?

We'll ask in the next house, I say.

It's ten to nine, and she looks a bit worried. I told my mother I'd be home by nine.

Just one coffee, and you can tell me more about the Legion?

Mrs Quinn raises one Roman eyebrow and looks at the clock on the wall. I pray that there'll be more people. Up on the balcony I see some of the lads. Annie the waitress brings the milky coffee we all love. One of the hard chaws from the balcony leers down and puts money in the jukebox and Rosemary Clooney starts singing 'You Belong to Me.' It goes, 'See the Pyramids along the Nile…'

I'm sitting there with my hands on the oilcloth, nearly touching Mary's. I haven't ever had a crush like this. I feel giddy. This is better than kneeling down beside her and saying the Rosary at the Legion meetings and smelling her scent.

Do you like this song? I ask her.

Oh, it's very nice. All about Egypt, is it?

Well, not really, it's about people in love, I think.

It stops, and Caterina Valente comes on with 'The Breeze and I'.

Will you come to the pictures with me on Saturday, Mary? I blurt out.

She gives me her lovely smile and says, No I can't, Bernard, and she looks a bit sad, like I shouldn't have asked that.

Why not? Do you have a boyfriend?

No, she laughs. I'm going to be a nun. She pauses. I'm entering the novitiate next year.

Are you serious? I ask. You're going to be a nun?

She blushes and says, I promised my mother.

But do you want to be a nun?

Yes, I do. I want to save the world from Communism.

I leave the Legion after that.

Oh, they are such good people, says my mother. Why can't you stick to them?

The Scouts are better, I say to her, and walk out. I still haven't forgiven her for that.

Forbidden Protestant fruit

As well as looking at the girls at the Adelphi and the Pavilion, Tommy Watson and Nick Heffernan and I go down the East pier at night. This pier is us teenagers' hunting ground. Contacts are made here and some lads have sex for the first time. Lots of hearts are broken.

She walks like Marilyn Monroe, says Tommy Watson.

Look at that waggle, says Nick Heffernan.

I am looking.

This amazing walk is strolling arm-in-arm with a friend in the navy blue raincoat of Glengara Park. A Protestant girls' school, forbidden fruit. Forbidden to the power of ten, says my cousin Con, who works in a bank. Excitement rises as we set off down the pier after them. Con has a bike, so he can't follow on foot. Just as well, because he's handsome. It's about seven o'clock in the evening and dark, for it's October.

They are walking quickly, and we are in full chase now. Will they turn at the bandstand? If they do, will we follow them back? There is something about the toss of the blonde hair when she takes off her beret, cheeky and exciting. And the way she swings her hips.

How old are they, about fourteen or fifteen? asks Tommy.

The big one looks about fifteen, I say. At nearly sixteen, I think I know something about girls.

They turn back and walk towards us.

Slow down, says Nick, then we can look at them in the light. As they get nearer the pool of white light under the double lamp standard, I'm desperate to see who the sexy one will look at. By this time I'm mesmerised.

They are giggling like mad and looking sideways at us. We stand like eejits in a huddle as if we have nowhere to go, stamping our feet in the cold.

She looks across and catches my eye. She flutters her eyelashes, grinning at the same time. My stomach turns.

Tommy's face says it all. She'll do it, he says.

But I can see his disappointment. He's seen who she looked at. I say, Let's follow them. Tommy hesitates, but follows. Off we go in pursuit. The sexy one looks around again, smiling back at us. Then Tommy says, If she was made of chocolate she'd eat herself. Nick kills himself laughing. The two girls meet up with more Glengara girls at the top of the pier. We slow down, outnumbered. They laugh and joke and look in our direction. I don't know where to look. Tommy keeps his eye on them.

They're going, says Tommy, and he waves. He's brave.

It is nearly nine o'clock, and they walk off towards Glenageary, a well-to-do and mostly Protestant suburb. Will they be back tomorrow? Some of the Glengara girls will report it if any of them go with Catholic boys. The fruit is just as forbidden in reverse.

Oranges and bananas, laughs Tommy when I tell him later in the Roman Café of my thoughts on the forbidden fruit, how it's more attractive.

What's so funny? I ask him a bit annoyed.

Well, the Prod girl is an Orange woman and you want her to meet your Catholic banana. He spills his coffee laughing. I decide not to tell him any more of my serious thoughts. Maybe I am a bit too earnest, as Mama says.

What did you mean, Tommy, when you said down the pier that she'll do it?

She'll eat your banana, he says, and they all die laughing. I just go scarlet. I'm a bit thick where these things are concerned.

Well, my banana is forbidden fruit for them too, I say.

We know this because last week we tried to get into a dance in the Methodist Church Hall. The minister asked us to leave. But nicely.

We are few in numbers, he said, and if one of our girls marries a Roman Catholic the children will be brought up as Roman Catholics, isn't that so?

We nodded our heads. That's what we have been taught.

He wasn't rude about it as we expected. So we decided not to be tough guys and gatecrash his dance.

Their numbers will drop, said Tommy afterwards.

They'll disappear eventually, added Nick.

None of us want that. We all get along fine. Protestants are part of our scene, and we'd miss them.

I think about my mother not being able to talk to me about girls. And Dada still hasn't, either. The Brothers and teachers only tell us to avoid impure thoughts, occasions of sin, bad company. Is Tommy bad company? He is. But we're lucky to have him.

The priests in confession mumble at us and ask how many times we've had impure thoughts and tell us our penance. Three Our Fathers, three Hail Marys and three Glory Be's. I ask Father Delaney in confession about my penis going hard. I really want to know. He says when that happens to take my Rosary beads in both hands and say a decade. Then he says, You might have to say two decades. I think I'll have to say a hundred. Particularly if I use two hands.

Show us the hairs, we ask Tommy after school. He has little bunches of hair in paper packets in an envelope. Girl hairs.

From you-know-where, says Tommy, and laughs.

I don't know where, because I've never seen any of those hairs. But I think I know.

Back at the top of the pier Nick and I are keeping watch. Con says it's too cold, he's going home. He's the only one with brains.

Then a group of girls cross the road up near the People's Park, the Glenageary end. That walk, that sway, is definitely among them. They stop, and the chattering and laughing make us very nervous. If only The Walk would look at me again. That'll be enough. For tonight. Her friend of last night walks over to us, looking back at the others and trying not to giggle. She looks at me.

My friend would like to go with you, she says.
I almost get sick with excitement. And fright.
Which one? I ask stupidly.
Joan. My friend from last night. You know, with the blonde hair. Will you go? she asks.
Down the pier? I ask like a proper eejit.
Yes.
What's her name?
It's Joan. I just told you. And yours?
Bearnárd. And em, this is Nicholas, I say.
I'm Jean. OK? I'll tell Joan. And she runs back to the rest of them.
Joan gives a little wave to her friends and walks – oh how she walks! – off towards the darkness. They call things after her I can't hear.

I'll see you in the Roman, I say to loyal Nick,
I walk after The Walk, admiring the swish of the coat. She looks back, grinning.

Hello, she says.
Hello, I say back, and we walk side-by-side towards the next pool of light.
I barely look at her, don't know what to say. We walk in silence.
Then she says, people will see us out here, don't you think?
Her accent is sort of half-English and half-Irish. Protestant. She swerves into the gateway leading to the Marble Arch, as we call it, a sort of shelter that's deserted. Except for courting couples. I

can't believe she's doing this on the first meeting.

It's dark, isn't it? she whispers. And takes my sleeve. There are other couples barely visible in the weak light coming from the seafront.

Which way do we go? she asks me. I can see her very blonde hair and her laughing eyes. We stop.

In here, I say, and we step behind a pillar.
There's a smell of piss and sea water. Will she stay here? She stands close to me with her back to the pillar, and I can feel and smell her breath. Maybe it is a Protestant smell? No, you eejit, it's peppermint.
I don't know how we start to kiss. My nose gets in the way. Her mouth is wet and so is mine after the first second. Her breathing is strong, like she has just been running. I can't breathe at all and break off, and she says no. She puts her arms right round me and covers my mouth with hers. She is breathing very loudly now and I can feel myself hot down there and excited. My penis is like a rod. She rubs herself against me and I can feel the throbbing in my pants and think she must feel it too and isn't this terrible what will she think and all the time she is kissing and rubbing and breathing like she is going to burst. She stops and holds her head against my chest.

Am I awful? She asks. Do you think I'm terrible?
I feel confused and sort of tender. I put my arms around her again.

No, I don't. I think you're terrific, I say.
Nothing like this has happened to me before. Ever.

I have to go now, she smiles, takes off her beret and combs her hair.
We walk back up to the pier.

Will you be here tomorrow night? About eight? she asks me.

Yes. Yes I will, I say too quickly, and watch fascinated as that walk disappears into the dark.

In the Roman Café, Caterina Valente's 'The Breeze and I' is playing on the Jukebox. That's Joan's and my signature tune, I think. Nick's eyes shine as I tell him a bit of what has happened. As I describe her enthusiasm, the first jealous thought comes into my head. She must have done this before. With someone. I tell Nick.

Doesn't matter, says the practical Nick. She's yours now.

But she has chosen me. So she can unchoose me.

We meet whenever school work and sports and families allow us. Joan, or JD as we call her now with her surname, tells me that she is fourteen. She looks and talks like fifteen at least.

One sunny Saturday afternoon we go on the 59 bus to Killiney Hill. She follows me to a field on the side of the hill where Davey and I used to look for nests.

The growing hay smells sweet on the hillside above the sea, the rocks are hot.

Droning bees soften our silence. Shall I touch her? Our legs are intertwined, but our bodies are not. She lies with eyes shut, a smile at the corners of her mouth.

Propped on one elbow, I confuse myself. What do I do now? The heat is all about me and also within. She stirs and twists her arm under my chest, pulling me closer. She murmurs something. The heat swims in my head, trying to get out. And in. Her hand touches my trousers. She sort of sighs. I want to die with fright at the things I want to do – but do not know how.

She moves, starting it again, and we roll, now locked, crotch to crotch. Pressed tightly, moving slightly, for that is all it takes – the heat swelling, warm sticky heat on my stomach and my shirt sticking. A blinding pain of pleasure. She moves again, moans, then smiles. And I don't know why.

Ladies and women

My mother is walking towards me in Cross Avenue one afternoon, carrying two bulging shopping bags. Just then, a woman with three kids clinging to her skirts comes tumbling out onto the street.

Look at that poor woman with those children, my Ma says, stepping aside to avoid the scuffle.

Why do you say 'woman' sometimes and 'lady' other times, Mama? I ask her.
She thinks a bit.

When I'm carrying two large bags of potatoes up the road in each hand, I'm a woman, she says. When I'm going down the road with my handbag, my gloves on and my umbrella, then I'm a lady. And she gives me her little smile.

Are you a snob then, Mama, because you use words like 'drawing room' and 'lavatory'? None of my friends' parents say them.

Well, they were used in my family, and I like to keep these things up. But I am not a snob. I don't look down on people nor look up to them either, she says. That's what a snob is. I just try to keep our standards.

Home trouble and heroics

There's a fight at the Roman. If you could call it that. I'm in a terrible mood because Mama wouldn't let me go out and there was a big row, but I went anyway. Two of the Convent girls come running in the door saying that young fellas from Dublin are touching them and want to follow them home. Up I get, and with Nick alongside, I swagger out. Three Dublin fellas are waiting.

What's the problem, lads? I ask. The girls are giggling in the doorway with scared faces.
One of the lads comes right up to me with a nice grin on his face.

113

Ah, we were only coddin' the young wans, he says, and then he puts his hands on my shoulders. The next thing there's a smack, I'm spitting out my front teeth and my eyes are full of tears. They run away laughing.

Nick chases them for a few yards and comes back. But the worst is the Convent girls. They are tittering their heads off. I pick up the teeth, and Mrs Quinn shouts from the door, Come in here, you stupid boy.

My poor mother. She takes me down to Mr Brady, the dentist in Blackrock, again. He adds two front teeth to my plate. I walk around for a week with a three-tooth gap while he works on it. I stay in and do all my homework and get decent marks in the tests.

When JD can't go down the pier at night we meet in the back lanes near her home. She has a new bike. We talk, pass love notes and kiss up against walls. I have to remember to brush leaves and cobwebs off her back before she goes home. She tells me that her mother comes from Armagh in the North and will kill her if she finds out about us.

My family hates Roman Catholics, JD says, and grins at the thrill of that. It gives me a funny feeling to hear it, to be hated.

We don't hate Protestants, I say.

That's because you love me, she says, and pokes my trousers. I jump back, embarrassed.

Don't do that. Someone will see.

You've gone all red, she laughs.

We become more daring. She needs the excitement as much as I do. I scout her house. We have all seen a film where the chap climbs in the girl's window and they run away together. A drainpipe is fixed to the wall on the left of the big bay window under her bedroom.

I can climb up to your bedroom, I say.

You can't, she grins, but her eyes say you can.

When my brothers are fast asleep and Dada is snoring like Paddy Brock's mother pig, I climb out the bedroom window. I wheel Dada's bike out of the side entrance and down the garden without making a noise. Fifteen minutes later, the bike is hidden in the bushes of a driveway next to JD's house. It's after midnight. I can tell from the chimes of the Town Hall clock.

The drainpipe is easy. It's fixed tightly to the wall. One step out, and I'm over the gap onto the top of the bay window. I can see Joan's sleeping head by the light of the street lamp. The window is open. Her bedroom door is shut. I open the window wider. Glance at the road. No cars. No people, at nearly one o'clock in the morning. I whisper her name. She wakens immediately as if she is expecting me. I kneel down next to her and we whisper for an hour.

The next night I hide under her bed when we hear a noise – her father snoring in the next room. We don't ever talk about what will happen to us if he comes in and catches me.

One night I try to go inside her, but my trousers are around my knees because I have to be ready to get out of that window fast. JD is scared.

We make a noise. Her father comes into the room.

Are you awake, Joan? he asks.

No, Daddy, she mumbles.

I thought I heard you, he says.

He had. She had moaned too loudly. I am lying flat on my back under the bed, trying to fasten my fly buttons.

The frenchie

There are four bad boys in our class. We're the only ones who do more than just flirt on street corners. It's us who crowd into the

lavatory together at school to see our first French letter. The one
Tommy says is for me.

Eddie Quirk asks Tommy, Where do you put it?

What, the frenchie? says Tommy.

No you eejit, your willy, says Eddie.

Don't call me an eejit. Where do you think? says Tommy. Did
you fellas never see a dog or a horse doing it?

But animals are not like us, says Eddie Quirk. In her belly
button, then?

I hate this. Now I'm worried I'll be the eejit if I ask, is it really the
navel – or somewhere else?

All right, Tommy, I think I know, I say. The same place as I put
my finger?

Yes, of course, he says. Imagine your tool is a banana, right?
Your Catholic banana, remember? And he starts laughing again.

Shut up, lads, or we'll be found out, says Eddie Quirk.

Give me your thumb, says Tommy to me, and he starts to roll
the thing up it. That's how you do it. All the way up when it's
hard, like.

I take my half crown and buy the French letter from Tommy. It is
the only one. In the whole school – and maybe in the whole of
Dún Laoghaire.

<hr />

I tell JD what I've got and ask her if she'll try it. She says yes, but I
can see that she's nervous. We arrange to meet after school next
day on the flat granite boulders facing the sea on the Sandycove
seafront.

Will anyone be able to see us there? she asks.

Only if they are on Howth Head and have a telescope, I laugh.
She doesn't laugh.

All the next day I hear nothing that is said in class. My mind is

numb with thinking about what is going to happen. Brother
Clancy writes an algebra equation on the board. He points at me.

I'm sorry, sir, I don't know. My voice is a bit shaky. A giggle
comes from across the room.

Who's the bright spark? hisses Clancy. It is a bad day. I hate
school. I hate maths. I hate Brother Clancy. I stare out the window
and think of the granite boulders.

I leave Davey at his front gate and he looks worried.

Are you sick or what? he asks.
Am I in love, I wonder, is this what love does? A fella in a book
that Tommy showed us says that I'm in lust. That's it. I'm in lust.
One of the Seven Deadlies.
JD is late, and she's nervous. She was trying to avoid some kids
playing in the rock pools. Now we're both nervous. The level rock
that I remember is not so level. We put our coats down and try to
cover ourselves. JD does things with her gymslip and I'm trying to
work out how to get my trousers halfway down. My willy is
nervous. He's only half stiff. I can't get the rubber to roll on. Half
on, now. Can I put it in there? How will it reach? Will she help
me, does she know how? After all these months, we're
embarrassed. We don't know what to say. What do I do? What?
I'm almost there when I start slipping backwards on the slope.
Just then a boy's voice yells, Hey fellas, come and look here.
At that moment, I come. Joan's face is angry. The kids are yelling
now and laughing.

They're havin' a coort, yells the young fella.

Would you eff off, I shout, trying to get my trousers up from
around my knees. I don't remember saying goodbye to JD. I have
failed. The big day has come – and I have come outside the
promised land. In a balloon.

Next day we laugh about it a bit, Joan and me. We decide to try again on Killiney Hill. On Saturday, if it's not raining. So Tommy shows me how to wash and roll up the frenchie.

It's easy, he says with his big grin. Look here. Hold that, and he takes out a real banana.

I hold it like it is my tool. He rolls it on.

Now roll it on the rest of the way. Not like that, you eejit. You're squashing it, he says.

The banana oozes out of the skin. It's over-ripe.

All right, all right. I've got it.

The night after when I climb the drainpipe I am so nervous that I fall. Once I'm in her room we talk, just talk. Just as well.

I knock a glass of water on the floor. We hear her father's feet hit the floor of his bedroom. He must have been awake.

I am out the window in seconds and jump off the top of the bay window into the flower garden. As the light floods out above me I run around the side of the house. I hear him shout, and I run round to the back garden and hide behind the first bush. In minutes, the back door opens and he shouts.

I know you are there, you bugger. And he comes towards the bush in his pyjamas, stripes shining in the moonlight.

I am up and running towards the high garden wall. Smooth plaster. No grip. But fright does it for me. I'm over that seven-foot wall and gasping on the ground on the other side in a flash. Olympic stuff. I don't see JD for three days.

My parents haven't said anything to the school, JD says. I told them that it was a boy from the Kingstown Grammar School talking to me in the garden, that's all.

If they do tell the school, I say, then your headmistress could speak to the guards and they'll tell my headmaster.

We're both very quiet then. We are in a lane where no windows overlook us. She is sitting on her bicycle and I'm holding the handlebars. It starts to drizzle.

I'd better be going, she says, and looks at me. I can see that she's worried now. So am I.

When will I see you? I say.

Let's leave it for a few days, she says. I have exams and I must work for them.

I wave goodbye.

Babies are the answer

I draw triangles on everything. Eternal triangles, I call them. JD on one side, school on another, and Irish history and the North on the third side. It's all I think about now, and there's no time for hobbies any more. JD is my hobby. Irish history is my hobby. School is a feckin' nuisance, but I can't ignore it. Home is just there – behind it all.

There's a funny thing we notice about the Christian Brothers. And even Mr O'Malley. They're great on the past, but they won't talk about what has to be done next. The baddies and the British are in the North, and nobody is saying anything about them. Why not?

The Church and Mr de Valera say that we can leave the North alone, he says. The Catholic parents there will have more children than the Protestants, and we will outnumber them someday. Then the North will come back.

What'll the Protestants do then, Brother?

It'll all be gradual and they'll be made welcome in the Republic – just like all the thousands of Protestants who live here now. They know that they'll be safe.

We accept the obviousness of this. The Glengara girls rarely had more than one brother or sister.

And you boys do the same when the time comes. Have lots of Catholic children. Tommy Watson digs me in the ribs.

D'ya hear that? He says. No more frenchies for you.

Street angel, house devil and dustbin

I think my father is unhappy, an unhappy person. Always giving out to Mama about something or other. He's criticising her. Night after night, he finds fault. He never shouts, just sort of drones and stammers. She gets redder and redder and looks on the verge of tears. He criticises her tonight for making too many sandwiches and cakes for her friends.

And you're so charming to them, she says. You're a street angel and a house devil.

I am helpless. If I start to argue it'll turn into a fight and me doing the shouting. Mama begging me to stop. Then it's as if he's won. Why doesn't she let me defend her? She's weak like that. I hate giving in to him.

It's as if he's not satisfied with anything she's doing, or me either. He leaves Dermot and Patrick alone. Thomas is too small.

I think he hates his job. He tells Mama about the chancers at work and how the boss does nothing to stop them stealing things and going out to the bookies and the pub when they should be working.

I won't even take a paper clip from that office, he tells us all at supper one night. Then he asks me if I've finished my meal.

I look at my plate, and there's a piece of fat there that I don't want. He leans his fork over and takes it.

I'm the dustbin in this house, he says.

Dada quotes Julius Cæsar

One morning at breakfast time, something different happens. I start on about something I have learned about the North.

You should not have let him go to Belfast, says my father at breakfast. In front of me.

But, Dada, you encouraged him, Mama says.

Yes you did, Dada, I say. You said that you liked Belfast. Don't you remember?

He blows on his tea. We can all see that he wants to put it in his saucer, but Mama doesn't like that. He slurps a bit because it's hot. Then he stirs it twelve times because he knows that annoys Mama.

I don't know where all this political talk is leading, he says.
I burst out, It's necessary. Nobody is doing anything about the North. The English must get out. Don't you agree with that?
I look from one to the other. Neither says anything at first. Patrick and Thomas are playing some sort of private game where the wireless is. Dermot just watches.

Why don't you leave all this till after school, Bernard, till after your exams and then see? Mama asks me.
I look at Dada's stooped figure at the table.
He says, Politicians and blackguards ruin this country, north and south. You're not going to change that.
Is he talking to me? He is. He's looking at me.

So we must get rid of all those crooks and go back to the first *Dáil,* I say to him, all enthusiastic. This is what I've been reading.
Do you know what Julius Caesar said? Dada asks.
I shake my head, even though we're doing the play at school.

He said break the law *only* if you are going to seize power. But in all other cases observe it.
I stare at him. That's fantastic, I say, can I write that down? And I run out of the room to get my notebook. He knows these things about the Romans.

That's exactly what we must do, Dada, I say, sitting down at the table again. Do away with both governments and set up a new Parliament, like in 1918.
But he changes the subject.

Have you not read about Jim Larkin or James Connolly? He looks at me again.

No, I say, not yet.

Well, they were both socialists – you should know that. The only way this country will be free, he says, is when the Catholic gombeen men and the Freemasons, who are Protestants, have the power taken away from them, the power of money. And he finishes his tea.

I don't think this conversation is suitable at all, says Mama. Bernard has enough to think about without this Labour Party talk.

Well, I think p-p-politics is a waste of time, he says. You needn't b-b-bother your head with it. It'll turn out b-bad in the end, you'll see. He's stuttering because he's het up now.
Dada looks at me again.

I've been trying to get your m-mother to vote Labour for years, but she won't l-listen, he says.
He goes out to the hall and puts on his hat, coat and bicycle clips.
I get up and follow him.
I can't believe this. He talked to me. About Mama. He's asking me to agree with him about something. Politics? I'll find out more about these labour people.
I watch him go, stooping over the bike. I hope to God he doesn't miss his train.

The FCA
More trouble comes. One afternoon a teacher tells us to get our parents' permission so that we'd be able to join the *Fórsa Cosanta Áitúil*, the Local Defence Force.
I run home after school like a kid. We are going to be trained to use a rifle. To defend our country. This is the best news ever. I blurt it all out to Mama. But she's ahead of me. She must have spies.

Do you know, Bernard, what goes on next to the Army camp? she asks. The Butlin's Holiday Camp is next door to it. I've been told all about it. All those girls from England and Scotland come over here looking for boys.

My heart drops. It's the Boy Scouts all over again.

What's that got to do with me joining the FCA, I ask. Nearly half the class is joining, Mama. I raise my voice. Uniforms are free. We are going to be trained to defend the country.

But the summer camp is next door to Butlin's, she says, and I've heard about the FCA men meeting the girls from England at night. They have no morals. We used to live in England, and I know that their girls are different.

I go out to the back garden and throw stones and half bricks at the garden wall as hard as I can. I must wait for Dada to come in. And give her time to change her mind.

I ask Dada when he comes in, but it's already after eight o'clock.

Dada, I have to tell them tomorrow at school.

I'm not interfering. If Mama says no, it's no. She's bringing you up, he says.

You don't take any interest in us, I shout at him.

Now don't say that, Mama says, Dada works very hard for all of us.

You're just as bad. You are always saying that Papa took no interest in his sons, and look what happened to them. Well, I'm going to be worse! I slam out of the room. Nothing will change her mind.

I sit in the drawing room and my book shakes in my hands.

Glengara Raid

When did you have your first boyfriend, Mama? I ask her one day when we are alone.

She doesn't answer straight away.

Now tell me the truth, I say, and give her a nudge. I'm drying the dishes at the sink beside her.

She gets her little triangular smile and says, Nineteen.

Christian Brothers' College

Monkstown Park

SECONDARY DEPARTMENT

Master *Bernard J. Ryan*

Term *Summer* 1953 Class *Leaving Cert. I*

General Conduct *V.G.* Application *Excellent* Attendance *Excellent*

SUBJECT	MARKS	MAX.	REMARKS
Religious Knowledge	64	100	
Irish	35	"	
Latin	60	"	
Greek	—	—	*General Result.*
French	—	—	
English	71	"	*Honours*
Arithmetic	71	"	
Algebra	44	"	
Geometry	72	"	
Geography	58	"	
History	45	"	
Science	28	"	
Drawing	88	"	

Next Term Begins   3   IX   53

Signed *H. C. Normoyle*

Headmaster

1953 school report

Ah no, Mama, I say. So old?

Well you see, I was always busy helping my mother with my brothers and sisters. And I worked hard at school. We weren't allowed boyfriends.

But boys get interested earlier, don't they? I ask her.

Well, working class boys do. But boys like you who go to school till they're eighteen shouldn't. You have to get your Leaving Certificate. And go to university if your marks are good enough. She stops washing a saucepan and wipes the steam off the window. If we can afford it, she says. Then she gets real serious.

I have heard that you were seen talking to girls from Glengara

124

Park, she says. She turns around and looks at me. She waits for me to answer.

I only talk to them sometimes, Mama, I say, when I'm with the other lads.

You are not to go out with Protestant girls, Bernard. It just stores up trouble for later on.

I only talk to them, I say. She looks at me like she doesn't believe that.

Now I do something mad. Completely mad. JD is losing interest in me. All my reading about Irish politics is making me restless, too. And I want to impress her some way, but how?

Then Tommy, Nick and I saw a picture about this Englishman. He climbs into castles and things and leaves notes saying that he is avenging a wrong and will be back. I think of Glengara. I can impress JD and do something about Ireland, all at the same time. Kill two birds – and maybe myself along with them.

I take Dada's bike again and ride the three miles to JD's school, then climb the high wall at two in the morning with a little tin of white paint and a brush. Moonlight helps, and the breeze rustling the leaves drowns out any noise. I am a commando now, a cat burglar, dark clothes and all.

I spread my speech paper on the window sill of the Common Room. 'People of Ireland, Protestant, Presbyterian and Catholic, we call on you to salute the Republic proclaimed in Arms in 1916, the Republic of All Ireland, North and South…'

I do my best to prevent the paint dribbles from running down the windowpane. Fourteen more lines, and my speech is finished, my arm tired by now. With my hanky I wipe away all my finger marks. There'll be ructions in the morning. The speech calls on all these Protestants who love talking about England like it is their country, to think about their loyalties. London and Belfast aren't the capitals, Dublin is. Ireland welcomes them as misguided, but forgiven. And so on. Great stuff, I think to myself. And JD, she'll be thrilled. She'll know who did it.

Trouble is, so does everybody else. After school the next day, Detective Sergeant Cassidy stops me on George's Street. Come with me to the station, me boyo, he says, and takes my arm. Everybody's staring. Will somebody tell Mama? This isn't supposed to happen. He shows me into a bare room with brown and cream walls and a fierce smell of cigarettes. Brown lino on the floor, and bars on the dirty windows. It's too big for a cell, I think.

Show me your hands, he says.

I can see white paint under a fingernail. He looks at it.

Even if that wasn't there, me boyo, the whole school knows you did it. Your little lady friend's pals have heard your opinions often enough.

What are you talking about? I ask him. The chaps in the pictures never admit it first go.

You painted your proclamation, or whatever you like to call it, on the windows at Glengara School last night, and I don't need to trouble the fingerprint lads with this, now do I?

He smiles for the first time. He is big and red-faced and doesn't give us lads a hard time like some of the Guards do. Heroes don't deny their actions. But I'm a scared hero now.

Will I go to jail? I ask.

Is that what you want? To go to jail for Ireland? He's laughing now. No need to laugh, I think. This is trouble, and I'll take the consequences. It's not supposed to end like this. How is it supposed to end? With mystery and investigations and a bit in the newspaper.

I did it and I'm proud of it, I say staring at him. I am very serious and straight-faced. But my stomach is all tied up and sick. Then he gets serious too.

A lot of those girls are frightened, he says. Some of them come from the North. You signed yourself 'The IRA'. He looks at me.

Is there anybody else involved?

No. Just me, I say.

He stares and then says, I think this matter will go no further if you apologise and if you tell me that you won't act the feckin' eejit again. He waits to see what I'll say.

I say nothing. My head is numb.

I've arranged for you to go up to the school and apologise to the Headmistress. I'll phone her now and make an appointment for after school tomorrow. Her name is Atkinson, Miss Atkinson. His hand is above the telephone. Are you going to apologise?

Yes. I will, I say.

He finishes speaking on the phone and says to me, half-past four tomorrow afternoon, right? Go straight from school, mind.

I get up to go.

The IRA is dead and buried. Stay out of trouble, Mr Ryan, Cassidy says.

O'Riain, I say back to him. And stare. I think he knows I'm on the verge of tears. Of frustration.

O'Riain, he says, and smiles again.

I don't sleep well. Next afternoon at half past four, all the day girls are supposed to have gone home. But bunches of them hang around the main gate, giggling and waiting. I step out from behind a tree. There's a fit of giggles and little screams, and they point and stare like I have two heads. No sign of JD.

I panic. Will I just run away? I can't. It'll be worse.

I march past them, looking straight ahead and up the drive of the school, big old trees on either side. Faces fill the windows of the boarders' dormitories – laughing faces.

A teacher comes out onto the steps and says in a snooty voice,
This way please, just like in the pictures.
I go up the stone steps. The teacher says, In there, and points. Miss
Atkinson is in a room sitting at a desk. She looks up and says,
Good afternoon.
I clear my throat and hope that I don't get sick on her shiny floor.
    Good afternoon, I say.
My stomach is like a big air bubble. She stares at me. Her glasses
glint in the grey light coming in the long sash windows.
    I'm here to apologise to you for frightening anybody by what I
did, I say.
She says nothing.
    And it won't happen again. I can hear my own voice sort of far away.
    And the damage to our property? She says.
    Yes, I say. I mean no, I'm sorry for that too.
Silence while she stares out the window. I'm Irish too, she says.
But I do not think your behaviour will advance your cause. Most
of the teachers and the girls were either indifferent or frightened
by your prank.
She looks sharply at me. It was a prank, wasn't it?
    Well, Miss Atkinson, I meant the words, but I shouldn't have
done this.
Now I'm really miserable, but I can see that she is not very angry.
    I accept your apology, she says. Sergeant Cassidy tells me that
you are from a respectable family. And you go to a good school.
She stops and looks at her desk.
    One other matter. We know that you are seeing one of our girls.
That must cease.
She says 'cease' instead of 'stop'. I nod my head.
    She has exams to do, and I'm sure you do too, she says.
She doesn't say anything about me being a Catholic or anything. I
don't know what to say now.

Have I your promise about not seeing Joan? She asks.
My mind has nothing in it. Nothing. I can't say anything. I am
trapped. She waits.

Can I see her just once then, please? I hear my own voice saying.
Her mouth is in a straight line. No, you may not. She looks out
the window and back at me again.

———

Next day, I meet Joan in a muddy back lane with rain drizzling
down. She says everybody knew who did it, and asks why did I do
that. I can tell that she didn't think much of it at all. I give her my
note saying that I've promised not to see her again, but that I'll
never forget her. We hold hands for a second, and she's gone. Next
week I see her with Brian Devereaux, a Protestant boy that all the
girls are after. He looks nervously at me. He is good-looking. I
turn and walk away. I feel sick. My stomach is sick a lot of the
time these days.

Breakfast down

The blood is dark blobs on my right hand now. It's almost stopped
dripping. I can hear their voices from the dining room, all talking
at once. Mama is still crying. I am terrified by what I've done.
Somebody is sweeping up the broken dishes. My father's voice is
rumbling away and Dermot is saying something to them in a
nearly-crying voice.
I've just upended the breakfast table. All over Dada. All over the
Protestant girl. But that's all over, anyway.
I am tired like I've run a race. And its only half-eight in the
morning. I push the skin around the gashes in my hand. There is a
sharp pain. Must be a piece of the teapot in there still. I take my
penknife in my left hand, lick the blade clean, and poke around in
the cut. Out it comes, a little piece of white Delft. His teapot. He

should get an aluminium one now. In case he starts his shite again. I'll smash that too. If he ever goes on about me again in front of me and my brothers, I'll smash more than a teapot.

But I'm sorry when I think of Mama's face and Patrick's and Thomas's. I remember them all right. Their breakfast on the floor, the yelling, the noise. I hate him now.

I need Elastoplast. The dining room door is still closed, and there's a crack in the bottom panel where I kicked it. I walk into the bathroom and bolt the door, run the cold tap in the basin and stick my hand under it. Then I turn the tap off and soak a piece of Mama's cotton wool in Mercurochrome and dab it on each cut. There are seven of them. Christ. I'm like a feckin' one-handed stigmata. But I know I mustn't say things like that.

I dry my hand in lavatory paper and look for the Elastoplast. There's none in the medicine chest or on the window sill or on the floor. Feck that. Mama hates me to say that word, but there's no feckin' Elastoplast. What'm I going to do?

There's a bandage that Mama has washed, so I wrap it round and round my hand. Can't go to school like this.

Then I hear Mama at the front door telling Davey O'Brien that I'll be late for school, that I've had an accident. Would he please go on without me, she says.

He'll know. Mama can't change her face. Her poor face. I start to cry again. Quietly. What have I done? This family is mad. We don't know how to talk. We row over everything. He complains about me like I'm not there.

And she argues back. Though she starts it so often. I could scream at her, she's so stupid. But they're my family and I've nowhere else to go. I'm feeling angry again now.

I'll go down to the library, that's what I'll do. There's a knock on the bathroom door, and Patrick's voice. Can I come in Bernard, please?

I unbolt the door. What?

Can I do a number one?

Come in and shut the door.

Then Thomas appears. Can I come in too?

I squash them both in and bolt the door again.

Where's Dada? I ask.

Gone to work, says Patrick. What's wrong with your hand?

They both gawk at it with their mouths open. The Mercurochrome is coming through the bandage, and maybe blood too.

What did that? Thomas asks.

His teapot. Who cleaned up?

We did, and Dermot helped too, they say.

I'm going down to the library. Tell Mama, will you?

They nod their heads real seriously. Then Patrick says, Dada was real mean to you.

I tell them they're going to be very late for school.

They say, We don't want to go to school today.

Ask Mama then, I say, and I unbolt the door to let them out. I listen, and walk down the hall and out of the house.

Only Dermot goes to school that day. I don't know what he'll tell his teachers, and I don't care. They are not going to speak about me again at the table or anywhere. In front of me like I'm not there. Halfway down the road I think about my terrible temper. Maybe I'm like Uncle Joe or Papa, who everybody is afraid of. I don't want people to be afraid of me like those two old bollixes.

7

The Irish Republican Army

THE LADS ARE AT it again, shouts an old man, waving his paper as he staggers out of Easons on to the main street in Dún Laoghaire. I stare at him as others join him.

'Armagh Barracks cleaned out!'; 'Not a pull-through left!' say the headlines.

The Sunday papers in June 1954 carry the biggest headlines I've ever seen. A Bedford truck pulled up outside Gough Barracks, the largest British Army barracks in Northern Ireland. Two men walked up to the British Army guard, put a gun in his ribs, and invited him to walk with them to the guardhouse. There the rest of the soldiers on duty were informed that they were now prisoners of the Irish Republican Army. Would they please lie down and allow themselves to be tied up?

This they did, whether out of astonishment or the heat of the day, we don't know. The IRA was supposed to have died in the late forties, and these soldiers have never heard of it. Neither has the rest of Ireland.

The lads loaded the lorry with Lee-Enfield rifles, Bren guns, Sten guns and thousands of rounds of ammunition. 'The armoury was emptied,' cry the papers. British personnel confirm this before

London stops them talking to the press. A statement signed on behalf of the Republican Movement says that an active service unit of the IRA was responsible.

But I thought the IRA was finished, I say to my mother. I am all excited, and she seems uncertain how to answer.

Well, I think it joined with Mr de Valera when he went into Parliament, she says.

Then who are these guys? I demand. They say they want to liberate Ireland, north and south.

It's all a big Irish mystery. I read and re-read the statement made by the Republican spokesman. It is written in the style of the noble words of the proclamation of the Republic in 1916. All the stories I've ever heard about Ireland tumble about in my head. Whoever pulled off this raid and writes these statements, signed P O'Neill, to the papers, is doing the same thing again. Ireland is still occupied by the British in the North. So it's the same fight for freedom that we've been taught about.

But we all think it's over. The South is free, they say, and they call it Ireland. It's like they want to forget about the North and our people up there.

They can't, Mama, I say.

Can't what?

Forget about the North. I'm going to find out who did this and join them.

Ah now, Bernard, don't be silly, she says. You've got your schoolwork and your exams and your whole life ahead of you. She is very upset. I think that we are both thinking of the Scouts and the Cadets. But I'm older now and I'm determined. It's always been 'no' and this time it's going to be 'yes'. It's everyone's duty to free their country. I have never been so thrilled about anything.

Next day I'm in Dublin to buy a school book at Easons. On the way to catch my bus I see the poster tied to a pillar of the GPO. 'UNITED IRISHMAN' it says at the top. A young girl is standing next to it under the portico of the Post Office. Under that, it says:

READ ALL ABOUT IT
The Inside Story
Of
The Armagh Raid

Who are you? I ask her with my money in my outstretched palm. She smiles and says, I'm selling these, and she hands me a small newspaper.

Does it tell you how to join?
She looks at me with a bit of a grin and says, Yes.
I ask no more questions and pay my money.
The entire story is printed inside. And a whole lot about the Republican Movement, like it has never gone away. All about its recent history and the unbroken succession since 1913. Like the Church talks about the Popes.
There is a name and contact telephone number.
I call next Monday.

My name is Éamonn, a voice says in a strong Dublin accent. He asks me a few questions. Then, Meet me at …
I like Éamonn immediately. He's small with dark, lively eyes. Mischievous, Mama would say. He says he's the recruiting officer. For three months I and about twenty others of all ages attend Induction Classes. Éamonn takes us through Irish history up to the 1916 rebellion. We'd done that at school and I'd read stacks about it. But what most of us do not know is the role played by those who are in power now. Like de Valera and his government. Éamonn opens our eyes.

We are not supposed to tell anyone that we are joining the IRA. It's an illegal organisation. The Offences Against the State Act was passed in 1940 to intern, jail, and if necessary execute for certain offences. But I can't keep my mouth shut. I tell Mama everything. I know that she's interested but hates anything like bad company. This beats the Scouts and the FCA into a cocked hat. She doesn't want her son killed or going to jail. I can see she knows she can't stop me any more.

One day Éamonn comes to the house about something and meets Mama. When I come in later she looks at me in an odd way.

That Mr Thomson seems to be a very nice man. What is he doing with these people?

She says 'these people' like they are the dustbin men. I explain that 'these people' are clerks, respectable shop assistants, and even civil servants. The last impresses her, but not enough.

I hope that this is just a phase, she says. I can see she doesn't believe that, though. But I'm almost a man now and will be leaving school soon.

The second time she meets Éamonn, she says, It's your fault that he's joined the IRA.

He's very influenced by you.

Éamonn leans towards her. Mrs Ryan, or is it Mrs O'Riain? Look at it this way. Supposing Bearnárd was out robbing banks, that'd be terrible. But he's an idealist. He's doing something good.

Well, I don't know about that, she frowns. And I can see that you're older than he is. I hope you will see that he doesn't get into trouble.

We'll do our very best, ma'am.

And, he says to me afterwards with a grin, I couldn't tell your mother that all we can offer is imprisonment or death. We laugh at the obviousness of that. That's what I want to hear. That is the sacrifice.

Éamonn

Gangsters and murderers

There is great camaraderie amongst us. Most of the lads are working-class from the city, with a sprinkling of country fellows. I am the only one from the 'south side'.

Will you come with me? I ask Brian Bateson, my Protestant friend from Clarinda Park in Dun Laoghaire. Protestants like Brian are aware of being Irish and not 'British', like some of them say. They're aware that the first Republicans were Protestant and Presbyterian, who did not want English rule. Inspired by the French Revolution, they rose against the English in 1798 and died for their trouble. Brian is a real exception to the Prod pro-British type. He has Northern Presbyterian ancestors on his mother's side. She will not talk about it, though.

She says she'd thought I was a nice well-brought up boy. But now that I'm talking to her only son about gangsters and murderers she forbids him to see me. Brian is torn by all this.

He comes to a few meetings, but pulls out when his mother gets sick with worry when he comes home late. It's hard for Protestants like that to see beyond all the stuff that they have been brought up with. For years afterwards, Éamonn asks after that grand lad.

I try to recruit one more friend. Andrew is a cynic. We meet in the Roman Café.

What do you do up in the mountains, anyway? he asks. I tell him a bit about it.

I can tell you for nothing, he says, that you're wasting your time. My cousins in Belfast say that Catholics there don't want to know. They say that the RUC and the B Specials will eat the IRA for breakfast; and that means you. Me join? Not a chance.

He goes back to eyeing a cheeky girl at the next table. But she is looking at me. I'm a bit fed-up with Andrew so I smile back. As we leave, her friend asks me if I want a date with her. I say yes. Her name is Sinéad.

During my induction training, a second raid takes place. Eight volunteers are captured at the Army barracks in Omagh, County Tyrone. A gun battle breaks out and two Tommies are injured.

You would have been liable for the death penalty, says the judge, if a soldier had died. They get ten years each in Belfast jail.

The euphoria after Armagh has died down. That was a glorious deed, the lads were audacious, the Brits made to look foolish, and nobody got caught or hurt.

But Omagh is different. This is serious stuff. Éamonn's phone doesn't stop ringing. Recruits almost queue up to join.

I walk in the rain and drizzle of October nights through the back streets of Dublin to the next secret meeting place. I stop at street corners to see if I'm being followed. I jump off buses before they've stopped. I duck down back alleys and get lost. I get into trouble for being late. I think of James Cagney in the pictures and love it all. But in the North itself the reaction is quiet. I only hear this from a Northerner in the induction class. He is surprised and sad that his fellow Catholics in the North are keeping their heads down.

Don't say anything, though, he says. We'll wake up sooner or later.

I don't tell him what Andrew had said to me.

Dada is up when I get home, making his last cup of tea. I want to tell him some of this. I am surprised when he sits down in his armchair with the one broken arm and listens. He doesn't look at me. But he listens. He finishes his tea.

Divide and rule, he says, that's how all empires do it. I must go to bed now, though.

And he gives me a sideways glance. He doesn't tell me to stop all this.

I am thrilled skinny that he's listening to me for the first time since I was six years old.

Eighteenth birthday vow

A weak light bulb hangs from the middle of the low ceiling. Water is dripping on a pile of coal in a corner.

Right lads, says Éamonn's voice, get in line. Volunteers – attention! he says. But quietly.

My shoes crunch the coal slack. No smiles. I am quaking. Éamonn makes a speech about why we are here. Then he says, Repeat after me: 'I swear to uphold the Irish Republic as declared in 1916, to work for an all-Ireland Parliament, and to overthrow both the existing puppet states – by force of arms if necessary.'

We repeat the words. One lad shouts them out loud. Another barely whispers. My voice cracks like a girl's.

It's my eighteenth birthday. The coal glistens in the corners, and cobwebs sway white in the weak electric light. I love every man there and I can feel that they love me too.

Everybody with one thing in common, a secret shared in the shadows.

We speak of Ireland as though she is a princess. An *aisling* or vision. The poets of old had been forbidden by the English to write or speak of Ireland. It was only a province, and that was that. So poems and songs sprang up about a beautiful woman who was in dire distress and who had been abandoned by her lovers or her children. And then came the rescuers. They rose up to defend her against storms and destruction, emerging bloody but victorious. I wondered how the English never saw through all this.

Well, says Éamonn, The poets and ballad makers used Irish to get the message across.

Ah, sure, the English never bothered to learn Irish.

Training in the mountains at weekends and in people's houses on weeknights is a cloak-and-dagger affair. Now this is the trouble with me. I can't keep my mouth shut. I want everyone to know that the liberation of the North is at hand. I forget that the Special Branch is watching our every move. And here I am, telling everybody that will listen, and some that won't, that I am a member of the IRA and would they like to support us, please?

It won't last, you'll see, Dada says to Mama.

Meccano, stamps, the Scouts, he forgot about them all. But I can tell he's interested in my politics. He sees I'm serious, and now I am almost a man.

De Valera is a bloody hypocrite, he says one night, putting his paper down, and I perk up my ears.

Why is that, Dada? I ask, all eager.

Well, he locked up all his old comrades when it suited him. I don't believe a word out of him.

He doesn't look at Mama because she's annoyed now. So he looks at me.

We call him the Devil of Éire, did you know that? And he laughs at the play on de Valera's name.

———

I buy a navy-blue trench coat and a beret to match. The stereotypical IRA man. I go so far as to buy leather leggings from an Army surplus store and wear them with my army boots on the bus going to secret training meetings. If I tied a notice on my back and front it couldn't make it easier for the Special Branch. The frustrated Boy Scout and FCA cadet is bursting out of his cocoon. A right eejit.

Preparation for war

Now it's your turn. Dismantle and reassemble this Thompson gun in 25 seconds, says the Training Officer. My hands shake, and it takes me 32 seconds.

Do it again. And again. If it jams and you are under fire, this know-how can save your life, he says.

I long to be under fire.

But there is a shortage of ammunition so we can't practise shooting. One weekend, after a night crossing mountains and bogs in the rain, we camp under dripping pine trees, make a fire with dry wood that one lad carried, and drink tea with three sugars and eat our sandwiches. Mama had made mine. I had told her that I'm training now.

I'm sure she won't say anything because she knows her sisters will be shocked and the neighbours' reaction will be worse. And Dada talks to no one, anyway. Most people still believe the propaganda spread in the forties that the IRA are killers of women and children. If they could see us, they'd be amazed. Clerks, civil servants, plumbers, artisans, postmen, bus drivers, and one ex-seminarian.

After our break we follow the officer up the mist-covered mountainside in single file. A maze of barbed wire and obstacles made of poles and oil drums appear. All that day we are crawling, running, jumping and clambering over rocks and trudging through bog water till we nearly drop.

This is what the Sperrin Mountains are like, says a man who walks out of the mist.

He's from Tyrone in the North, whispers the lad next to me. He's one of the hard men.

So ye'd better be ready to dive into a boghole when the choppers come lookin' for ye, says the hard man from the North.

The lads from the North saw houses burnt down and people shot in the streets during the pogroms of the thirties and forties.

Discrimination everywhere, says Éamonn during a break from the assault course.

It makes me laugh, he says, when I hear the Brits complaining about South Africa. Economic and political apartheid has been going on in the Six Counties for three hundred years, sure.

I am tired and wet. We shoulder our rifles, crook our Thompsons and Stens under our arms, and head down the mountain. A van is waiting on a boreen for the arms. We split up into twos and threes and go on walking over hills and through government forests to isolated bus stops where suburbs lap against the slopes. Tired and happy I am.

You look exhausted, says Mama, and puts a plate of mashed potato with two eggs down in front of me.

Thanks, Ma, I say, noticing the two eggs. And what have you been doing?

I've been thinking, she says. I would not let you join the Boy Scouts or the FCA. And now look at you. You've left school, got your Leaving Certificate, and now you've got a grand job in Caltex, and Sinéad's a grand girl. You are a man.
She turns and looks at me.

I wish now that I'd let you join those other things, she says. That's why you are in this business now.
She couldn't bring herself to say 'the IRA'.

Ah no, Mama, I say, Ever since O'Malley, do you remember, I have been going to do this.
She looks away and says nothing.

Missing the call

Something is in the wind. A kind of suppressed excitement infects the Army HQ staff. Early in December, Éamonn tells the Dublin Company commanding officers to be ready for the call. The campaign is about to be launched. Everything we have been training for is about to happen. I swell with pride, and tears come into my eyes.

I ask, Could you give us the date, O/C? We never say 'sir' — a left-over from the days of the socialist Irish Citizen Army of James Connolly.

No, I can't. Just don't go out at night, d'you hear? Unless you absolutely have to. And don't go far. If you really have to leave your home, tell someone where we can find you.
My parents don't have a phone. Then a couple of days later I am asked out to dinner by Ann Ormond at the swanky Marine Hotel in Dun Laoghaire. Her family are wealthy horsey people — but I

like Ann anyway, so I take a chance. And I don't tell Sinéad. My parents don't approve because the family is Protestant, so I don't tell them either where I'm going.

Ann has organised a five-course meal. Her brother and sister are there. They don't approve of Ann's going out with me. I'm a Catholic. With all the talk, the food and the posh atmosphere, I do not notice the time passing.

When I get home at ten o'clock I immediately feel the tension.

Éamonn was here looking for you, says Mama. She stares at me. What's going on? she asks.

Did he leave a message, any message? I am frantic. How long ago was he here? Can I catch him? I am halfway out the door again.

No, no, he's gone for ages. He was here about nine. She looks at Dada. He looks at me with an expression of concern that I do not remember ever seeing before.

What's wrong? he asks. He's half-deaf, so he can't hear us.

I have made the worst mistake of my life, I say.

Everything I've been living for. For the sake of an evening out with a girl. How can I be so stupid? I run all the way down to the bus stop. No good. Éamonn's gone.

First thing in the morning, I am in the *United Irishman* offices beseeching Pasha, the newspaper's manager, for information. He looks really sorry for me.

I don't know where anyone is, he says in his strangled voice. He's stone deaf.

Please, Pasha, you must know how I can contact the lads.

I am desperate now. Pasha's old collie stands up from under the desk and starts howling. Pasha takes a piece of paper and writes an address on it.

Andy McGann, he says.

I am out the door and running.

Thank God, Andy you're here. I missed Éamonn last night, I gasp it all out. Where must I go?

He shakes his head. He is a serious and severe man. It is said that he is the Chief of Staff. He looks out the window, all cobwebs. And shakes his head again.

Now I am begging, beseeching. He is torn.

I can't now, he says. They are assembled already. The police know that something is happening. If I send you there now it could destroy everything. And then, almost to himself, he says it again: Everything.

He is not unkind, I realise afterwards, and he is right. But I don't accept it then. He ushers me gently but firmly from his office, saying, Go home and wait to be contacted.

I don't ever get over the stigma of that mistake. Two years of training – and all gone for the sake of supper with a girl. Because she flattered me.

That night in December 1956, twelve active service columns go into action throughout the six counties, attacking radar stations, blowing up bridges and British Army installations. Headlines circle the world. It is the biggest military action to be taken against British Forces in Ireland since the War of Independence in 1921. And I was not at home waiting for the call.

8

Gentlemen terrorists

MY PARENTS KNOW the enormity of it all. The radio talks about the massive mobilisation of the British and the RUC and the paramilitary B Specials. Nobody has been killed. Yet. A few soldiers have been slightly injured. No IRA men have been captured.

The announcement from the Republican Movement calls on the British to get out or face the consequences. Then it calls on all Irishmen serving in the RUC to resign within three days and to hand in their weapons. I sit in a safe house on the north side of the city with a few of the lads, and we ask ourselves, Why give those fellas, the police, that chance? Ninety per cent of them are Protestant and Loyalist, and enjoy keeping the Catholics in their place.

But, I think, some of the people that I met in Belfast two years ago are probably in the police. I agree with the Republican gesture.

It's principled, I say.

Principled, me bollix, says Barney, blinking through the thick glasses that have prevented him from doing his bit. They'll just go ahead and fortify the feckin' barracks.

And they did. Two of our lads died soon afterwards when attacking them.

To the North

In late January Éamonn says, Are you ready this time? No mots
now? And grins.

It's no feckin' laughing matter, I reply, hurt by his reference to
the girl, and he says sorry.

This is going to be a good one, with any luck, says Éamonn. Get
yourself disguised and take the train to this address.
I buy a trilby with a snappy brim and a beige raincoat. I think I am
Humphrey Bogart. But no trench coat this time. I have learnt a
little, at least.

This looks lovely on you, sir, says a funny little man in Cleary's
with twinkling glasses and no chin. Look at yourself in the mirror.
I see a tough expression, thick lips and unsure eyes. My
confidence is low. I still dream at nights that Éamonn is knocking
at our door: Where is he, Mrs Ryan? You've hidden him, haven't
you, he's saying. Where is he? Mama is crying and saying, You can't
have him. He's gone away. For a long time.

I look around my Caltex office for the last time, go home and re-
pack my little rucksack under the bed, hide it down the road
behind a hedge in the dark, and look at Dada before going to bed.
He'll be gone before me in the morning. Will I ever see him again?
I say goodbye to Mama in the morning, just as I always do, and
walk out. I had seen Sinéad the day before. I told her I'd be busy
training lads for a few days and I'd call for her when I'd finished.
I'm getting really fond of her. And Mama likes her too.

She's bright – like an imp, Mama says.
The train to Leitrim is a slow one, and has a bar. I stare out the
window at the hedges and cows. At last the great adventure has
begun.

I'll have a sherry, I say to the barman.

146

It's the only drink I know. He gives me a funny look. If the cops ask him he'll say, Yeh. There was a funny-lookin' young fella, about nineteen, wearing a Humphrey Bogart hat and drinking sherry. He sounded like he was from Dalkey or Monkstown or somewhere like that.

That's him, the cops will say.

What happens next is upsetting and frustrating. Local men and women in Leitrim near the border move me from house to house. One woman laughs straight out at my trilby. I give it to her husband. He gives me one of his caps in return.

Now you look more like one of us – just so long as you keep your mouth shut, he says.

They laugh, and slap me on the back.

Take care of yourself now, and God Bless, she says, blessing me just like a priest would. Come back safe now.

I think they feel sorry for this Dublin fish out of water that looks like he is born yesterday. The day before, really.

A bomb in a priest's boot

Whatever has been planned for this area doesn't come off, because I'm told to go on to Donegal. The narrow-gauge rail car runs up beautiful valleys with great brown mountains guarding them. I hardly see a house or a person, just sheep.

Ballybofey is close to the Donegal-Tyrone border, and I go to the house of Mr Bree. Fergus from Dublin is already there. A unit will be formed around us. The postman's wife, a tall and beautiful Donegal woman, says she hates no one except the British who tortured her husband in the forties when he was captured in an arms raid.

He wouldn't harm a fly, says Val his daughter, and smiles at her own boldness.

Val's beautiful too. She brings us our meals in the loft where we are hidden. She puts down a tray made of the sides of a wooden box, with our mugs of tea and slices of soda bread. There are always layers of butter on them. I remember Mama giving us 'bread and scrape' as she called it. Scrape it on and scrape it off again. It's so expensive.

At teatime we hear voices downstairs. Val will not come up if there are visitors. When she arrives half an hour later we say we don't like butter very much, so would she leave it off please from now on? She looks at us like we are a wee bit mad.

I'm getting a crush on her and try to make her stay behind and talk. But she's shy and a bit in awe of these city slickers. She always finds an excuse to go back down the ladder, her cheeks burning. I think about her at night. That's the kind of wife I want when Ireland is free. I don't think of Sinéad at all.

The weeks pass by, and four more of the lads arrive from different parts of the country. Now we are seven. Just enough. We collect gelignite and weapons from a dump on a farm. We're ready for the raid.

I ask Mrs Bree to arrange for a sympathetic priest to hear our confessions. She is a tough woman and a believer. But she wouldn't let any of the lads slip out to Mass on Sundays. You'll be spotted inside two minutes, she had said. God will understand why you can't be there.

Why are the bishops condemning us from the pulpit, Mrs Bree? one lad asked.

They always support the government of the day, she told him. They did the same in my husband's time – and now those fellas are all heroes, with their Old IRA pensions.

The priest parks his car in a quiet spot on the road to the border.

Comrade-in-arms – Billy in 1997

He tells me that he's got our gelignite in the back of his car. They
never stop me at the roadblocks, sure, he says.
I climb into the back seat of the old Ford. Close to the bomb in
the boot. The priest sits in the front seat.

How many priests carry high explosives around in their cars,
Father?

Ah now, not many, he laughs – but very quietly. He turns to look
at me. I believe it was you who asked for me to be here tonight?

Yes, Father. All the lads will want to go, I say.

How long is it since your last confession, my son?

Is it three weeks? Time isn't normal on the run. It stands still, like we are not in the real world at all. All we do is wait. Wait for news, wait for a contact, and wait for orders. The campaign has been crippled by arrests on both sides of the border. But the worst is, the people of the North haven't risen, they haven't responded to the action, the arrests, and the deaths.

I think it's four weeks, Father.

Go on, my son.

He's only a few years older than me, I think, and I'm his 'son'. I look at the priest in the front seat and remember Pierce saying, That girl is a cause of confession. We all grinned in unison, thinking the same thoughts – for Val is a fine-looking girl, with long legs and dark hair to dream about.

I think about her now, so I say, I've cursed a few times...

Did you take the Lord's name in vain?

No, Father, not that. Never, I say.

For I never have. A long pause. I clean the steam off the side window with the sleeve of my khaki British Army blouse, and can see the other lads waiting under the trees, stamping their feet and beating their arms from the cold.

Is there anything else, my son? This is an important night, he says. His eyes shine in the weak light. Damn right it's an important night. Which would I prefer – to be killed outright with a bullet or spend the next ten years in jail? What if we kill one of them and get caught? They've said they'll execute us for that.

'High upon the gallows tree, in the cause of Liberty', goes the song. Don't think about it. Get this over with and concentrate on the operation.

I look at the priest wrapping his Rosary beads round and round his fingers. He is a Republican and one of the few risking severe punishment if he is caught with us. They'll send him to Africa to look after black babies.

Anything else…?

Will I tell him that I have impure thoughts? About Val Bree? I can't. He'll know who it is if it's in the last four weeks and me locked up in that house morning noon and night. It'll scandalise the poor man.

I had impure thoughts about a girl in Dublin, Father.

Never mind that now. I want you to say a sincere Act of Contrition.

And the Latin words fall off his lips like a song. *Ego te absolvo.* I get out of the car and say, Thanks Father.

God bless now and be very careful tonight.

And yourself, Father. What'll they do to you if they catch you? I give him a grin and call the next man to confess.

We crouch down on an old humpbacked bridge between Strabane in the North and the Donegal border. A building across the river is manned by the para-military B Specials. The outpost stands out against the clear night sky. We are seven men Or boys. Pierce is twenty-two, I think. We have scuttled a few hundred yards from where the car dropped us. I carry the bomb. We lie there in silence, weapons cradled, and listen and watch. A curlew cries. Then another answers.

Right, I whisper. No sound and no moving. I'm placing the gelly. It's a small bomb of six or seven sticks and an ordinary detonator with a slow-burning fuse long enough for me to light it and get back in position behind the parapet. No problem. It's just to attract attention. A buttress gives me cover and I place the bomb against it, and some large stones on top. A head comes over the edge of the bridge.

Don't blow the feckin' bridge, Bearnárd. We're up here.

Get the fuck down, you eejit, I say to him.

This will make a big bang. The idea is to bring the B Specials out to investigate the explosion and ambush the bastards. I listen. No sound.

Are you ready?

Feckin' ready, says a Cork voice. That's Tomás, a good lad and second-in-charge.

Load weapons quietly and be ready to fire, I say. Five rifle bolts slowly open and shut. Safety-catches on, I say.

I light the fuse. And crawl back on the bridge, looking at my watch. Two minutes. Metal clanks against stone. I jump out of my skin, near enough.

Quiet, I whisper. I sound like Pasha — strangled. Every one of us is nervous. No, frightened. Only one man has seen action before — Tomás. Once.

The bang is deafening. It cracks my head open. Bits of stone fall all around us. The noise echoes off the hills. I'm surprised I can hear that with the ringing in my ears. Then silence. Lights come on in Strabane. It's two o'clock in the morning. The light in the barracks doesn't change. Someone clicks his safety off.

Not yet, I whisper. There's a flash and a bang over to our left, a hundred yards from the barracks. They must have an outpost there that our Intelligence didn't report or know about. The only two men we had in Strabane were arrested last week.

More flashes from the right. Bullets whang off the parapet and into some willow trees along the river.

They don't know where we are. Hold your fire and pray they come. All OK in the rear?

Pierce says OK. He is watching the Donegal road. The Guards might come from there, or not. More shots seem to hit some oil drums away to our left on the banks of the river. Silence. We wait. They're not coming.

I'm relieved and sick with disappointment at the same time. Am I never going to see action? There's a jinx on me. Bullets whack the side of the bridge again and one of the lads starts to rise up in front of me. I can see his arse as he starts to straighten up.

Get down, for Jesus sake, I say, and pull him down. He's frightened, and I've just said Jesus for the first time ever in anger. Our time is up. The Guards will cut us off if the RUC has called them. But the B Specials and the RUC are not coming, not falling into our ambush. The evening papers will report an abortive attempt to blow up the bridge.

I'll fire a round or two, Pierce. You start back. Now. Here, swap weapons.

I take his Lee-Enfield. My father's words arrive in my head. It's harder to live for Ireland than to die for her, he says. Do I really want to die?

The lights are all on in the police post now.

Resting on the right-hand parapet I aim at the biggest window, a small yellow square. One shot, re-load, then a second, and a third. I imagine the sound of breaking glass. Answering shots ring out and hit the oil drums again. Time to go.

I follow the path back through the dark swishing trees as a wind springs up. I am alive. I am so relieved I'm dizzy with it. I'd better wipe this smile off my face before I reach the car. We're all supposed to be annoyed, angry with the bastards who wouldn't come out and fight.

Mountjoy

Operations cease for a few months for regrouping. The dismay at the lack of response from the Northerners is real. We know that economic conditions in the North are seriously better than the South. The dole is higher, food is mostly cheaper, and the repression of Catholics has eased. And the '56 uprising in Budapest and the aftermath of suffering, death and destruction are fresh in all our minds. Nobody wants anything like that here.

'38 Men Arrested in Glencree,' shout the Dublin papers.

On a training exercise in the Wicklow Mountains, armed Special Branch detectives surround our entire unit of young lads in early morning mist. I am the O/C.

Shit luck lands us in Glencree. John Garfield, a Headquarters man, has come out with us to exercise his leg, which had been shot up in December. We stop at midnight.

How is the leg, John? I ask him. His limp has been getting worse.

The leg's hurting, he says, I can't carry on.

Do you want to go back then? We can go on. I can ask two of my lads to go with you.

Séamus, one of the rising stars in our unit, Tony, Andy and the others gather round in the light of the stars.

We could go back through Glencree, somebody says.

That's fine by me, says John. It's not so far.

We gather round to consult our ordinance survey maps to work out the route. Glencree is a favourite destination for a moderate route march.

The rest of the lads are pulling on their fags in cupped hands, talking quietly, resting from the hard climb. Big grins greet the change in plan.

Jaysus, says one, I'm knackered. Thank God for John's gammy leg. The Special Branch never know how lucky they were. Thirty or forty of them rise out of the early morning mist all around us as we near the ruined building where we are headed.

Halt, stop where you are! Halt! Halt! all of you, they roar.

I can hear the yells from all about us. We are low down, close to the stream in skirmish lines. They are above us.

I am dazed by the suddenness of it. A voice shouts, Drop your weapons.

Are they armed? If I give the order to run, will they shoot? I can't risk them firing on my unarmed lads. This is so unexpected that I believe anything can happen.

Don't run lads, I shout, don't run. We're unarmed! I yell. We stop in our tracks. There seem to be as many Specials as us. They search us and find maps and hunting knives. One bayonet. Nothing else.

No resistance, lads, I say. We play this by ear. They've got nothing on us.

Two waiting lorries take us to the Bridewell holding cells behind the Four Courts in Dublin City centre. Next morning we are called into court one by one. We speak in Irish. Giving our names only, we then say that we refuse to recognise the right of this court to try us. All questions put to us are met with silence. Such is the sympathy for the 'gentlemen terrorists' in the South that the first two judges refuse to sentence us. One judge addresses McMadden, head of the Special Branch, who is the chief State witness: Am I to understand that besides some maps and penknives, which any sensible hiker would carry, these men had one bayonet, and this leads you to the conclusion that they are terrorists?

Yes, your Honour, says McMadden.

Well, in that case, Inspector, you and your men had better be in Glenmalure next weekend to catch me and my family – who will be considerably better equipped. Case dismissed.

Back we go on remand. Inspector McMadden is furious. His orders are to get us behind bars. The Irish politicians have given undertakings to the British to stop this guerrilla campaign. But they have to be wary of public opinion in the South, which is turning our way.

We laugh at McMadden and sing rebel songs in the Black Maria going to and from court and to the holding cells. Passers-by bang on the sides of the vans and shout, 'Up the Republic', 'Long live the IRA' and 'Where can we join up, lads?'

Then they find a judge willing to try us. He is the first judge to address us in Irish, conducting each of the thirty-eight cases in our native tongue, then sentencing us to two months in Mountjoy Jail. A right Gaelegóir bastard. On the sixth of June 1957 we join fifty or so comrades already in the 'Joy.

<hr />

My mother changes like Saul on the road to Damascus. On her first visit to the prison she is in a fighting mood. I can't understand de Valera, she says – the 'Mr' has been dropped – doesn't he realise that you were all unarmed and were only training?

I am proud of her. I look sideways at Dada. He looks dazed. And Sinéad looks a bit shocked by it all.

Were y-y-you in charge then? he asks, looking at me with a little smile like he's asking me would I like a biscuit.

Yes, I'm in charge of this unit and look where I have landed us up, I say to them.

I'm sure it's not your fault, she says.

Well, Ma, it's like this. de Valera hates us. I want you please to go home, and under my mattress you'll find back issues of *The United Irishman*. I want you both to read them. Please. You'll read about what Dev got up to during the last war, how he executed his own ex-comrades and locked up hundreds in a place called the Curragh military camp down in Kildare. Read them, and then we can talk more next time you visit.

The warder is pointing at the clock on the wall. Our thirty minutes is nearly up. My father looks at me and smiles a bemused sort of smile. He looks a bit proud as well. I am against the government – which his socialist heart distrusts instinctively – and also de Valera, whom he detests as a hypocrite and a rogue.

What do you think, Dada? I ask him. The warder looks away, out of the small barred window of the visiting room.

As long as you don't get yourself killed as well, and he laughs a little at his own joke. But I can see he's enjoying this.

But I might one of these days when we get out of here, I say back to him.

Ah now, there's no need to go that far, he says.

Now you and your friends are just protesting – isn't that all? says Mama.

It's not a question but a statement. She's great at rationalising, turning a negative into a positive. It's a long way from the Scouts. They're looking after us all right in here, though I just need some things, and I hand her a list.

The warder comes over, reads it and hands it back to Mama. Dada has a sort of permanent smile on his face now, like he can't believe what's happening and life has got a bit of excitement at last.

A thing of beauty

We are treated as political prisoners, allowed to wear the motley uniforms that we were captured in, and we are supposed to get non-prison food.

The thing of beauty is in the 'Joy forever. That's what my father says to me on their second visit. He rarely speaks, but when he does, he loves wordplay.

Do you think Keats would mind? he asks.

It's his way of making peace with me.

Sinéad and I have been getting fonder of each other in the past weeks back in Dublin. Now she just stares at me with a look that says she thinks we are all eejits. But nice ones. On the third visit they bring extra food because the prison stuff is shite. And also soap powder – and best of all, the little wind-up record player that the Governor is allowing us for good behaviour.

You can have one record only. To begin with, says Prentice, the head screw.

I had asked Mama to bring in Ravel's 'Bolero'. The lads think it will be rebel songs or something Irish at least.

The long June evening lies softly on the silent prison when I put the record on. As the rhythm rises in crescendo, the acoustics of D wing's high stone walls carry Ravel beyond our ears to dreams of outside, of freedom, of foreign places. The melody crashes to its finale. Silence. Then hands begin to clap from the cells.

Whitewashed stone walls, a vaulted brick ceiling, a bed, a bucket, a table and a chair is each man's world for nineteen dim-dark hours a day. They let us out for three hours in the morning and two in the evening. So we read, lie on our beds, think of girlfriends and wives, stare at the ceiling, and make Celtic crosses and models with dead matches.

Are you having a fag, Gerry? Give us your match then.

Everyone has to sing or recite a poem or tell a story at least once a week. I learn Brendan Behan's song 'The Old Triangle'. He composed it in D wing in 1943, when hundreds of IRA prisoners were here:

> Now a hungry feelin' comes o'er me stealin'
> All the mice were squealin' in my prison cell
> And the ould triangle was going jingle jangle
> All along the banks of the Royal Canal.
>
> Up in the female prison are 75 women
> And among them I wish I did dwell,
> Then that ould triangle would go jingle jangle
> All along the banks of the Royal Canal.

The triangle of the title hangs from the roof at the central hub of the prison, from which radiate the five tall cell blocks. It is a huge triangle, an equilateral tubular steel instrument, with each side about four feet long. It is like its smaller cousin used in orchestras. The warders beat it with a steel bar to announce morning rising, breakfast, dinner, tea and lights-out. It is the marker of our days and nights. It rules our lives.

Thirty-five years maximum

The de Valera government invokes the Detention Without Trial law from the forties. Now, in the fifties, the European Court in Strasbourg pronounces it to be in conflict with basic human rights. No matter. As every political prisoner's sentence expires, they are taken to the Curragh Military camp in County Kildare, the Free State Army's main encampment, which has been re-opened for us. The maximum possible sojourn is thirty-five years. At about this time we read about the Minister of Justice in South Africa, John Vorster, introducing a 'draconian' law, detention without trial for ninety days. The world is up in arms. But they ignore what is happening in Ireland. We aren't black.

The letters to the editor of the *Irish Times* are fifty per cent in favour of hanging us, and the rest of leaving us to rot. The other two dailies are split between those against us and those who think that we are indeed the true inheritors of the Republican tradition. People in the South are now questioning the status quo. But the North is quiet. There, nationalists, the Catholics, have their heads down and turned away. This cuts the ground from under us.

When the six-month men are released, they're re-arrested immediately at the gates, put in lorries, and taken off to the Curragh Camp.

The thirty-eight of us who are last in will likewise be re-arrested and taken to the Curragh for indefinite internment as soon as our sentences are up in four weeks time.

HQ staff decides that we should attempt an escape. If even a few manage to get out and away, it will be a great propaganda victory. It will boost morale, which has taken a bit of a knock with the mass arrests and reduced armed actions in the North. It will help with the by-elections too, which Sinn Féin is contesting.

Mountjoy is a tough jail to crack, though. Only a few lags have ever ducked out the gate in the past two centuries. And no politicals.

But enough of us had read *Escape from Colditz* and *The Wooden Horse* and other great escape stories to know what to do. More or less.

Escape

Civilian clothes quietly replace army jackets during visits. Trousers and boots are allegedly worn out. Money is smuggled in – enough for bus fares and a packet of fags each.

You're getting' tired of wearin' that cowboy stuff? asks one of the screws.

Ah yes, someone replies. I'm looking forward to my own clothes now.

Steady, patient comrades are selected to record every movement of the warders.

Look out for anything that will help us get out before they take us to the Curragh, we tell the men. Make notes of what you see around the place. Look out for any equipment that we can use to get over the walls.

Then comes a bit of luck.

Eddie Fagan kicks a ball down into a hollow next to the barred basement windows of D wing and looks in.

You won't believe it, lads, but there's steel scaffolding down there and all the knuckle joints and everything we need to build a ladder.

We look at him, thinking it's a joke, and he grins.

That used to be my game – scaffolding, he says. But, he adds, there's five half-inch bars on the window that we'll have to get through.

The plan takes shape. Scaffolding will get us to the top of the wall. Strips of bed linen will get us down the thirty feet on the other side. Our legs will get us across no man's land to the back gardens and to the street. We can see the buses passing in the street from our lookout post at the top of D wing.

The scaffolding is underneath our feet, says Albie. And it's our cell.

How do we get to it? asks Billy.

Through the floor there, says Eddie. It's the only way.

Albie Murphy and two others share the three-man cell on the ground floor. That night they prise up six floorboards. There is a two-foot space and then brickwork. Curved like the top of an arch. Eddie says, yes, he had seen arches through the window bars.

Since the day we arrived, there has been a 56lb weight lying around in the yard. Some of the lads used it for exercising. Now it's brought in quietly to Albie's cell.

We ask the head warder for permission to have Irish dancing as well as music.

OK, he says, but only between five and six when we're having our tea.

We can't believe our luck. We set up the record player outside Albie's cell and play jigs and reels and hornpipes at full volume from 5 o'clock till six. The lads who can dance, jump about in the heaviest hobnailed boots we've got between us. Irish dance is all in the feet, so the noise is terrific. It reverberates not only through D wing but the other wings as well. The lags, the burglars and thieves, complain.

Ah sure they'll be gone out of here to that other place in a few weeks, the screws tell them. Let them enjoy themselves while they can.

No such privileges exist in the Curragh Military Internment Camp.

We tie twisted lengths of tough prison sheet to the weight. The other end is tied around the midriff of one of the strongest men. When the music and dancing begin and all the lookouts are in position, the floorboards come up and he lifts the weight above his head and throws it down with all his strength onto the brickwork below. The building shakes. Just before the end of a dance record, the signal is given to stop dropping the weight. Music back on, the lads start pounding again. After three evenings of this there is a hole only six or seven inches deep, and a lot of dust. On the fifth night the weight goes through the bricks and one of the lads is almost cut in half by the lump of iron heading for the bowels of the prison in uninterrupted flight. Down goes the team of bar cutters and scaffold men.

Eddie finds enough steel to assemble a ladder. Speed is vital to get enough scaffolding out before the alarm goes up on the day.

The window bars are the last obstacles. They are half an inch thick. On her last visit, I'd given my Ma a ten-inch-high Celtic cross made with dead matchsticks. I put a note in her hand. 'To my mother, on her birthday, July 14th 1957. From your loving son Bearnárd. Cross of Matches constructed in four days.' Boasting as well.

On the back of the note it said: 'Find secret drawer in base of cross. Note for Sinéad in it. Handle with care!' Thomas found the note. It asked my Ma to put a hacksaw and blades in two separate packets of soap powder.

The next week, she and Sinéad arrive with the goods, their eyes bright, voices brittle with excitement. That night, while the rest of us sleep, Albie and his two cellmates go below and slave away at the bars. We give them extra potatoes for this the next day.

We need these spuds *before* we bleedin' work, says Albie.

On the appointed afternoon, the twenty-four chosen by the Army Council in the Curragh say quiet farewells to the rest of the Glencree men. My lads. I want to bring them all.

Now the fourteen of you that's left have to look and sound like the whole thirty-eight of us for as long as possible, says John Garfield.

The last dance is struck up. We say goodbye to the fourteen and down the hole we go. Eddie is supervising the poles in a nervous sort of way. I remove the five window bars, each of which was held in place by soap. Right outside the window, rows of healthy potato plants stand at almost full height. It's the last week of August and Ireland's national plants – never mind the shamrock! – are tall and healthy.

Lie down in the praties, lads, head to toe. No shoving, keep your heads down and no talking. Wait till you're told to move. Nerves are taut. The signal is given. The game is on.

Eddie and his men stand up and carry the pieces of steel out and lay them down on the gravel beneath the wall. I see Eddie's hands shaking. The steel knuckles are tightened around the poles and the four-legged ladder is ready.

Joe MacIleany and I start to climb. At the top, we wait. Nothing, no shouts or whistles. I look over the wall. Nobody. I look to the left and can see the arse of a guard sticking out, one of the card players. I give the signal. Four lads climb up.

They pause with their heads just below the top of the wall, their

163

faces white. The next four begin their climb, carefully placing their feet so as not to jerk the ladder.

Then it happens. A steel knuckle snaps loose. It's the top rung with the four lads on it. The whole contraption starts to collapse, screeching its way down the wall. More knuckles give way under the strain. The noise is terrible. The ladder disappears beneath us, the lads in a heap amid cries of pain. Joe and I are stranded on the top of the wall. The shout from below is clear.

Get off that fuckin' wall or I'll shoot!

I turn with great care towards the voice. A guard is pointing a pistol, the little black hole of the spout is huge. His hand is shaking.

Get back, will ya, he shouts again.

Joe shouts down, We can't. The ladder is broken. We're not armed, and he tries to raise his hands and nearly falls off the thirty-foot wall. Joe and I look at each other, the same thought in our minds. Do we jump and make a run for it? Our legs, our backs will break. Or we'll get shot.

There are four of them below us now, and whistles going, and then the old prison siren starts. The biggest jailbreak in Irish history is over.

Second 'escape'

They confiscate every personal possession we have, including toothpaste. All privileges are halted. Double the number of guards patrol in the few hours a day that they allow us out. It's like the sun has gone forever. A few days later, we find some old newspapers in a corner. There's a description of two EOKA prisoners who'd escaped from the British on Cyprus. They told the Brits that they wanted to give up their fight for Cypriot unity with Greece, and if they let them out they'd show them an arms cache. When they got to the spot they ducked and ran. I showed the report to John Garfield.

164

We could try that, I say. Or some variation of it, and get a few out.

One of the warders is a sympathetic courier, and permission is given from the Curragh in forty-eight hours. The instructions are that I'm to approach the head warder and ask to see Inspector McMadden. The Special Branch have told all of us that they are ready to let us go if we are prepared to sign out. This is a way of undermining morale and neutralising Republicans. If you sign a statement that you will recognise the Southern Government and not join any illegal organisations in future, they'll release you. Of course, you can't rejoin. It is surrender – and they know it. McMadden takes the bait and says they'll let me out on two conditions. One, that I'll take them to a cache, and two, that I'll lead them to Charlie Murtagh and Seán Curren.

Back inside, we want to call the whole thing off. These are the only two Army General Staff members to have evaded the swoop that netted the more than two hundred men currently in the Curragh. They are on the run, and keeping the guerrilla campaign going.

What can we get away with? John asks.

We can show them an old arms dump, I say. Then make contact with Charlie and Seán, arrange a rendezvous, and shake off the Specials.

Jays, they'll stick to you like shite to a cow's arse.

I'll only make physical contact when I'm two hundred per cent sure I've shaken them, I say.

We impose two counter-conditions. I am not signing any paper, and they will have to release eight others with me. Otherwise, I say, people will be suspicious of me on my own. In the minds of the police, this makes sense. I am giving up, but if they are to catch the big fish, nobody must suspect what I'm doing. They agree to let four out with me. McMadden is worried. I sense that they are under pressure to crack our solidarity.

Lying awake that night, the thought that anyone will use the dreaded word 'informer' against me almost makes me give up the whole risky business. I know the worst that can happen will be that they'll tumble to what we are up to, re-arrest us, and slam us in the Curragh. But there is one greater fear. They might outwit me and catch the two most wanted men. HQ is prepared to gamble getting the five of us out. So five of us walk out. The other four go off home to lie low, and I take the Specials to a recently abandoned dump in Stradbrooke. The lady of the house is furious and tells the Special Branch to go to hell.

There's nothing here, says a detective after searching.
I express surprise and annoyance. They threaten to give me a beating, and send me straight to the Curragh. I keep quiet and start hoping that they'll call the whole thing off. But the temptation to get the two leaders, the country's most wanted men, is too great. They let me go again, with fresh instructions on how to contact them and set the trap for Seán and Charlie.
I see Sinéad almost every day. I look at her and think, this is only for a week or two. That makes me want her even more.

If you love me you'll resign from your Army, she says.
I do love you, but this is my life, I say.
I go over it all again, as this isn't the first time she has done this. It's not her fault, I say to myself. Her father hates Republicans and the IRA and her mother is not interested in politics. But Sinéad comes around, and everything is fine with us again.
Three months in total behind high walls, and I appreciate the smell of grass being cut, a bread van passing with fresh loaves, motor cars and girls. Just people in ordinary clothes – but mostly girls, and especially Sinéad.
My parents don't know what's going on either. The newspapers have surmised that a gradual releasing policy has started.
Everybody is fooled. I can't breathe a word of the plan to anybody.

You've done your bit now, Bernard, Mama says. I'll see if Caltex will take you back.

Ah, it's a bit soon, I say. Let me think about it, Ma.

I make contact with my two leaders. Shaking off the Special Branch when the prize is IRA leaders on the run is not easy. On the appointed day, I shake them off by jumping on and off buses at speed. That and disguises. When I reckon I've lost them, I take off a dark raincoat and a fawn one is underneath. Wearing a cloth cap, I take the bus for the foothills and climb to the rendezvous with an hour to spare.

Charlie and Seán appear on time. They have been watching me with binoculars to make sure I am not being followed.

Tell us how you did it, Charlie says. We had bets that half the Peelers in Dublin would be on your tail.

And that they'd catch you and string you up, laughs Seán. We're glad we lost the money.

I look through incoming mist and rain at Dublin below us. The city gradually disappears. We slosh our way up and over the mountain. A farmer meets us with tea and shelter.

You're going to Cavan, Charlie says. Wait there for more instructions. We have something big planned. You'll have your own active service unit. You'll have a very good local man, from Fermanagh, as your 2 i/c.

We talk into the night, throwing damp turf onto the fire and sending fairy-light sparks up the black chimney.

I say a whole Rosary that night kneeling at my bed; thanks for helping me to shake the cops and for Charlie and Seán not being caught.

It's not their war

Next morning, they grin and shake hands, saying goodbye in the driving rain. I'm not ready for this. I feel I'm not good enough.

But it's a huge chance to prove myself. I run down to a waiting black Ford Prefect driven by a local farmer. He passes me on, and three cars later I arrive at a mountain cottage on the border.

You'll be stayin' with a good man. His name is Danny and he is a pig smuggler, only he can't run pigs into the North now because your activities have disrupted all that. But he smiles, says, God bless the work, and drives off into the muddy darkness.

I bang on a lighted window when there's no answer to my knocking.

Sorry about that, says a friendly face with hair sticking out in all directions. I was playing the accordion here. Practising for the *fleadh* on Saturday night, y'know.

Next morning, I sit with Danny in his cottage on the mountainside. He tells me about the good old days running rashers on the hoof into the North.

Come outside and I'll show you the route we used to take, he says.

I slosh along behind him through a gate and up a hill. The wind nearly takes my head off. Danny points. You can see the road running beside that little stream there. Then he swings around like a weather vane. Over there, he points again, is the road the British patrols come along. He looks at me to see how I'm taking this. It's my first look at our target area.

Can anyone see us from here, Danny? I ask. We're right on top of a hill.

No. They'll just think I'm looking for sheep.

Who will they think is *with* you? I persist, but he ignores me. Immigration has taken the bulk of the people from around these parts. Two figures on a hilltop when there should only be one will cause tongues to wag, I fear.

We sit down on the grass. It is dry now from all the wind. We look at the road in the distance. Windscreens flash. I imagine the flash of the Land Rovers and Saracen scout cars in a week's time.

The flash of rifles, a Bren gun. The return flashes of the soldiers. That evening we head down the mountain in Danny's van. He hasn't had pigs in it for years, but it smells like there are twenty in the back.

We are going to meet Phil McManus in Mickey Tom Jack McGowan's B&B in Swad – Swanlinbar to you, says Danny. It's a safe house, and Mickey is even safer. Phil is an Ulsterman from Fermanagh with a mop of red hair and a grin of good humour. We like each other straight away. He is my second-in-command in charge of the column. Danny is our guide into the North. Seven more of the lads are due up in a few days from Cork.

How soon can Mickey… what's his name again? I ask.

Mickey Tom Jack. There's so many McGowans around here we have to name them like that, you see, Danny grins.

How soon can he show us the arms, do you think? Phil asks, anticipating my question.

In a day or two. We'll ask him tonight, says Danny. We spend some hours with maps, planning and discussing with the local lads. Then Phil goes off to his safe house for the night. We arrange to meet the next day. Going back up the mountain, Danny and I bounce and splash in his van. It grinds over rocks and potholes in the boreen. Around a sharp corner, a light appears. A man is waving a torch for us to stop. I see the glint of his visor. A guard. I pull my cap over my eyes. He is on my side of the road.

Is that you, Mr Cahill?

It is, says Danny.

How are ye then? And he turns the torch into the cab. I put my left hand up to my face.

Sorry, sir, says the cop, shining the light on the floor and into the back where the ghosts of the pigs are.

You haven't fixed that headlamp yet, I see. That's why I stopped you. This is the third time now, the guard says.

Ah sure, I'm sorry guard. I'll have it fixed for definite tomorrow. I've been a bit short.

The Guard takes another close look at me, then waves us on.

We're in shit, Danny boy. He knows I'm not local. What the fuck is this about the light?

We are in more than pig shit now, I think.

Can we go back by a different route, Danny? He'll be on the radio by now. Where can I sleep?

Well, there's the outhouse…

No, Danny, not there. Another safe house? I ask him.

D'you think…?

Yes I do. They can raid you tonight. And I know they are looking for me, since I gave them the slip in Dublin.

That night I sleep in a cousin's roof – attic, we'd say in Dublin. This is a hotel for rats and spiders. I stiffen at every sound. I imagine the spiders spinning silent webs in the night and trussing me up like Gulliver, the product of another Irishman's imaginings. I lie awake.

What hope have we now? The guards are patrolling the length of the border in the Free State. The other side is swarming with RUC and B Specials and British troops.

How many of us are there left on the outside? I try to calculate. Over two hundred are in the Curragh now, and about the same in Belfast and English jails. Would there be forty, fifty left outside? If that. A dozen or so would be fully trained.

There was only a handful that defied the Empire on Easter Monday 1916. They lasted a week. But then Michael Collins brought the Brits to a standstill five years later with only two or three hundred dedicated men and women guerrillas. So why do I doubt us now?

170

I know the reason. The people in the North haven't risen up since the Campaign began in December. And it's now six months down the line. Two of the lads are dead and hundreds in jail. No swarms of volunteers are coming south to be trained, no protest meetings are being organised. It's all been left up to us from the South. There are times in history when people are just too tired or apathetic to fight. Or can't see the point.

I know, I say to myself. Give them a few more martyrs and they'll rise up. We must succeed with this operation – and we can take no risks now, with the cops all over the place.

Danny's cousin takes a note down to the others. We postpone the job. They could raid us any time. They could capture the precious arms. Phil and I decide to split up. I'll go to Mickey Tom Jack's place, and Phil will head off immediately to another town. As he is from the North, he can't go home. His house is under continual surveillance. This decision proves to be Phil's death warrant. Four months later he blew himself to pieces with a bomb under a bridge.

I move in under cover of darkness with Mickey Tom Jack. We are bitterly disappointed. This op was to kick-start the campaign again. The lads in Cork are told to lie low.

The Army is reduced now to hit-and-run sabotage raids over the border, the line that cuts villages, pubs and houses in two. There is nowhere in the North we can safely stay longer than forty-eight hours. And now the guards and the Free State Army are closing in on us from the South, too.

I've never seen so many Peelers, says Mickey, looking out at a police car on the wet street.

What is it, Mickey? Why is there not support for us in the North?

Ah well, you see, Bearnárd, there's no call for this sort of action up there. He pauses and looks a bit uncomfortable. The idea for

this campaign was born in Dublin and Cork, he goes on. You
didn't know that? Not in Belfast or even Derry. It's not their idea,
their baby. They say, What do these guys down south know?
He pauses to see how I am taking this. I am an officer and from
Dublin. But I am also only twenty years of age, still wet behind my
ears, and Mickey Tom Jack is fifty if he's a day.

Go on, I say.

So you see, it's not their war. Ah now, I don't mean to say they
don't appreciate the lads dying and going to jail and all. But some
of them question the motives and the methods like, don't you
know.

He stops for breath. It's as if a veil is being pulled back from a
picture. It leaves me feeling empty. Just empty.

Apart from the Mickeys, the Dannys, and other great individuals
in the North who are doing their best, there are few active
supporters. Without civilian support you can forget it, all the
great guerrilla leaders say. That Cuban guy Castro is fighting in his
mountains, and General Grivas and EOKA in Cyprus. Hanging on
by the skin of their teeth, they are.

It looks like a shit situation from where I'm sitting, looking out at
Mickey's backyard with the rain pouring down again. The elation
of 'escaping' from the 'Joy, of seeing Charlie and Seán and giving
the Special Branch the slip, is slowly drowning in the rivers of
water in the yard below me.

---

*Can the mind split into two separate paths? Working independently of each
other? How do you know when the mind withdraws from reality? Or
creates two realities?*

*My mind must have split about then. One half wanted to go on, to stay on
the run for as long as possible, and stay out of jail.*

But the other half gave up, just rolled over and accepted defeat.

I made a phone call. I made it to McMadden. Or somebody close to him.
When or how I made the call, I still do not know. It can only have been
from a callbox in the town.
But I had McMadden's number. He had given it to me when I had to find
Charlie and Seán and set up their capture.
Something gave way in my head that night in Swad. Because I told
McMadden, or somebody, where I was hiding. And to come and get me.
Phil would be safely away from the town and into another county. It was
only me that they would get.
But at the same time, the other mind-path was planning my escape when
the police raided Mickey Tom Jack's house. That part knew that a raid was
coming, and proceeded to work out a plan to avoid arrest. To escape. The
plans ran parallel.
The call set one track in motion.

Escape – or break my neck

Mickey, I've seen where I want to go if they raid us, I say. Can I
break the window in the bathroom upstairs?

We sat with tea cups and sandwiches in my bedroom where none
of his family could hear or see us.

You can break what you like, Bearnárd, but why would you go
out that one? It's three storeys up.

Because I want to climb on the roof and go across to the
border.

The border cut through the edge of Swad.

What? says Mickey and stares at me.

I've given it careful thought, I say. If I break the window loudly,
the police will think I'm coming down the drainpipe. But I'll
climb onto the roof and make my way along the ridge, around the
chimney pots, until I reach the other side of the border and take
my chances there.

Mickey says it's a great plan and that it may well work. He and I are excited now. He leans out the back window and shows me the house that's near the border.

You can climb down into Gogarty's back yard easily enough. I'll talk to Gogarty, and he'll keep his ears and his eyes open for you.

I can hold them up with this, he says. We have moved to his bedroom. He puts a hand under the pillow and pulls out a Webley .45, the revolver that British Army officers used in the First World War.

No, you can't, Mickey. You know the rule, I say. I smile at his determination to hold off the armed Special Branch. No shooting in the South. You remember?

I do, I do, he says.

In his day, fourteen years before, the IRA had resisted arrest with arms. Several guards were killed and volunteers were executed by hanging. Now orders are strict. No armed action south of the border.

Later that night, the banging wakes me up. The knocking sounds like they are going to break the door down. I run into Mickey's room. His wife has her teeth out on a stool. Mickey has the .45 in his fist.

Are you sure now, Bearnárd? His blood is up.

Please no, Mickey, hide it – don't let them find it now.

The banging gets louder.

Thank you, ma'am, and you, Mickey – I'm going to smash your window now.

I run up to the bathroom and break out two panes from the lower part of the window, then lower the upper sash and look out.

I catch sight of a figure running across the yard two houses away. They are falling for it. My adrenaline gets me up and out to the downpipe on the right. I have checked it. Old iron, solid as a lamppost. I climb to the top of the roof. Four squad cars look small on the street. Townspeople, hands folded across their chests, stand in little groups. Nobody is looking up. I feel a surge of excitement. I am getting away.

Where is the other person that phoned Dublin? Is that half of my mind in suspense?

I start to ease like a crab along the slates, keeping a grip on the roof ridge. A chimney blocks my way. I ease down, and up the other side. Another peep over. Nobody is looking up yet. I repeat this four more times. The next chimney is smaller. I grasp it, and the plaster and the bricks come away in my hand. I am losing my balance.

The noise in the wee small hours is horrific. I hear shouting from up the street. A powerful light shines upwards. I want to knock the whole chimney down onto the cops. I look to the North and it's all in darkness. No cops. No RUC. But for that feckin' chimney, I'd have made it.

The police spotlight steadies on my face.

Come down, Bearnárd, calls a voice. We see you.

It's McMadden's side-kick, Detective Sergeant Small. He plays the good cop.

I'll stay up here all night, I think. Freedom is up here.

But yet I had made the phone call that brought the police to end that freedom.

I take a long time to get back to the gutter above the broken window. Without the adrenaline, I'm scared stiff of the three-storey drop. But I manage it. A cop is waiting to pull me in at the bathroom window. I shake off his arm, and he lets me go as if he's been stung.

Down in the hall, Mickey Tom Jack and his wife are standing in their pyjamas. I'm glad she has her teeth back in. About six police surround them. McMadden and Small are there.

I thank Mickey and his wife. Sorry about your window.

He smiles at me. We're both thinking of the hidden-again Webley .45 and the Custer's last stand he could have made.

They grab me then – down the steps, across the street, and into a car. I hear shouts from the people and 'Up the IRA!'.

McMadden is in front with the driver.

What the fuck did you think you were doing on that roof?

I nearly made it, I say.

You nearly made what? He turns around in the seat with a furious expression.

The border, I say.

Small looks at me with a disbelieving face. The driver is listening, so they say no more.

Get us the fuck out of here, McMadden says to the driver.

Out on the dark country roads I try to imagine the Curragh. All I can see are the faces of my comrades who will be there, waiting.

Are you hungry? asks Small in a quiet voice.

Very, I say.

He takes a greaseproof paper packet from the back window and hands it to me.

Eat this, he says quietly.

Two rounds of ham sandwiches.

About halfway to Dublin, the Inspector turns around. Have a look there, Bill, My wife made me some sandwiches.

The prisoner must have eaten them, says Small, with a straight face.

Are you guarding the fucking bastard or what? McMadden shouts.

Sorry, sir, says Small and stares straight ahead.

Back in Dublin in the Bridewell, they let me sleep. But not for long. At about eight o'clock I am taken to an office.

Now, Bearnárd, what's going on? Where are Charlie and Seán? Well?

McMadden has calmed down, but his eyes are cold and furious. I tell him that he must be mad to think I'd ever hand over a comrade, least of all Charlie or Seán.

Is that right, you bastard, he says.

Silence. We stare at each other.

But you gave yourself up, he says. I am silent.

So what were you up to in Swanlinbar then?

Can't tell you that, I say.

Do you want to give it all up now, give up the IRA?

No. I want to go to the Curragh.

And all that running about on the roof, what was that about? he asks.

I say nothing.

I don't know the answer to that, either. The two competing strands in my head are becoming one. All I can remember now is that I'd tried to escape.

And now I suppose you want to leave the country? McMadden says.

No.

What do you mean 'no'? What *do* you want? he asks.

I told you I want to go to the Camp. I stare at them.

What? They both say at once. They still don't believe me.

Why did you phone us? Small asks.

I don't know.

You phone us, and when we arrive you almost kill yourself and one of our men trying to escape, says McMadden, now very annoyed. Are you mad or what?

177

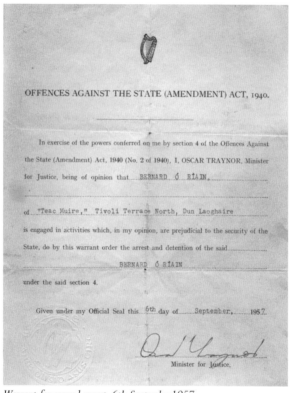

OFFENCES AGAINST THE STATE (AMENDMENT) ACT, 1940.

In exercise of the powers conferred on me by section 4 of the Offences Against the State (Amendment) Act, 1940 (No. 2 of 1940), I, OSCAR TRAYNOR, Minister for Justice, being of opinion that BERNARD Ó RÍAIN,

of "Teac Muire," Tivoli Terrace North, Dun Laoghaire

is engaged in activities which, in my opinion, are prejudicial to the security of the State, do by this warrant order the arrest and detention of the said BERNARD Ó RÍAIN

under the said section 4.

Given under my Official Seal this 6th day of September, 1957.

Minister for Justice.

Warrant for second arrest, 6th September 1957

I tell them that I am too tired to talk and will they take me to the Curragh Camp. I do not want to go home. That is not a place I want to live in again. My friends, comrades are in the Curragh. That is safe. That is home.

Why had I done these two things in parallel? They are impulses that I cannot explain. As far as I know, the Special Branch never talk about it all because they have egg on their faces. And I never tell my comrades about this. They believe – and I believe – that the guard who stopped Danny's van because of his broken headlight called in the Special Branch. That I then tried to escape and was caught because of the chimney falling down.

Half of my mind still believes that. What was going on in my mind at that time? The comparative safety of the Curragh versus almost certain death on active service in the North or a jail sentence in Belfast for ten years? Cowardice? Fear? Is it as simple as that?

The question that hangs like a man from a gutter is, what would have happened if the chimney had *not* fallen down? I'd have made it into the North – and then?

9

The Curragh Internment Camp

WE WANT YOU TO stop walking around the perimeter like a caged animal, says Tomás MacCartan – our IRA O/C – to me after my first week. The guards think you are an escape artist, and we want them to relax. Get a hobby and take it easy.

Little do they know that I am in fact glad to be here with my pals. I learn how to make leather wallets, billfolds and Rosary bead cases. My family brings in the materials and we make our own tools. Billy Keegan introduces me to the writings of Hemingway, Faulkner, Steinbeck, Runyon, Kafka and Proust. And to jazz. The former sticks, the jazz does not.

Debates about Ireland, socialism and communism rage. The latter are discussed only when walking the perimeter because the vast majority of Republicans are convinced Catholics. James Connolly's socialism has yet to make its comeback.

They allow us out after dark to see the first Sputnik pass overhead in 1957. Next day, roly-poly Free State Army Sergeant Foley is re-named Sputnik. His face is redder now, and he smiles with pride. The Monday rissoles, left-overs kneaded into meatballs, get the same name, and are tried out for their flight capabilities. A shower of Irish sputniks splatters the floor and walls of the canteen. Ten of us get no food for twenty-four hours for our test-pilot efforts.

Mist mingles with sheets of rain and we huddle around the iron pot-bellied stoves in the wooden huts. When the wind howls, rain comes in the cracks. The lads either look for a place at the stove or read in bed. Or sleep. Nobody fights for a warm place. It's first come, first served.

Spring comes late. Curlews cry over the rain-soaked plain. A man moves slowly on a bicycle on the far horizon, black coat dark as puddles. Damp smells rise, and the midday sun soon has the land steaming. Earth freshly turned in the Camp garden plot smells heavy and fresh. This soil has not been dug since the potato famine, and was turned over to sheep and horses when the people had gone.

At times I walk alone, but mostly with Billy. Round and round the perimeter fence. It's at least a mile in circumference. I do want to get out, to see Sinéad, to have freedom again. But on the other hand I have my friends here. I do not want to give them up. I am appreciated here. I am a somebody.

Fatal contacts

I watch Andy McGuire making a ring for his girlfriend out of a British sovereign. I write and ask Mama if she can find one. She brings me one on the next visit.

I've had this for years, she says. This must be the rainy day!

Andy teaches me. The painstaking process starts with drilling a small hole in the coin. After three weeks, the ring is beautiful.

Will I give it to Sinéad? I am missing her more than ever.

You're just horny, says Séamus Costigan, the cynic. I am, of course, but it's not just that.

I wish we could have our wives and girls in here, like the married quarters in their army, I say, pointing at a guard.

It's well for you, says Séamus, you have a girl. What about us that don't? What do we do for the next thirty-five years?

Pull your wire, somone mutters.

Seán Ryan accuses Séamus of being a misogynist. It is my first meeting with the word. Séamus is crusty, for a nineteen-year-old. He had said something disparaging about the lads who talk about girls all the time. He's not criticising women, Billy smiles, but the men who are obsessed by them.

Am I obsessed? I think of my girl when the lights go out at night and before we get up at six in the morning. They don't put as much bromide in the tea as they should.

To calm our appetites it is, says the chaplain in confession. I know it's difficult, my son, when you are in the Army. Or in jail. But think of the saints and say a prayer for me.

From the way he says that, I know he has the same problem. Must be hard for him in confession with women telling him what they do. I think of the word 'misogynist'. But how could men hate women? I love my Ma. And I love Sinéad. She's been my girlfriend now for over a year, and visits me with my parents and brothers. We sign our monthly letters 'all my love'. So I do love her, and she loves me.

But now I'm not sure any more. She told me in her last letter that she went out with another fellow. Paul. My heart did a loop. He wants her to break it off with me.

If he loves you he will sign out, Paul had said. At least she says he said this. I'll teach him with a smack on his gob, I decide. My neat and tidy, busy little world falls apart. I need Sinéad. She mustn't go out with this guy. She must wait for me. Like all the other

CORAS IOMPAIR EIREANN
(ROAD PASSENGER SECTION)   CH 004708

THROUGH _Return_ TICKET
(INSERT SINGLE OR RETURN)

FROM _Curragh Camp_

TO _Dublin_

WARRANT No. _7050_

FARE. £ _: 11/ 0_

DATE _3 . 9 . 53_

CONDUCTOR _Jo Regan_

SERVICE No. _327_

EXCHANGE No.

TRANSFER AT

Valid date of issue only for Outward Journey and one month for Return Journey.
Break of Journey not permitted. Issued subject to Board's Rules and Regulations.
To be retained for Inspection and given up on demand.

Return bus ticket to Curragh Camp

wives and girlfriends. Well, except one – John Garfield's girl married a Sinn Féiner who hadn't been arrested yet. We were scandalised by that.

But, says Sinéad on her next visit, you told me yourself that they could keep you in here for the next thirty-five years if they want.

No, it won't be anything like that, I say, maybe five years at the most.

That was the considered estimate by our own leaders. Her eyes tell me the story. She fidgets in her chair and Mama says to Dada, Let's leave them alone now.

I feel angry with Sinéad. My world is falling apart and it's because of her. She's not listening to me – I can see that.

God bless, Bernard, says my Ma and they leave the visitors' hut. She still pronounces my name 'Bernid', her old way. Sure, why not? The lads saying it in the Irish way is enough. Dada looks back, and it's a look of real understanding. I want to thank him, but he is gone. I turn to my girl.

Let's wait and see, she says. I don't like Paul all that much, anyway. She pauses then. My father likes him, though, because he's got a good job.

I see the hesitation in her eyes. Suddenly they fill with tears.

Daddy never leaves me alone. He says he'll throw me out. He says to Mammy that he'll throw her out too if she supports me. Our whole house is upset now. Sinéad blows her nose and the guard looks away.

I think I'll kill myself, she says in a small voice.

What did you say, Sinéad?

Nothing. I'm just upset by all this. Daddy says I should never have started with an IRA man, that I need my head read. She smiles then through her tears.

Those words haunt me: 'I think I'll kill myself.' And Paul. He haunts me too from now on. I try to imagine his face in the ceiling of the hut. I can see it. I drag it slowly down, kicking it to the table with the leather knives. But I can't, I can't kill him. I'll have to do something else.

<hr />

What's wrong? asks Billy

Will I tell him? My pride says no, and I ignore the worry that's now eating my insides.

I can't sleep, and wait for the next letter. I can't get her out of my head. Billy and the lads who share our nightly chat around the stove look at me sideways. I don't talk or eat very much, and I stop my leatherwork. Reading is the only escape. I must get out. I must stop this other guy. She's my girl.

I feel ill all the time. I'm listless, stop walking around the fence with Billy. I am panicky. I imagine Billy speaks to the O/C about me. Then the Camp doctor puts me under observation in the clinic hut that is apart from the others. I don't smoke – I never have – but still I ask him for cigarettes. I inhale deeply to knock myself out at night. So that I can sleep. I think of McMadden. What if I contact him? I'll tell him I'm finished with the IRA, that I want to get married and go and live in England.

What's wrong with you? asks the military doctor. I can't find anything physically wrong, what's upsetting you?

It's my girlfriend, I say.

Will he understand better than the priest will?

What about her? he asks.

She won't wait. And she says that she might kill herself.

Ah sure, young girls often say things like that. If they don't get their own way, he laughs. Why don't you just forget her?

I want to get out of here, I say.

He stares at me. He can see that I mean it.

Do you want me to talk to the Commandant then?

The Commandant comes in. I tell him I can't stay here a day longer. He comes back the next day and says McMadden wants to see me.

The only thing I cling to is not signing out. I'll show him a letter of resignation from the Army if he wants, I tell him, but that's all. I tell Éamonn and I go to see MacCartan and tell him the whole story too. He suspects most of it. I tell him that I'm letting him and all the lads down. He is very upset but says he understands.

I'm sorry, he says, that we ever allowed that bastard McMadden anywhere near you in Mountjoy. That was a fatal contact.

I cry in MacCartan's hut and then in my own. I am in shock, and so are Billy and the lads.

Next thing, I am sitting at a table in the military compound with McMadden, and Small's there too.

What are you up to now, Bearnárd? McMadden asks.

I'm not up to anything. I want out, that's all. I'll resign and go to England.

We've seen your letters to your lady friend, Small says. He waits and then says, Sorry for your troubles.

Don't be sorry, I snap at him. Just let me go.

He pushes a grubby typewritten sheet across the table. I read it. It is the infamous signing-out paper. I push it back.

I told the Commandant I wouldn't sign that.

OK, McMadden says, all smarmy. He looks at Small.

But will you just answer a few questions, then? He asks

What questions? I ask.

Is there a split inside? You know, are there factions that want to give up the campaign and others who want to continue, some who want to escape and others who think it's too risky?

I know that there are, but I laugh at him and say that the lads are solid as a rock.

And are there any more like you that want to come out, have had enough?

I don't know of one, I tell him. And I don't.

I say, I just want out. I'm telling you nothing.

I am angry and frightened and tired at the same time. Where is this going?

After muttering something to Small, he asks to see my letter of resignation from the Army. I show it to him.

'To the O/C Dublin Brigade

I hereby resign as a Volunteer in the Irish Republican Army for personal reasons.

I cannot remain in jail any longer, nor can I face going inside again. I remain faithful to the ideals and objectives of the Republican Movement.

Yours sincerely,

Bearnárd S O'Riain'

McMadden pushes the letter back.

You can't say that. We can't let you out with that.

I am angry now.

I'll go back then, I say, and stand up, shaking. They look startled.

What do you expect us to do, just release you? Just like that? McMadden says.

Yes, I say.

They look worried, like this is not what they expected.

If this is another trick... Small starts to say.

It's not. You've seen my private letters. And don't think you can use my leaving here for your propaganda. I'm no use to anyone now. Not the Movement. Not you.

But what am I saying? I'm letting my dislike of McMadden and his bullying get the better of me. Better shut up.

Sit down and wait here, Small says. They go outside.

A Free State Army captain comes in. Your friend, Billy, says that you want him to look after your stuff. What about your clothes?

I only want to take what's in the hospital, I say.

I sit in silence. Outside, the soldiers are laughing about something. Then I see eyes gawking through the window – a green cap above them. Like I'm in the zoo. I turn my chair around and face the door.

This is my last chance to go back inside. To my comrades, my books, my leatherwork.

Is this what I want? To go back? Or to get out? No, to go back to my friends. To hell with Paul and Sinéad.

Yes, yes, yes.

Small comes back into the room and stands looking at me. We'll take you to the bus stop, he says quietly. They've got your stuff.

I look at him, and he takes my elbow. He seems to know what's in my head. I let him lead me out and across the yard to a police car. McMadden is already inside it. Small opens the door and I get in, and the world closes on my head. My little case is on the seat. They stop fifty yards from where the bus is waiting.

Will you just sign this then? Small asks me. It's a torn-off piece of a notebook and it says: 'I undertake to resign from any illegal organisation and not to join any others in the future.'

Well, will you sign it for us then? Small says.

It's not the same as my letter, but near enough, I think. I sign it, get out and walk to the bus. But deep down I know that I've signed out. The conductor looks at me funny and asks for the travel voucher that the Captain has given me. It says 'Through Return Ticket'. 'Return' it says.

I know now that I have to get out of Ireland.

Elopement

I remember nothing of the journey or my arrival home. I am numb.

Next day, Pasha jumps up from his desk in the *United Irishman* office in Gardiner Street. His eyes are moist and his old dog starts yowling. I give him my letter, let him read it, and try to stay calm. He can't talk properly at the best of times, but now he fails altogether. He just sort of waves his arms as if to say, Why? I can't begin to tell him, so I just grab his hand, shake it, and run out of there.

What do you want to do now, Bernard? asks Mama, Why don't you go away to rest a while? She is hurting for me.

They say in the papers that the campaign is nearly over, she says. Will the rest of the men be coming out now?

I have told them in the past of the stigma of signing out. But she doesn't care, as long as I'm safe.

Yes, Mama, I'll go away for a bit.

They don't know what to say, and they all leave me alone.

Now I want action. I'll convince Sinéad that we must elope. We'll get married in Scotland, Gretna Green. My empty head fills with plans. My girl's eyes light up like a child's at Christmas when I tell her.

My father will go mad, she says. But my mother will be on our side.

Her eyes are sparkling with the thrill of it all.

What about Paul? I ask.

Oh, he doesn't matter now that you are here, she says. And Mammy says we must stay with Auntie Molly. She lives in Wales. She knows all about us. Her eyes are shining. It's contagious.

Are you excited? I ask her.

Oh yes. We'll be like Romeo and Juliet.

Two days later I meet her at the bus stop in Blackrock with our little suitcases, and we elope to Wales.

On the back of my return ticket to the Curragh Camp, I had written:

Dún Laoghaire	9.15	Mailboat
Holyhead	1.00	
Holyhead	1.35	Train to L'pool
Bangor	2.09	
Bangor	2.15	
Rhyl	3.35	

My father's timetable lessons have stuck. Sinéad's Aunt Molly in Rhyl has written to her saying that she must bring her swain over to stay with her. I have to look that word up. She hates Sinéad's father for his treatment of her sister. The father who says that I am a gangster and a murderer.

She's a great romantic and reads novels about true love, says Sinéad. She told me on the phone that we can live with her as long as we like, and we can get jobs and all. She's never been married.

She's a romantic spinster.

We sail on the mailboat and tell ourselves that we'll get married in a registry office. Aunt Molly cries at the railway station and smiles at the same time. Rhyl looks like a picture postcard.

We stay in all day. On the first day we decide that we'll have lots of children. Sinéad tries on the gold ring. By the second day, it's down to four children. We only go out for walks after dark. It's exciting when we see a Bobby standing with his arms behind his back. Are they looking for us? On the third day, two policemen call. We hear the voices. Aunt Molly is outraged. How dare that brother-in-law of hers, and so on. She's a good actress. They go away. But the search is on. Aunt Molly has put two single mattresses on the floor of her lounge for us. But we don't do anything much at night.

I want to be a virgin when I get married, says Sinéad, I promised Mammy.

But what do you think? I ask. We are going to get married, so why don't we practise a bit?

She laughs at that but says, No we must wait.

Next day we don't talk about children at all, and don't say much. It's raining and dark.

The Welsh police call at the door again on the fifth day, and Aunt Molly says she's not heard a thing. For five days and nights we only walk in the garden. No sex, only doing everything except the 'real thing', as Tommy would say. I'm twenty-one and still don't know how to do it properly. True Irish Catholic sexual constipation. Fired only three shots in frustation and never in bed. The young lads on the rocks behind the pier had put me off my aim with JD. We look at each other instead, and it all sinks in.

This is not right, is it? I ask her.

The next morning it's raining and dark. I watch the rain lashing against the windowpanes. Like it did in Donegal. In the warmth of the bed I imagine Val beside me, and it makes me blush. I see her in a white dress brushing her long brown hair. She looks around in my half-dream and smiles. Her eyes are not on me, but on something far away. Then I look at Sinéad asleep beside me, her face like a child's. This is the end, I say to myself. I must take this girl home to her parents.

This is not right, is it? I ask her when she wakes.

Her eyes are big, and there are dark rings under them. Neither of us is sleeping properly. It's not just the rain clouds that are hanging over us. We are like the babes in the wood. Lost and frightened.

I'm not waiting for the woodsman to rescue us, I say suddenly. I am standing at the sash window, watching the rain streaming down it.

What? she asks.

The fellow that rescued the babes in the wood. I'm going to be him, the woodsman.

You mean we can go back home?

She suddenly looks calm. I can see the relief. She can go home.

And me? I must leave Ireland.

Aunt Molly cries when I say we are going back to Dublin.

We're not in love really, we explain to her. We just thought we were.

But you'll still be friends? she asks.

We don't look at each other when we say, Yes, Aunt Molly.

The cops are expecting us at Dún Laoghaire pier. They just nod, and one turns away to make his phone call. I take Sinéad up the steps to her front door and say goodbye. We have tears in our eyes. I don't ever see her again.

Coming of age

I can't keep up, Dada says when I tell them what has happened. But he smiles a sad little smile. What are you going to do now?

It's the first time he has ever asked me that question. I'm nearly twenty-two, and I think he sees me as a man now.

I talk to him that day for hours. Mama brings us loads of tea and sandwiches and leaves us alone. She has never seen her eldest son and her husband talking like this. She walks into the drawing room, sees the two of us sitting side-by-side, with me talking into his good ear, and she just stands there with the tea. We look up at her. And there it is, her funny happy smile.

We talk about Dermot's studies, Maybe he'll be a priest, Dada says. And Patrick now in the Christian Brothers. Imagine. He's locked up now too. And Thomas? I ask.

Oh I don't know, Dada says, he's g-grand, and he nods his head. I can see that his four sons will always be a mystery to my father. Though now I think he may just understand me. A bit.

Leaving Ireland

Mama and Dada walk down to the mailboat pier with me in late September. It's a nine-fifteen sailing, so it's still light.

I am happy for you, Bernard, that you are leaving all this behind you. It's been too much for one person. You will be able to come back when all the trouble is over, won't you?

She had seen most of her brothers leave on this boat, but they never came back to live in Ireland. She knows I need to go, but she is frightened too. I can see her trying to remember all sorts of things to say.

Go to Mass now, won't you? Never give up the faith. Your faith. It'll stand you in good stead.

I look at Dada. He doesn't know what to say. Can't get a word in. He's looking at me like he really does care. Sort of mesmerised.

Where's Dermot? I ask. I've forgotten him for the moment.

He's got an exam tomorrow, so I said he's to study, says Mama. It is then that I miss him. Patrick is with the Brothers. Thomas is only eleven, and loves coming down to the boat. Like we all do. He's all excited that his big brother is going away. But this time it's not a day trip.

I think of what my Ma has just said about coming back. I have not the faintest idea of what that means. I realise that I have not even thought about coming back. But I mustn't let them see that.

I'll be home for Christmas, I say. I put my arms around Thomas, who is tall already. His brown eyes are full of my adventures to come – just over the horizon there, beyond Howth.

Dada and I have never hugged before. Not even in jail. And I can't shake his hand – never done that before either. He sort of takes my arms in both hands and I pretend he's Mama and put both mine around his shoulders. I feel how rounded they are. It's that desk he's sat at all his life.

I grab Mama, and she's sobbing, then the boat's siren howls, and Thomas is looking at Dada in surprise.

I pick up my case and shout back at them, See you at Christmas! I pull out my hanky and wave. My loose change falls out with it. It clinks on the planks and some falls through into the water below. I look up, and my mother has started forward to help me. The ticket collector holds his hand up.

No. You can't follow him, ma'am, he says.

The boat leaves the harbour with me on it for the second time in two weeks. Strollers at the end of the piers wave to us as they always do, casually, as if they're saying, We know that you'll be back.

I am leaning over the stern. The lights of the East Pier sparkle in the wake, and the rising wind stings my eyes. There are stars galore, and they seem to glisten more than usual. The warning light flashes from the Mugglins rocks. The faint shapes of the church spires and the Town Hall are still visible against the lights of the town. A lifetime lies among those winks of light and blobs of darkness. How will I manage to live in another country without the people back there? Easily, I think, it's like a holiday that's over, and you're tired of the place and the people.

But no, it's not really like that. I will miss them for the rest of my life. I will go back. But what was it Mama said walking down Tivoli Terrace? That she was glad I am going abroad as it will keep me safe. From being killed in the North, she meant. Better in London or somewhere else, than dead in Ireland.

My parents' faces are swimming in the wetness in my eyes – and Billy's and the rest of them, too. They are there forever. No matter what. But leaving Ireland is the only way I'm going to be free again.

Irish Mail train to London

PART TWO

10

London launching pad

LONDON IS A megalopolis. It goes on for dozens of miles. Excitement's in the air.

At least, there is for a lad who arrives from Ireland with twenty-two-inch trouser bottoms while the locals are stalking around in stovepipes. I have them reduced to twenty inches and imagine the world is agog at such daring.

I gape at the signs in the Brixton boarding house windows saying 'No Blacks, Irish or Dogs'. It's a sort of compliment in a funny way. You can see all kinds of things, hear any kind of music, taste food from everywhere and learn anything you want to in this city. My life speeds up like the chair-o-planes at the carnival. I enrol in Spanish night classes. I want to go to Spain to continue what Hemingway started in the Curragh Camp. And I go to a dancing school in Balham to loosen up. The German dance teacher takes my virginity with ease.

Life in London is overwhelming. I stay with Andrew's mother in south London. She still makes sandwiches like she did in Dún Laoghaire.

The bread and water here are not as good, she says, and smiles at me. So don't get arrested over here and go to jail.

What's wrong with the bread and water then? I ask.

They mill the goodness out of the flour so the bread is like cotton wool. The water is full of the chalk of the white cliffs of Dover, she says. So it's hard.

I put an extra spoon of sugar in my tea and eat the sandwich. It's all fine by me. Andrew says it's about time that I left the IRA. I try to explain that the way I left was not right at all.

What does it matter, he says. Those eejits are still in jail and you are at the centre of the world. Anyway, I'm glad you don't believe that stuff any more.

Those eejits are my friends, Andrew. And I believe more than ever that they are right. I just don't have the stomach for jail. I want them to succeed the next time. I stare hard at him. And they will, I say.

And what about Sinéad?

She's at home again, and I heard that she got her job back, I tell him.

He grins that grin that girls love and says, Well, don't worry. When I'm over there next I'll look her up.

I feel that old twinge of jealousy.

I look for a job with meals for free. Saves a fortune, the Irish lads say. I go for an interview at the Savoy Hotel in the Strand. I rehearse what my Ma taught me. She taught me many things. How to dress with a clean hanky in my trouser pocket, a tie with no food stains, pressed trousers and brushed jacket, polished shoes; how to address the boss's secretary or receptionist, and how to greet the boss himself.

Say, How do you do? Never: Pleased to meet you. Only speak when spoken to. If he asks you are there any questions, then have them ready. If he doesn't ask you then you say, Excuse me, Mr So-and-so, may I ask a question?

After just one letter to say that I've arrived safely and so on, my first postcard home reads: 'Landed a job as a clerk in the office at the Savoy Hotel on the Strand. Meals all free. Thank you, Mama. *Le grádh*, with love, B.'

The waiters are almost all Italian. My job is to catch them stealing. They falsify restaurant bills by ordering wine and food for the customers, then not delivering them all, or changing them.

Fill one foolscap page with names a month, O'Riain, says Barker, the office manager. If it's less than that I will not be happy with you. If more, the Italians will be less than ecstatic. I don't know which will be the worse for you.

I learn Italian swear words – like *stronso*. Arsehole. Barker gets his pageful – and I avoid wearing cement boots in the Thames. But I am often called a *stronso*.

Friday and Saturday nights Andrew and I go drinking.

You've a lot of catching up to do, he says.

I had never been drunk in Ireland – didn't like the taste of beer, Guinness or whiskey. Only sherry and the white wine that Sinéad and I drank together.

I catch up fast and turn into an emotional drunk. Looking in a bathroom mirror at a party in Earls Court one drunken Saturday night, I am muttering to myself. Another Irishman having a piss says, What are you running away from?

From him, I shout, and smash my fist into the mirror. I sit on the edge of the bath, pulling pieces of mirror out of my hand. Just like six long years ago. Then it had been Dada's teapot. Now it is my image of myself. I hate what I've become. A failure. The owner of the flat comes in with his friends and throws me down the stairs. I recall thinking his stair carpet is threadbare. As I try to rise, they throw me down the stone front steps.

And don't come back, Paddy, one shouts.

Typical, another voice adds.

I sit on the kerb. A sudden eruption comes from the basement where another party is in full swing. Three or four men come charging up the area steps. One big guy stops and points at me.

There's a fellow countryman if ever I saw one, he laughs and carries on down the street singing 'The Wild Rover' at the top of his voice. It's Richard Harris.

So, a filmstar talked to me, I think. Well – at me, anyway. Time to move on.

After three months of the wild life, ignoring Italian curses and listening to Manuel of the Mountains and his syrupy Spanish music in an Italian spaghetti joint, I start saving for a three-month hitch-hiking trip to France, Spain and Morocco.

Andrew and I go on a whiskey bender one weekend. I cry, I rage, I smash a door down. Why had I let my friends down? Why had I left the Curragh? For that selfish little girl who said that she loved me. Who said that she couldn't wait any longer. Who said that she'd end her life rather than 'go on like this'. Girls are bad news.

When I sober up I glare in the mirror and say, It's all your own fault, you feckin' eejit. You can't blame Sinéad. You knew what you were doing, and now just live with it. Definitely time to move on. It'll be better over the next hill.

<hr>

I know some French from school, which helps the Spanish I am learning at night school. We have just mastered the present tense when our teacher has to stop to have a baby, and they can't find a replacement. So I set off for Europe without the other tenses. The weight of my rucksack is double the value of my funds. It weighs 56 lbs. My money totals £28 to last me the three months. The Irish tricolour flashes on my rucksack, but it doesn't impress the French. In France, every nationality stops to give lifts – except the French. I dump half the contents of my bag with a Franciscan priest in a Paris church.

Late at night, I knock on the door of a darkened youth hostel in Bordeaux. A hunchback opens it and growls.

Do you have a bed, please? I ask.

It's too late, says Quasimodo, as he tries to close the door. I drop my rucksack in the gap and smile.

Please, I threaten.

He grunts at me and lurches into the common room by the light of a candle. In the light of another candle stuck in a bottle I see a gaunt face.

Rasher! says a gravel voice, What the fuck are you doin' here?

Can I ask you the same, Ronnie?

It is Ronnie Drew, who was in the same class as me at the Christian Brothers.

Certainly you can ask all you like, he says. The truth is, I got fed up with Seville, broke me guitar on a wall outside Madrid, and now I'm tryin' to get home with no money.

We threaten Quasimodo with Irish imprecations and he brings us a bottle of *vin* very *ordinaire*.

How are the rest of the lads down there? I ask Ronnie. Tony White had gone to teach English and Pat McMahon to learn to be a matador.

Well, Tony is still teaching. And Pat hasn't been killed by a bull yet, but he's tryin' hard.

And the flamenco? Did you learn that? I ask.

Ah Jaysus, it's marvellous, Rasher — and the gypsies, the Gitanos, are a rare breed of men. And the women. Smashin'. He pauses. But I can't make enough money on the teachin'. So I left, and here I feckin' well am. He grins across the stump of the candle.

I imagine little Spanish boys and girls speaking in Ronnie's Dún Laoghaire accent. Not to mention the swear words. Then I 'lend' him the three half-crowns that I am keeping for emergencies. He wants to start a ballad group in Ireland. A year later, he's started The Dubliners. My investment, I like to think. Fair play to Ronnie, whenever we meet in London or Dublin, he buys the first pint in remembrance of 'them half-crowns'.

Spain

Irun on the Spanish-French border beats even my high hopes of Spain. Not even Hemingway conveyed the noise, the colour and the sheer exuberance of the place. The French are asleep by comparison. Wine is a peseta a glass, and bread a peseta for a hard little roll. It doesn't matter to me how hard, it is Spanish.
Africa starts at the Pyrenees, the English say. They do not mean just the climate, they mean the backwardness too. Evidence of the Civil War lingers like stale dust in an abandoned house. Half-empty villages, tired, hungry faces and wrecked bridges recall *For Whom the Bell Tolls*. A busload of Franco Youth stops for me outside Madrid. We sing their marching songs all the way to Alicante on the Mediterranean coast.
Huge, colourful posters announce a *corrida* on the city's feast day. I know from Papa Hemingway that top matadors will be fighting on such a day. I have devoured *Death in the Afternoon,* his book on the bullfight.
Inside the arena, the buzz of excitement is intense. The sun picks out the bright colours of the women's shawls. Many wear mantillas and combs in their hair. Cigar smoke mingles with their perfume. The guy next to me is squirting wine from a leather bag. I ask him in my present-tense Spanish who will be fighting. He offers me his wineskin. I hesitate, so he demonstrates and hands me the bag. I squirt red wine, *vino tinto*, down my chin and on my

shirt. They crack up laughing and insist that I practise.

Today is a very special day, Señor. It is a *mano a mano* between the two greatest *toreros* in all Spain.

Heads nod and grin. I can understand more than I can speak.

Who are they?

Luis Miguel Dominguin and Antonio Ordóñez, I am told.

The miracle is made manifest. I have budgeted for one bullfight in Spain and have landed in on this.

Dominguin's young brother-in-law, Ordóñez, has challenged him to a duel to establish who is truly number one. They will travel all over Spain this summer, fighting it out. We will see both matadors at their best.

The *Olé's* are passionate, proud. They fight three bulls each. More bulls' ears are cut off for Ordóñez in recognition of his bravery and skill, and so he is the winner. Both are carried around the ring on the shoulders of their followers. The guys around me splash tears of joy on my face and shirt. Walking out of the bullring, their arms around my shoulders, I feel I am at home. I'm high on Spanish comradeship, *tinto* and euphoria well into the night. I awake in a public park next morning with a police baton gently tickling my wine-stained shirt. Time to move on.

~

A French guy makes amends for his countrymen's negligence by taking me all the way to Tangiers in Morocco from Málaga in Andalusia, across the straits of Gibraltar I hitch south across the desert highway as far as Marrakesh. There is the smell of sand, dust and dried camel-dung fires in the villages. The smell of Africa, like a fragrance. It is another world.

Back through Fez and Tangiers, eating kebabs and couscous, I sail back to Algeciras in Spain. On the road north I sit on my rucksack under a small tree in a Spanish village. The August sun tries hard to beat me. Only one car passes every half-hour or so, and they are all full.

I keep shifting around in the small black shadow of the tree and sipping warm water from my bottle. An old woman in black approaches. She merges with the shadow and asks me who I am and what I am doing. I tell her I am making *autostop*. She nods, gestures to me to wait a moment, and walks back inside her dark house that is shuttered against the sun. No cars pass.

She returns with a potato omelette, a hunk of bread, and a tumbler of red wine. A little girl in a red frock puts a wooden box down and solemnly hands me a fork.

I use all the Spanish I can find to thank her.

I am in love with Spain, with the clack-a-clack of the language, their laughter, their boisterous bars, their wine. I want to marry a Spanish girl and have kids that run around the plazas at eleven o'clock at night.

Back in London Town, back with Mr Barker who has not been able to replace my talent for filling a page with the names of erring Luigis and Domenicos, I plan my next adventure.

Finding Uncle Jack

Where is Uncle Jack? I ask Mama when I go home to Dublin for a break.

In Buenos Aires, my Ma says.

Why are you frowning, Mama? Is there another family secret here? Teasing her now.

Papa cut him off because he deserted from the Royal Navy, she says.

Uncle Jack jumps in my estimation. Straight away.

Mama tells me what happened. Many wounded British sailors had been hospitalised after the Battle of the River Plate in 1940. Jack, terrified by the slaughter, like many others, never returned to his comax ship.

Mama had tried to censor the stories of Jack's escapades, telling us he'd eloped with an Irish heiress whose father had threatened to shoot him.

He used to write to my mother of his exploits on the pampas, riding with the *gauchos,* and winning tango competitions in the dance halls of Buenos Aires. He was a romantic rebel, like Errol Flynn or Zorro, and my very own uncle.

Armed with his last known address, and a photo of him with wife and sons, I set out in his footsteps. I eat, drink and sleep the adventure of finding Uncle Jack.

How do I join the Merchant Navy? I ask a Cockney friend back in London.

Go down the docks, mate, and ask about.

Right. I scour the London docks for more than three weeks, asking for a job as an Able Seaman. Nothing doing. Only jobs as stewards. A sissy job, I think.

The idea of going to sea is intimidating. Nobody I know has ever done it.

Smells of diesel and stale sea water are intoxicating. Foreign flags, faces, languages, clamour and noise are the drumbeat of my imagination.

No vacancies for ABs, lad, they all say. Why don't you go as a winger?

A winger turns out to be a steward, so called because in the days of sail, young boys were taken under the wing of older men. And a lot more besides.

I swallow my pride after almost four weeks already spent on a fruitless search for a 'man's job'. I apply at the Blue Star Line offices.

Told you there's no jobs, says the recruiter.

I'll work as a winger, I say.

Experience?

Worked at the Savoy.

He asks no more questions, assuming that I had waited tables there. How long will it take before they find out the truth?

In a tumult of expectation I make plans for Jack and me. My fascination with things Spanish is in overdrive, Jack will know all the right people, I'll meet sensational South American girls, and get started on making my fortune.

Another postcard crosses the Irish Sea from my London launching pad: 'Got a job as a steward on a ship to South America. Will find Uncle Jack. P.S. All meals included.'

Archie is the head steward, a kind though imperious old queen.

I've worked on the Queen Mary, you know, he tells us at the drop of a spoon. Then he gazes at my ship's papers, a sculpted eyebrow raised. Oh, the Savoy is it?

Yes and no, Archie. I only worked as a clerk – but I have to get to Buenos Aires to see my uncle, I say.

A slight smile flickers.

The nerve, he says.

He teaches me the ropes, serving three simple meals a day to company execs and officers while we are in dry dock, refitting.

You're lucky, Paddy. When we sail, you'll be ready to serve at those corner tables next to the doors where they put the naff passengers.

Lunch and dinner are a nightmare. The Captain comes down to the saloon and everyone is on their best behaviour.

Take this pad, Tiger, and write it down, says Archie. And stop panicking, you fool.

Tears and dust

In Buenos Aires, shore leave granted, I head to the Embassy for help, as a key word in Uncle Jack's address is unclear. Miss Cleary makes some calls.

I think we've found him, she says. I'll take you.

Intrigued by the stories of Jack's escapades, she chats on the bus. Sure, he sounds like a grand lad. I'm looking forward to meeting him, too.

My anticipation is at fever pitch, my thoughts a kaleidoscopic jumble. This man hasn't seen a member of his family for twenty years. Will I give him all the news from Ireland first? Or ask him what he is doing, what his plans are, and could I fit in with them, can I get lodgings near his home, a job, Spanish lessons, learn to dance the tango?

The bus rattles through the outer reaches of the city, where dust devils hunt down the dirt roads between half-built houses, football fields, little shops and old cars. My embassy friend turns to a woman sitting behind us and asks directions.

She is getting off at our stop and will help us, Miss Cleary says. The area is poor. Does Jack live here? Must be a mistake.

The little lady, dressed all in black, stands with us on the dusty roadside as the bus grinds away in the wind. My new friend gives her the piece of paper with Jack's name and address. She stares at it. Then she looks up, her eyes filling with tears as she says something in Spanish. I know – I just know in that dreadful moment – what it is she is saying.

I am Señora Mullett. My husband died two weeks ago.

Uncle Jack's widow looks at me. You are his family, yes? she asks.

I am, I say.

We stand holding each other for a long time. I cry with them, for the loneliness of this woman, for her Jack and my Jack. I have come to love the idea of this man, his laughing photo, his exploits, and his promise. And it is all gone like the swirl of the dust in the wind.

In her little house built of concrete blocks, Maria, my aunt, cries again as she shows us photos, offers us tea. That is what Jack liked, she says, tea. I still have some left.

Her young sons come in one by one and stare at us big-eyed. They are confused, seeing a man from their father's country. One sobs, and that starts us all off again. I am embarrassed, I feel helpless. Death seems much closer here than when I had seen Papa dead. He was old, grumpy – and had forbidden his daughters to answer Jack's letters because he'd 'deserted'. Jack's laughing face – young and open – is staring at us from his pictures.

But I am all too aware he had lost his devil-may-care life. He was trapped by poverty and six mouths to feed. Maria told us how hard he had worked, all the jobs and businesses he had tried. He'd ended up like my father. Except Jack was already dead.

Back in London after a third voyage, I meet Billy Keegan and Tony Hayden, my mates from the Curragh. They want to find out how to get a job at sea.

What happened after I left the Camp? I want to know.

Nothing much, we were released a few months after you, says Billy.

If only I had waited, I say.

Ah no, sure we know what happened, says Tony.

I have ruined my life, I say, as I cannot undo that.

Don't be an eejit, Tony says, nobody blames you. They look at each other. Well, maybe Séamus Conron, and they laugh.

You did what you had to do, Billy says.

But it is a huge relief that they are here with me at all. I'd imagined the lads never wanting to talk to me again.

11

Double love in Manchester

I BREAK OFF MY affair with the sea. I need a new love. I find two.
I am invited to a party in Manchester. I meet Katy, a lovely Irish
girl, and decide to stay. I find work with a Greek shipping firm.
Alan Larke sits opposite my desk. He is a working-class lad from
Moss Side. He looks like Buddy Holly and all the girls are after
him. We become mates. He tells me all about Manchester United,
Matt Busby and the Munich air crash. I say I'm not interested. I
pull his working-class leg and say that rugby is my game.

Will you come to Old Trafford to see the first game of the
season? he asks.

Will you come with me to see *The Hostage* by Brendan Behan if I
do?

The theatre is for toffs, he says, like you with your la-di-da Irish
accent. And anyway, he laughs, it's all that rebel Irish stuff.

Like your football is only for workers and hooligans, I say.
We both give way and shake on the deal.
By half-time at Old Trafford I am hoarse from shouting. Alan has
filled me with the history of the Busby Babes. I am a goner. 'We'
beat Chelsea 3–2 that day in 1961.

By the time we take our seats in the Playhouse I have brainwashed him about the IRA and given him the background to Behan and his play.

It's a powerful piece of theatre. He comes out in a daze.

Theatre is marvellous, he says, absobloodylutely marvellous. But do you still believe in the IRA then? Alan asks in the pub afterwards.

Yes, I do. Though I left it and Ireland, the reason for its existence is still there. The English ruling class – *not* people like you – will not let Ireland go unless they are forced, I say like a pedant.

We have huge debates but never fall out over it.

He joins a repertory company and a few years later is directing plays of his own. I remain a fanatical United supporter.

One fine morning, Nicky Du Valois walks into our office and is given a desk and a typewriter. She grins and says, Hello there.

This one's for you, whispers Alan emphatically. He has heard her accent.

Middle-class you English call it, I believe? I say. Or is it upper-middle?

Call it what you like, that one's not for me.

She is smartly dressed, has a sexy figure and a perky personality. Next day I invite her out to lunch. She is impressed with the *Nuits St George's*.

You've broken the rule, she says. Red wine with fish. Do you break many rules?

I just like them both, I say.

She is in need of breaking rules. Her life needs spicing up and I am a candidate to do that for her.

I am flattered that this girl likes me. She is a cut above. But all my Irish ambivalence where the English are concerned comes into play. I have grown up in Ireland with the belief that if a shoe brush is made in England it has to be better than the one made at home.

I am swept along by a feeling of rising above my station. She is unique in my experience, fun, attractive, and hungry for adventure. She talks about Spain, South America and Belgium, and she is fluent in French and Spanish. She wants to go back to Spain. Katy, on the other hand, wants to settle down, have a family in Ireland. But so do I. My ambition at school had always been to have a loving wife and children. Like my parents. In spite of all the shite at home.

Yet for now, I am enjoying this person with whom I have little in common. We speak the same language, more or less, but that is all. I break it off with Katy. She does not know about my affair at the office, the lunches, and my rising fascination with Nicky. I swing between remorse at what I am doing to Katy, and the allure and excitement of this smart, funny, adventurous English girl. This English exotic tugs against Katy who was raised with the same hang-ups, guilt, angst, eccentricities and humour as me. But my ever-hungry ego is seduced by the captivating stranger.

I am in love with Nicky. And undeniably in lust. Her father wants her to get a degree in French literature – and he wants her out of the country. He can see what is happening between his daughter and me.

Will you come to France with me? She throws me her tantalising grin. I simply have to go. You can get work there, you know.

Pourquoi pas? Why not? I say, airing the schoolboy stuff. A few weeks later, I follow Nicky to Grenoble in the French Alps. It's two months since we've met. This is going steady with a difference. It's almost like being engaged. The adventure has begun.

A French stone in my shoe

A Greek director at work calls me in before I leave and tells me that if I want to get married I can have a job in West Africa with

213

free accommodation and all the trimmings. I promise to remember the offer. Exciting stuff. Africa again, after my taste of Morocco.

I take five trains from the north of England to the south of France, where I'll be meeting up with Nicky. I find myself talking to my father about the size of the engines, where the coaches have been made, as if he is with me. He gave all us children his love for trains. During the walk from the station in Grenoble I am assailed by the smells of France. Coffee, bread, garlic, wine and Gauloises. Plane trees are scattering their leaves over the boulevards. But this euphoria is short-lived.

The door of Nicky's apartment is whipped open by Waltraud, a German student who shares with Nicky. She looks at me with the apprehension of somebody who's startled, who has something to hide.

Come in, how are you? Waltraud asks.

I put down my rucksack and she hands me a mug of coffee, glancing at the wall clock as she asks, How was the journey? Then the front door bursts open and a good-looking guy comes in rather breathlessly. She introduces him as Nicky's friend in that awkward way of somebody who wishes they were someplace else. I know immediately. Nicky is involved with this attractive lad, and he has blundered in on me. He also looks anxious and starts to ask Waltraud something in French. She waves his words away and says, Come back later, Jean-Paul.

Then Nicky arrives. She grins in a funny embarrassed way and Jean-Paul disappears. We go out for a drink, I wait a decent interval. Like five minutes.

No, Jean-Paul is just a friend, Nicky grins. I am to learn that the grin is a nervous habit that signals she is not telling all the truth. It all blows over, but I know something has happened. Waltraud's none-too-subtle whispering performance had told me so. The incident is a tiny stone in my shoe.

Is history going to repeat itself in this new romance? The liaison in Manchester that I ended does not, at this moment, count. I remember only JD, my Protestant girlfiend, and Sinéad. They both dropped me.

Yet Nicky is just doing what all her generation of university students in England or France or Germany would do. Not in Ireland or Spain, though. I am not in control of my life with Nicky. But I know I'll get over it.

⚫

After six months in France we hitch-hike through Italy, Yugoslavia, across the mountains and winter snow into Austria, and back to Manchester. Nicky's spirit of enterprise, not to say daring, has me convinced that this is my partner for life. A life of adventure and travel together.

The English visitor

Mama says in her letters that they are dying to meet my girl. I send a telegram to say I'm bringing Nicky over to meet them. They still don't have a telephone.

But I am the Wild Goose, the one who Mama dreads coming back and getting involved with the IRA again.

I know where your heart lies, she says in a letter.

So do I. It's a cold day when Nicky and I come down the gangplank off the mailboat at Dún Laoghaire. A chill breeze blows across the planks of the pier. The smell of salt rain is in the air.

I see two or three Special Branch detectives. They nod in recognition.

Howareya, Bearnárd, one says. Stayin' long?

Their report will go to Dublin Castle. So-and-so is back. Keep an eye on him.

Who are those men? Nicky asks, IRA men?

No, they are Special Branch, I laugh. Just keeping an eye on things.

Would you go back to the IRA?

They wouldn't have me, I say.

Dada makes a big fuss of Nicky He pours the tea. Mama loves Nicky's sense of humour and fun.

You remind me of my years living in Cambridge, Mama says. They go off to the kitchen, swapping stories, Mama tying her green apron back on.

I whisper in Mama's ear, but loud enough for Nicky to hear. She's a Protestant too, Mama.

Oh now, Mama says, and smiles, embarrassed. These days it doesn't seem to matter as much.

Nicky says she will not mind becoming a Roman Catholic. I can see my Ma totting up in her head the possible score of new little Catholics.

I take Nicky on the bus into town. She is included in somebody's conversation, her opinion asked.

Are they always so friendly? she asks.

I buy her an engagement ring in O'Connell Street. We are happy.

Can we go up there? she asks, pointing to Nelson on top of his pillar.

From up beside the Admiral, we can see the mountains. But the happiness I felt on the street below is blown away by memories of days and nights in those mountains with the lads.

I ignore the subtle signs of worry from Mama and Dada. They have sent these signals all my life, no matter what I am doing. Why should this be any different?

We all like Nicky, Mama says, very much. She is such fun. But are you sure that she is right for you? She has her worried face on, like before.

I reply as I have in the past. She's the one for me, Mama. I'm going to take her to Spain and then we'll travel all over. I'm sure, Mama.

She looks over at Dada, who decides to poke the fire. I wish he'd join in this. I know that he likes Nicky.

What do you think, Dada? I ask him as Mama leaves the room.

W-w-well you know, she's a grand girl, he says. B-but will you be happy when the f-f-fires have died down? And he gives a little grin.

Thanks, Dada, I say. I learnt from you how to keep a fire burning.

He still has the poker in his hand.

Dada just smiles at me. He points to his little aluminium teapot in its green cosy that Mama knitted. It's not Delft these days.

I'm wetting the tea, he says, would you like some?

Yes please, Da, and I smile back at him, even though I don't want any tea.

I look at the teapot and my father. He's so small and mild. Not the distant stranger of six or seven years ago.

Do you remember that breakfast, Dada?

Will I ever f-f-forget it, he says. He stares out the window. Unsure.

But I go on, as much for his sake as for my own. I'm sorry about that, for what I did, I say.

Silence.

I must have been hard to handle.

Ah, not as hard as Thomas is now, he says.

I want to finish up with my bit. Then Thomas. Why did you buy an aluminium teapot? I ask.

He turns around and smiles. Sure I always wanted one, and Mama said there wasn't enough money before.

He glances at the closed dining-room door, lowers his voice and says, I'm glad you broke that other one. He is smiling at me.

Thomas can wait till later. We talk a long time that day. The prodigal son and his Da.

Forged French varsity canteen pass, 1962

⁂

Next day, when Nicky is out at the shops, Mama asks if I have seen any IRA men.

You don't have to worry about me, Ma, I say. The IRA won't have me back.

Oh, I don't believe that.

I met one of your old friends from the Curragh, Dermot says. He is asking for you.

There you are, you see, says Mama.

My head is with the lads, my ex-comrades, but my heart has gone elsewhere. Though the campaign is over and many have left Ireland, like me, there is still a hard core of believers. The movement is in turmoil and there is severe soul-searching. The socialist route proposed by James Connolly all those years ago is again being advanced. Mama and Dada put on their hats and coats and we all walk down to Goggin's Pub the better to discuss it.

What's the use of a green f-flag flying over Belfast City Hall if the f-f factory-owners still pay dirt wages and landlords f-fleece the people with rack rents? asks Dada.

Why can't you say an 'f' word, Dada? says Thomas.

Oh now stop that, Thomas, says Mama. But she has her triangular smile.

Nationalism is a type of curse, says Dermot in that reasonable way of his.

I look at him and think how I hated him a few years ago. Now he has his own life in Dublin, studying to be an accountant. He is the *de facto* eldest now living at home – and in peace. I can feel an argument coming on. I suspect that he is a more advanced thinker than I am, and I don't much like the feeling. He has that look on his face that says, you are behind the times, brother.

Now let's not get onto politics, Mama says. Bernard is only here for a few more days, Dermot. She knows the signs. Nicky listens, not interrupting.

That's all right, Mama. I'm not coming back to live. Not for a few years, anyway.

I still believe that 'some day' I'll come home to live. But not yet. After a week, I board the boat with Nicky – time to move on. Again.

Spanish bulls and English bull

Nicky is finishing her education in Manchester under her very concerned parents' eyes. The last thing they want as a son-in-law is this Irish Catholic who has no qualifications and a jail record for terrorism.

I'm fed up living at home and studying, she says. Why don't we go to Pamplona in Spain? And you can run with the bulls, like we've talked about so much.

You're on, I say.

My parents will go mad, she laughs.

She is clever, knows of my fascination with all things Spanish. And the bulls. And scoring over her parents.

We go to Spain with the unconcealed disapproval of her parents. Their opposition is petrol on the fire, as far as Nicky is concerned. In July we hitch-hike to Pamplona for the *fiesta* of the bulls. Papa Hemingway prepared me for this during those long wet winter hours under the 40-watt bulb in the Curragh, and I can't wait to meet him there.

But the town is buzzing with the news of his death. I am sadly disappointed. I even know his favourite bar and favourite chair. Spaniards stand around with their darkly handsome, tragic faces and stare about in awe. But nonetheless, all around us the party is in full swing, the town in an uproar. Every other male is dressed in white with a red sash and neckerchief, brass bands bash, flutes lead the singing, and dancing crowds are everywhere. It's the greatest party in the world. The excitement, the danger, the madness of it all is overwhelming.

I have missed the first running. Now we are victims of wild rumour. The bars are abuzz with stories of the first run, photos in the paper show bodies on the cobblestones beneath the hooves of 600-kilogram fighting bulls, with men in hospital beds happily giving interviews and statistics of the wounded.

This is bad news. By watching the first one I'd have been armed with the 'how to' for the next morning. My stomach tightens. One internal voice says, These locals know what they're doing – you don't, and the other replies, What did you come here for then? Sleep does not come easy. I toss and turn. Sneaking out at 5.30, running shoes in hand, my stomach is in a knot. In the dawn light, silent figures in white shirts and trousers and scarlet sashes stride towards the old town, Spaniards of all ages with a mission. I am swept along, quite unable to turn back.

I'll just watch closely what they do and do the same, I say to myself. Simple. The photos show guys running up the narrow streets, along with the bulls; it is about 1 000 metres to the bullring. And I am fit and fast. Nothing to worry about.

It is 6.20 – forty minutes to go. The balconies hanging from the tall old buildings are crowded with excited, chattering women, children and the old ones. The heavy timber barricades blocking off the side streets are already packed with people, cameras at the ready. It's lonely being in a shouting, roaring crowd of strangers with nobody to share the rising smell of fear. I could climb out of this and nobody will know, says the frightened me. Yeah, but think of the admiration, the notoriety – that's what you like, is the persuasive reply. The fearful one mutters, But it's stupid, you could be killed or injured – and for what, your image? Yes. You'll never face yourself if you duck, so stop the shit and ask somebody what's going to happen.

Strange how fear speaks in the first person, and the ego in the third. I am standing in the crowd closest to the corrals, wanting, in spite of myself, to miss nothing. A local says that warning cannon shots will be fired and then the bulls will come. He does not say that no human can outrun a fighting bull, that the locals run for only twenty metres or so and then duck.

The tension in that narrow canyon is so thick I can barely move. I am overwhelmed by the shouts, the laughing and the yells. The first shot reverberates up the street. I wonder fleetingly why another group is waiting fifty metres further up and nobody in between. The second cannon shot cracks and a few faces, contorted with fear, run past. Then stabbing horns appear over the heads of the runners and they turn as one. Panic hits me and I run too.

The noise swirls about me, fear blurs my vision. I am going flat out. Then his voice, his face, his windmilling hands appear before me. He hangs over a wooden barrier, one hand pointing, pointing, mouth distorted, eyes staring, arms outstretched. I look over my shoulder.

Adrenaline sharpens my eyes as they process the scene behind me in a split second. Runners are on the ground, huddled in doorways. There is nobody between the bulls and me. I can see their eyes, saliva dripping from their mouths, all in slow motion, just two or three metres away.

The blow strikes hard the moment he drags me over the barrier. We fall to the ground, and a very upset Spaniard pummels me like a mother smacking a child that has narrowly escaped injury. He points to my ripped shirt and a large bruise that is purpling over my kidneys. Another second, another couple of centimetres, and my close encounter would have been a final one.

The bottle is green, frosted and beautiful, the beer bitingly bitter, the tension slowly releasing like a sigh now that it's over.

And nobody has been killed. But twenty-one are injured, three seriously. Paco, my rescuer, announces that he will go to heaven for saving me, and that I will too, being too foolish to deserve the other place. I run one more time, with Paco, this time correctly. We meet him and his mates every day, sell blackmarket tickets and go to see the *corridas*, the bullfights. Antonio Ordóñez is as astounding as he was in 1959. I devoured Hemingway's *Death in the Afternoon* in the Curragh. I understand the ritual that I am looking at in the ring. The noise of the village bands, the bright colours, the smells of wine and cigars and sweat all add to the drama. I love it all – except when I become stupidly drunk. My black wineskin is shiny with use. I mix my guilt-filled IRA memories with the drama of *For Whom the Bell Tolls,* and become either maudlin or aggressive.

Soon after appointing himself my guardian, Paco admonishes me. You are Irish. So you know how to drink? No. You do not, he says. You become drunk. Behold how we drink. Slowly. *Muy tranquilo.* And we remain standing and dancing for ten days, *amigo.*

I am ashamed. Why can't I be happy in a place that I love, with a girl that I love?

My fear of failure is not far beneath the surface. And being with the wrong partner – someone not right for me – is a form of failure.

I promise Nicky that I'll behave. Paco and I swear eternal friendship. I promise to return to Pamplona. But I lose his address. I will need his advice in the years to come, I know.

Nicky's brother Dick is lounging at a table with friends in a crowded bar on the main square. I want to leave. My sense of inferiority sneaks into my head when I see them and hear the la-de-da accents.

He'll be all right, Nicky says, looking at my face.
He isn't. We detested each other on sight back in England. He thinks his sister is mixing with a pleb. And an Irish one, to boot.

Ah Bernid, he smirks up at me. No attempt to pronounce my name correctly.
I look down at him, trying to be casual and superior myself, but nervous inside. Tell me, Dick, I say, pointing to a Spaniard. Would

you call that guy over there 'Bernid' if his name is Bernardo?

Of course not, he says. What are you driving at?

My name is Bearnárd, not 'Bernid', I say, taking myself too seriously.

Come on you fellows, let's enjoy ourselves and not fight, says Nicky.

I wish she'd back me up on my name. She never corrects her mother's pronunciation of it, either. Though her father, at least, gets it right. I go to the bar and bring back two tumblers of wine and some tapas. Nicky is gone.

Where's your sister? I ask Dick.

Oh, she's gone to the loo, he says. Then he leans across the table. Do you know that my wild sister is not for you?

His eyes are bloodshot, his lips sneering. My stomach turns over at the words with their nasal Cambridge drawl.

What was that? I ask.

You heard, he sneers. She is no good for an Irish Roman Catholic like you. You will hate her. I know what she was up to with the chaps in Cambridge. He sits back in his chair.

My mind falls over itself and I haven't even had a drink yet. A vision of the good-looking French guy in Grenoble comes back in a flash. So it's true? But in the same moment I'm furious with Dick for his arrogance, scared that what he's saying may be dead right – and I'm angry with Nicky for laying herself open to suspicion. All at the same time.

But I love Nicky. Fuck him. He is leering at me and knows that he has got under my skin. The table is wide, a mottled black and white marble, with circles of spilt wine on it. I reach across it, take him by his collar, and pull him hard towards me. I feel the power of my anger.

Oh no! cries Nicky arriving back. What are you doing?

I hit him full on the mouth. He goes down on the floor with bits of shrimp tail, paper napkins and cigarette stubs. He is moaning, his blonde hair in his eyes.

You turd, he says, as he tries to get up.

I am shaking, and run around the table to have another go.

Nicky grabs me and says, Please no, and pulls me away.

I am surprised at her strength. I look at him snivelling, and the anger drains away. It's gone in a moment. Now I remember the word he used.

What's a turd? I ask his sister as we head towards the door through disapproving Spanish faces.

What you call a shite, she says. Let's get out of here, and she pulls me away from where Dick's friends are trying to lift him back on his feet.

I tell her what he has said in a gasping rush, pushing through the crowds, one half of my mind clearly remembering his words and the other burying it deep in the vault of my memory.

Oh, he's just jealous, she says. Don't mind him. He's resentful that you ran with the bulls and he still hasn't.

The same sick feeling in the pit of my stomach that I felt in Grenoble is churning again. I am out of my depth with these people. How can they talk about each other like this? It's his own sister. And his friends were leering, listening. Not shocked at all. Am I just a simple yokel and they are simply more sophisticated? It's not Nicky's fault. She just has a shite for a brother. She's not a bit like him. At least he and I call each other the same thing, and I have learnt a new word. All that summer and autumn, Nicky and I travel Europe. We run out of money, do odd jobs, eat cheap meals, and sleep in fleapits and barns. We are happy, without responsibilities, and have the freedom of the open road. It is our true honeymoon although we do not know this at the time. I am totally in love with this adventurous, lively, funny and daring lady. Back in Manchester, the Greek directors confirm their offer, made when I left them, of a two-year tour of Sierra Leone with a free house, fully furnished. If we are married. We jump at it. We have no money and are in love, so we announce that we will marry and go. I am still a Catholic in name, and it isn't conceivable to marry except in a Catholic church. My parents will be devastated by anything else. So Nicky is instructed and converted. Her agnostic parents don't care as much about the religion as the thought of their daughter going to live in 'the white man's grave' of West Africa with this Irishman.

Forgetting the past

12

A cold wedding

TEN DAYS BEFORE WE are to get married, we are sitting in her father's Ford Cortina outside Andrew's mother's house in London, where I'm staying. I do not know how he came up. Perhaps I was having last-minute fears, premonitions. But I ask Nicky about Jean-Paul in Grenoble. Did he or didn't he, did she or didn't she? She denies it. Just some petting, that was all. Well, they had all been a little drunk. I press her. It gets worse. The final act is still denied, but it seems superfluous now.

One more question – I can't let go – and she gives that little grin. I know now what it signifies, and I reach over and slap her in the face. The sound is like a shot in the silence.

Mrs Bateson's voice rings out. Stop that at once! Come in now and let that girl go home.

<hr />

Nicky is crying. I apologise. I cannot believe that I've slapped her. I've never done such a thing in all the rows at home. You don't hit a girl.

But under the carpet the episode goes. We marry in the snow of that bleak winter of 1963.

Dermot stays with me the night before the wedding. Do you have much in common? he asks. Yes, I assure him, plenty.

Everybody puts on a brave face the next day. Even the mother of the bride. People just know when a marriage is not going to work. If they know the parties well enough, or even one of them, they can tell if they are marrying for the wrong reasons. They can sense incompatibility under the infatuation, the glitter and the razzmatazz.

My family prays for us and hopes that they are wrong and that Nicky and I will be happy. But Nicky's family, I suspect, are more resigned to failure. Well, Dick at least. He is his affable, drawly, sarcastic self, but otherwise he behaves.

The bride is glowing. She is happy to be going on a great adventure to a foreign land with the man she loves. I drink one too many and forget what I intend to say.

So my speech about the meeting of two cultures, of two religions, of two different ways of life, is lost. It was going to be an upbeat speech, stressing with humour and candour the positive aspects of the two of us, and promising our families and friends that we would not let them down despite the omen of it being the coldest winter day in recent history.

I see Alan Larke and my Manchester mates at the back of the hall. I raise my fist and shout, Long live Manchester United! Apart from my family, they are the only ones in the room that I feel anything for. I imagine the eyes of Nicky's parents lifting heavenwards in despair.

Five days later we land at Freetown, capital of Sierra Leone.

The white man's grave

The BOAC Viscount takes two days to get to Freetown. Years before, I had gone below to the engine room of an old steam mailboat with Dada in Dún Laoghaire. A stoker had opened the door to the furnace. I had fallen backwards with the blast of the heat and the fright of the flames. The same heat hits me as the door of the aircraft opens at Lungi airport. I raise my arm to ward it off. The air hostess laughs.

Get used to it, she says with a smile. I haven't.
I turn to help Nicky down the narrow steps.

I can hardly breathe, she says. But the excitement of the smiling black faces, the palm trees in the distance, the heat shimmering like liquid corrugated iron off the black tarmac, has us mesmerised. This is Africa. On the way to town on the bus and on the ferry to the mainland we ask questions.

Is it always like this?
A red-faced, middle-aged Englishman turns away as if he hasn't heard. Nicky and I make faces at each other and grin. A colourful local, no doubt. A French lady of uncertain age says, Yes it is like this always. She looks pale and sympathetic. Even at night, she adds. I frown. How can it be like this at night? We bump over sandy potholes.

First tour, is it? The Englishman has turned around in his seat.
Yes, I say.
Probably your last, he says. Not like it used to be. Good old days are gone. He turns back to glaring out the window of the bouncing bus. The French lady makes a *moue* behind his back and shrugs.

You will get used to it, she says. Most of us do. And she smiles, a little fringe of moisture on her upper lip.

Our first child is born ten months later in spite of the heat and humidity. It's not true that the tropics encourage sex. In fact, it is illicit sex that thrives – encouraged by the lazy and boring lives that many live in the countries that lie between the tropics of Cancer and Capricorn.

This is the graveyard of marriages, white marriages, says Frank, an Irishman, in the bar of the Paramount Hotel where we spend our first two days.

White men work hard and play hard, my friend says. Their women don't work, and there are too many randy bachelors around. Look over there.

In a corner of the bar, half-hidden by a couple of potted palms, fronds waving back and forth in the breeze of an overhead fan, is an attractive young woman in her mid-twenties with a white guy twice her age. She is fresh-faced and wears a light cotton frock. He is florid, has a double chin and bags under his eyes. I wonder if Scobie in Graham Greene's *The Heart of the Matter* had looked like that.

He's a divorced diamond miner, says Frank, and she's been out here almost a year now. Her husband spends a lot of time upcountry. So she's having it off with your man.

Won't happen to me, I say. We're in love.

How long are you married, did you say?

Six days.

Ah well, that's grand. He takes a pull on his beer. Keep it that way, he says. If you have a good woman, you've got to look after her in this place. Affairs are a plague out here.

The skin under his eyes is pale like a fish's belly, his eyes languid.

How long have you been here, Frank? I ask.

Too long.

Rocklands is the name of our first home. It was once a desirable address. About twenty years before. While Nicky views the old and dilapidated wreck through rosy specs, I see the cracked windowpanes, the broken cupboard doors, and the rust stain down the side of the bath, with its bent tap.

A delightful apparition suddenly appears.

My name is Sorry, says a piano smile that stretches across the blackest face I've ever seen. I forget the perspiration, the musty smell, the cockroaches wandering about underfoot, and take the man's hand.

Very gladdy to meet you sah, he says, and the smile doesn't slip a bit. You and madam are welcome.

It is our best welcome yet. The two Greeks and the English guy we'd met at the hotel have been friendly enough. But this guy is in a class of his own.

What do you do, Sorry? I ask.

I be your houseboy, cook and gadineh, sah, he says, pointing to the overgrown lawn. The smile stays on like a floodlight on a bright day.

I go fetch your bags now, he says, and off he goes.

Isn't he great? says Nicky. I love our new home.

For her, it is a home and not a sad old neglected lady fallen from grace.

Our Greek friend, Costa, appears, shooing Sorry, who staggers before him down the path to the front door. The weight of four suitcases has slightly dented that smile.

We're here for two years, Sorry, I call after his bent back.

I look for the air-conditioner. In the bedroom. The guys back in Manchester in the Greek company PZ, who'd lived on the Coast, told us what to expect, more or less, and what we are entitled to, what to avoid and what to insist on. I hadn't listened properly in the rush, but it is coming back to me now.

A torn mosquito net hangs from rusty wires over the double bed. I turn to Costa. He is looking embarrassed.

Yeh, OK, he says. I used to live here. They put all the new people, young ones, in here. But, he looks around, nobody has been here for six months. I'll speak to the boss, Dino.

We have met Dino briefly and he seems a good guy. But he shrugs and apologises and says that unfortunately the General Manager will not approve of an air-conditioner. Paint, yes, repairs he will organise. But no aircon. Heads shake and sympathetic noises are made.

Our first night we cannot sleep.

Look, I say to my wife, and point as I touch her arm in bed on our first night. A globule of sweat appears on her skin. I do it again, and another one glistens in the cobwebby 40-watt globe. But Nicky doesn't mind.

I'll organise Sorry to clean everything tomorrow, says my brave Nicky. She is in love with the place and with life.

That night, the geckoes sing, night birds compete, and howls ring out from the darkness. Sounds and sweat.

Sorry wakes us with tea. Milky and sweet. He has worked for the English.

Short black socks

Carter, the General Manager, sends for me on my third working day. I am wearing my new tropical gear of white shirt and shorts. I had not found the required long white socks in London, and so I'm waiting to buy them here. I have short black socks on and black shoes. Before going in, I ask John, the English accountant, about Carter.

He's a colonialist of the old school, he warns me. I hate him, he says.

So why are you here then? I ask him.

The Greek directors pay me well to watch the other Greeks, he smiles. Then he looks at my legs. By the way, I hope you are not going to wear short dark socks?

I explain that we are going shopping this week.

By dressing smartly we can stay ahead of the other Greeks and the foreigners in this town, says John. He does not have a hair out of place – he is one of those people who looks cool even on the hottest, most humid day.

I knock and enter Carter's office – and shiver, it's so cold.

Everything all right on the domestic front, O'Ryan?

O'Riain, sir. Pronounced O-Ree-an. Yes, we've got everything we need. Just a few spoons and forks missing.

Got a good boy, then?

Pardon, Mr Carter?

A boy. A houseboy, cook and bottle-washer.

Yes, a lad called Sorry. He says he always works at Rocklands for whoever lives there. Do you know him?

Good heavens, no. Just ask Papadopoulos, he'll know if he's all right.

Thank you. One thing, Mr Carter. We have no air-conditioning.

Really? He says in a distant manner. Not everybody here does, y'know. But first things first. We want you to run the supermarket downstairs with immediate effect.

I am startled.

Mr Zochonis in Manchester said I'd be a trader.

'Fraid not, my boy. Just sacked the supermarket manager and we have nobody else.

But sir, I have no experience running any kind of shop. I pause and smile, Except for shoplifting, of course.

That's the wrong thing to say.

Well, O'Ryan, Carter says with a frown, that's why we fired the last chappie. He stole things. Do you want to follow him home?

No sir, just joking.

Well, don't joke about that. Stealing is the plague of the Coast.

So, I meet two plagues in twenty-four hours that are not marked on our yellow vaccination certificates. Extra-marital affairs and theft can be added to cholera, yellow and blackwater fever.

Our friends are horrified by our 'quarters', as Rocklands is called.

It's our nest, and I love it, says Nicky.

It's a disgrace, says an Englishwoman, suitable for these Greeks out of Sparta, maybe, but not for one of us.

They tut-tut around the house and garden.

We'll lend you our garden boy, she says. Sort this mess out for you and show your chap what to do.

Must get an aircon though, old boy. Her husband frowns at me. No good for your wife, living like this.

I speak to Nicky. Though difficult, the nights are not impossible.

Don't know how anybody makes babies in this lot, my wife says, but we must try.

Brave girl.

I tell Dino that I'm going to talk to Carter. He looks a bit worried and says better not. That I should wait a few months and see how I get on in the supermarket. But to me this smacks of having the cart in front of the horse.

Then Carter's secretary calls me into his cool office.

I understand, sir, I say, that we are the only European staff without an aircon in our bedroom. We are prepared to put up with Rocklands. It's charming in some ways. But for my wife's sake and for the sake of a good night's sleep, I think we should have one now.

He stares out the window at the vultures flopping about on the iron roof on the opposite side of the street.

'Fraid it's not in the budget, O'Ryan. We can do nothing for the next three months, at least.

He looks at me and stands up. Try to make some profit in the supermarket and we'll see what we can do, hmmm?

I think of John Zochonis and the other Greek directors back in

Manchester shaking my hand and saying, We'll look after you, and you'll do well.

But Carter is dismissing me now. Then he looks down at my legs. Extraordinary sight you are, O'Ryan. My wife mentioned it. Hope you are getting regulation socks, hmmm?

It's the implied distrust, the 'we can treat you like shit until you prove you can sell the groceries' bit that gets me. And spicing it all up is maybe the fifth mispronunciation of my name.

I go straight back to Dino's office and recount the tale. No, Dino. I am very comfortable in these socks. As the one who doesn't yet qualify for an air-conditioner I do not qualify for long white socks either.

He stares and then begins to laugh. You know what, Bearnárd? He is sure to mention the socks to me again. He already has. I will tell him what you have said. And I will tell him that I agree with you. Then I hold out my hand, we grin, and shake on it.

Nicky goes to work for the Diamond Corporation as secretary to the MD.

At the first cocktail party, her boss and I are introduced.

Ah yes, you're with PZs, I believe. The Spartans looking after you, are they?

The ladies who are listening, smirk. Nicky says afterwards that they are bitches. And I decide the time has come for a little recognition. I'd been bowled over in Manchester when they'd offered me £1 000 per annum to go to the Coast. But now we know that it is no prize.

I knock on Carter's door.

We've been living without aircon now for four months, Mr Carter. We hear that there's a house available in Kema compound. His damp white hair sticks to his forehead in spite of the aircon whining on the wall. Yes, indeed, he says, with a vague wave of his hand, Dino said something about your socks. He frowns at them over the top of his spectacles. And my wife was just saying, O'Ryan, that her lettuce that you are flying in from Paris was badly wilted last Friday. Can you see to it next week, please?

I feel my temper rising. I don't understand this switch in subjects.

I'll put aside the best heads this Friday, I say, taking a deep breath. Mrs Carter just has to tell me how many.

I pause, and he takes a great interest in his ashtray.

And will I speak to the property manager, sir?

He waves his mottled brown hand. Go along with you. Just fix that froggie lettuce. And get some decent socks.

We miss Rocklands, but not too much. The new air-conditioned flat is heaven. I buy three pairs of regulation white socks.

Jungle child

Lunsar Missionary Hospital is the best place for having babies on the whole Coast, says our doctor friend. The nun in charge speaks on midwifery at conferences throughout Europe.

How far is it?

Two and a half hours on a goodish road. More and more European women are having their babies there.

The alternative is for Nicky to fly out to London, as most expat women do.

Let's go and see these two nuns, says Nicky. I don't want to leave you at a time like this.

I love her more than ever for that.

A Fiat 600 is not ideal for running over a hundred miles of corrugated roads. But I drive slowly and Nicky holds her tummy. Three hours later, Sister Columba and her young Irish co-worker in Lunsar meet us in the swept courtyard of a collection of iron huts. They are surrounded by the jungle. Monkeys gossip in the trees and swing down to the mesh windows to see who's arrived.

As soon as you feel… I hear a nun saying to Nicky, their voices trailing away into the ward and theatre to discuss the next steps. She is overdue now and the nuns say that they will induce the baby within the next two days.

Can you wait that long? asks Sister Columba.

Of course, smiles Nicky. I am proud of my lovely wife.
The village is a quarter of an hour away along a track through the bush. Monkeys announce my arrival. Hunger hasn't hit these parts yet, so the wildlife has survived.
Drums are beating. Smiles greet me. A toddler runs screaming, clutching at her mother's skirts, wide-eyed with terror. Never seen a white man before.
There are rumours of diamonds in these parts. Nicky's boss has said that if they are there his company will get them out. Just have to 'dash' the right people. And this community here looks like they need someone to give them work.
Back at the hospital, Sister Columba says the drums are for a female circumcision ceremony.

It'll kill me yet, she says, but with the help of God, we'll stop it.

Will diamonds help? I ask her.

No, they will not. We pray they don't find them. Everywhere else they do, killing and corruption follow, she says. These people need seed and ploughs and education. Not diamonds.

Sister Columba says I can watch. She says it'll be good for both of us. And the baby.

She will be induced after twenty-four hours, so we know when it is all going to happen.

I watch, fascinated. I hold Nicky's hand and squeeze like mad. The little pink doll appears, held aloft by the nun's red and runny hands. Tasha yells without any encouragement.

The nuns complete the procedure, wash up, and present Nicky with her firstborn. Even the monkeys are respectful and quiet. We could be in Europe – except for the fans, the ever-present fans.

I baptise you Natasha Celina Yamide, intones an Italian priest on his weekly visit.

When we discuss names, Nicky chooses Tasha. I love it. Russian and revolutionary and Tolstoyan.

I get to choose the second name, Celina, a girl I'd admired from afar who danced jigs and reels and spoke in lilting Donegal Irish. Ireland hovers like the ghost of a lost love, my *aisling*, my vision of her freedom still there. My infidelity to her is my sin.

West African custom is to call the first girl to arrive after a death Yamide. I have told the hospital staff that my granny has just died. The name makes everyone happy.

There are tearful farewells among the women.

I'll have my next one here too, Nicky says.

Take your time, take your time, the old nun calls out.

Stubborn and stupid

Friday and Saturday nights are party nights. The same people are there, week in, week out. The temperature drops by one degree from midday to midnight, and the humidity not at all. Beer is one solution. Cold Star beer, made locally.

One Friday night, the temperature rises even more when frayed tempers unravel. I get into an argument and a fight breaks out. It's not the Irish-English thing. It's about the way some of them speak about the 'natives' and how they boast of treating them. After the drunken bout I tell the company accountant, a Scot, that this is how some of the Anglo-Irish speak about the 'natives' – the Irish – in Ireland. We spend the last few drinks outdoing each other with tales of Sasanach treachery.

Let's guess how long they've been out here by the fish skin under their eyes, I say to Nicky at a party the next Saturday.

That's cruel. Let's go outside.

I take a quart bottle of beer from the aluminium basin of ice.

Haven't you had enough? she asks.

It just runs through me. I don't feel it, I say. Excuse me. I pee in the bushes of the front garden. An hour later I'm drunk. Again. The moon is the same moon we looked up at in the Curragh. The faces of my comrades come back, queuing for our food ration, walking round the perimeter. One word out of place from Nicky now and I'll explode. I'll be stuck with these memories for the rest of my life, I know.

Shouldn't we go now? The nanny will want to go to sleep too, Nicky says. And Tasha might be awake.

No, she'll be asleep. Just one more, I say.

Several drunken lads call me over to the bar to hear the latest Irish joke, and I must tell one in return. That's the custom this night and every party night. The beer is like water but the alcohol in it is not.

I insist on driving home. I always drive slowly when I'm drunk, I say.

That's not the point, Nicky says, throwing me a worried look. Why don't you let me drive? Please?

Stop nagging. Relax. We're nearly there.

This becomes a habit. SAS. Stubborn and Stupid. Next morning I apologise and hold my head in my hands. I can see the hurt on her face, each time a little more. I vaguely know, realise, that this can sap a marriage.

Fantasies for Father Fennelly

A strange thing creeps into our lives. I lose interest in sex. Well, not entirely. At night in bed I begin to think of Katy, the Irish girl in Manchester. All I can see is her body, and all I can remember is the sex that we had. My arousal is intense. Only going into the bathroom and masturbating can satisfy it.

Shame floods me when I look at my attractive wife. I feel confused and guilty.

We have stopped going to Mass. The old habits are almost dead. But now I have a problem that I do not know how to solve. I think of the two Irish priests I know socially from the supermarket and the Club. They are popular with the English non-Catholics, too.

Can't stand these Protestant missionaries, says an Englishman from the High Commission, they make me feel like a sinner. Do they ever smile? Now take Father Fennelly, for instance. He'll down a beer with the best of us. Plays a mean hand of poker, too. Next time I see Father Fennelly, I ask him what time confessions are at the parish church.

Why don't you come around to the house? he says. It's quiet there – and no queues.

I'm going to see the priest, Nicky, I say.

What for? she asks.

Well, about my drinking. And just things in general.

I take time off and see him at about three o'clock. Father Fennelly asks if I would like a cup of tea or maybe a beer? He raises bushy eyebrows over a red face. A tired face.

That's partly why I'm here, Father. The beer.

Sure, I like a drop meself, but it can be difficult for a married man.

He sighs and says thank you to his cook, who puts down a tray of tea. We say no more about the beer and stir in the sugar instead. He asks a few general questions.

This is better than a confession box, Father, I say, smiling at him rather nervously, but I don't know where to begin.

Anywhere you like, Bearnárd. I see you spell your name the Irish way. That's grand, and he sips his tea like a man more used to drinking from a glass.

Well, I'll start with the beer, Father. I hardly drank a drop in Ireland, but I went mad in London, and ever since. It's like a compulsion when I pass number three. I start to get memories of Ireland and just want to forget them. I'm drunk in no time. But my body keeps going, y'know, and the head is gone. I don't know what I'm doing or saying from then on. I pause.

He just looks at me and waits.

It's hard on my wife. Nicky. She's English. They're not like us. I wait again. He appears to be half-asleep, but his hands are holding the arms of his chair.

You might think its funny coming from a priest, he says, but I think that a mixed marriage of two cultures is sometimes worse than one with two religions.

I've never heard that before, I say.

Well, I've seen it so often out here. The expats intermarry with each other. A young Frenchman falls in love with one of the few secretaries out from the UK because they have little choice. Religion is not so important any more, the Lord knows, but what a Frenchman and a young lass from Lancashire think about food are very different.

He gazes at the palm trees rustling in the afternoon breeze.

The English and Irish are like stepbrothers and sisters y'now, he goes on. We've known each other for eight hundred years. We're like family. But estranged family. It has paid the powers-that-be to keep us from understanding each other. There is underlying contempt, almost, for the Irish from the English upper and middle classes, he says. Contempt for a subject race. And the Irish – we don't trust perfidious Albion.

Last time I heard that, Father, was from my father. He would love what you're saying. He likes, or I should say he respects, a lot about them, but it's the ruling class he detests.

And you've married into that class? He raises an eyebrow.

Yes, I have. A pause. And I try too hard to convert her to our ways.

Look, he says. She became a Catholic so that you could marry in a Catholic Church. So leave her alone about the rest. As you grow older, please God you will become more tolerant of each other. Now. What about that beer? I have a trick that might work for you. A bishop down in Nigeria many years ago said to me, look at yourself in the mirror, Frank, when you are drunk – and again the next day. Well, I did. I was so horrified that I stopped for about eight years. Try that.

We look at each other. I am completely relaxed now. So the next bit is easy.

I've gone off sex with my wife, Father.

More tea? I won't offer you a beer, he says.

Yes, please, and I get up to pour.

Ah sure, a lot of men go off sex after their wives give birth – although it's usually the other way round.

Well, she has also gone off it a bit. The baby is making her tired, I can understand that. But I keep thinking of the Irish girl I was in love with when I met Nicky. And she has noticed this, and it worries her.

242

Do you think that you should have married this Irish girl then?

No, I fell in love with Nicky and out of love with the other one. I just wanted to be with Nicky.

We both fiddle with our teacups and spoons. Will he know about this sort of thing? We were told at school that priests have to study for seven years because there is so much about life that they have to learn.

Perhaps deep down you feel that you should have married one of your own, he says. Because of what you told me about your politics in Ireland. That's understandable. But this will pass. He pauses again, then looks at me.

Do you still pray?

No, Father, I say, hardly ever any more.

Do you still have the faith?

I don't have it like I used to. I respect people like you, but there are lots that I don't. I suppose I've just grown away from it all. But I still try to do what's right and to avoid what's not, I finish a bit lamely.

He surprises me then. That's common down the ages, Bearnárd, he says. It's not a recent thing at all. Ireland is very narrow, you know.

Yes, I say. I never met a priest like you back there, never, Father.

Africa teaches you tolerance, he says, a thing in short supply at home. He puts his cup down. And about the sex, he says, I want you to put that other girl out of your mind altogether. She is gone out of your life. Your young wife has given up a lot for you, and she loves you. Don't go letting her down now. When those thoughts come into your mind, think of something else entirely. Like football. Who's your team?

Manchester United, I say.

Well then. I fancy Liverpool meself.

We laugh, and he holds out his hand.

243

That night when I think of the Irish girl in bed and want to go to the bathroom, I switch to the priest's idea. I think about a great match at Old Trafford.

After a while, Nicky mumbles, half asleep. What are you laughing at?

United has just screwed Liverpool, I mumble back.

Nappies, the highlife and leaving Sparta

Our daughter has gorgeous red hair – well, sort of ginger – and freckles, and a pudgy face that goes red with the sun and any form of excitement. Like when she's hungry, has pooed in her nappy, has wind, or is tired and wants to sleep. Nicky is an attentive and loving mother. I help with changing nappies if I'm there, and also with getting Tasha to sleep. I do this by putting her on my hip and dancing the West African high-life. With or without a record on the record player. The two-step shuffle is easy. This is my job at nights. To high-life my daughter to sleep.

We put her in her cot and spend ages tucking in her mosquito net. One night, a mozzie gets in, and we are distraught at the big red bites all over her body the next morning.

There it is, Nicky points to the wall. The insect can hardly fly it is so full of blood. I squash it, and Tasha's blood stains my hand.

Kingsway, our opposition in Freetown, has hit on a novel way to checkmate their opposition. Mike Hollard invites us for supper. He says I am wasted with the Greeks and he wants me to apply to Unilever for a job at Kingsway. I am flattered. He spells out the conditions of service. The salary will more than double, and instead of twenty-four-month tours on the Coast without a break, we will go home every year. His wife Sally shows us around their company house. There's a vacancy in Nigeria, Mike says. All our houses are like this. Superior in every way.

Next day, I go to see Dino, my immediate boss at PZ.

Can we talk? I say.

Sure, close the door.

He picks up the phone and orders Greek coffee.

What are the chances of a salary increase and one of the houses in a cooler spot, Dino?

I knew that sooner or later you'd be comparing what some of the other expats get here. At Kingsway, for example, he smiles. He knows. Nothing stays secret for long in this little community.

I tell him a few of the differences, the substantial perks, and so on.

Most of our people are Greek, he says. They come from villages in Sparta where most of the Manchester directors come from. I am from Athens, and I would never accept these conditions. To them this is heaven. If we pay you what you want, there will be a riot. So we may be forced to lose you.

Chilly days in London Town

Why are you so angry? asks Nicky.

Why are you *not* angry? I am furious, upset and want to pack up and leave here. Now.

We are at the bottom of her parents' garden in Ealing, London. As soon as her mother saw Tasha, she said, Huh, an Irish child. In the silence that followed she elaborated for us. Look at the red hair and freckles. Ha. And she lit another cigarette.

Tasha is not a beautiful baby. Her face is chubby and red. She's just in from the tropics and is a mere fifteen months old. Why did we not just laugh? Because this sally is the latest in a long line of sarcasm levelled at me.

To be fair, Nicky's father followed his wife into the kitchen and remonstrated with her. But I was enraged and went down the garden to escape.

Nicky is caught between a powerful mother and me, her husband. It's tough on her. And we are staying with her parents.

Leave it to Daddy. He'll talk to Mummy, she says.

It's the last straw, I say.

I have failed to handle this woman, and she has the upper hand now. My anger is a mixture of knowing that I am being got at through our child, and my total inexperience with this kind of attack. I have never before come across clever innuendo that is impossible to answer without appearing to be oversensitive or to lack a sense of humour. The remarks have the appearance of being casual, while I know damned well they're not. But my deep dismay is with Nicky. How can she not stick up for Tasha?

Mike Hollard has arranged interviews in London with Unilever, Kingsway's holding company. I'm accepted on a package that is some three hundred per cent better than PZ's.

No congrats from Ma-in-law.

Look how you've let yourself and my daughter be treated for two years, she says. I told you that you two were rushing into things with those Greeks.

They weren't so bad and we couldn't have got started without their offer, I say. We had nothing. We couldn't have got married. That was not the right thing to say. She hated the Greeks for giving us the chance to get married.

Richard, Nicky's father, speaks up. Now, Marjorie, they wouldn't have this job if they hadn't gone out there in the first place. So we must congratulate them both, I think.

The tension in the house is horrible. Her father was caught having an affair a few years back. He's scared of his wife too. I look at

Nicky and see her desire to keep the peace. The whole family treads carefully around Marjorie.

Let's go to Scandinavia, I say next day to Nicky, before we go to Ireland. It's on our list, I remind her.

She doesn't answer.

I unroll the map of Europe on which I have traced our three major pre-nuptial hitch-hiking journeys.

How can we do such a thing? she says.

Well, your mother *has* offered to look after Tasha for a while.

The old enthusiasm that I'd loved so much in Nicky is not there. Indeed, Marjorie has offered. And Richard has pointed out that we have both worked for two years without a break in the steamy heart-of-not-quite-darkness. We need a break, he says.

I can't understand the failure to light up of Nicky's eyes. We'd always promised ourselves to travel through Norway, Sweden and Finland.

The Land of the Midnight Sun is calling, I cajole.

But my wife is changing. She's now a mother. And I cannot see it. I start to see her as part of her own family set-up, conservative and unquestioning.

Dick returns to town and moves into his room. We are now under the same roof.

Ah, Bernard. How long will you lot be here for? This he says with a wide smile that is supposed to make the innuendo OK to anybody listening. I, basic lad that I am, want to punch him.

Richard looks embarrassed but says nothing. Dick is his mother's favourite. The remarks from her mother and Dick lead to another row between Nicky and me.

We go down to the end of the garden again. Silence.

Why are there no daisies in the lawn? I ask.

247

My mother kills them. She says they're weeds, Nicky explains.
I turn to her, feeling like a weed myself.

Who are you going to support, them or me?

They are my family, Nicky protests.

I am your family too, I say.

She looks defiant and unhappy at the same time. But I don't
handle it well. She needs support in this, not this whose-side-are-
you-on stuff.

Let's go to Ireland sooner, I say.

Yes, please, she sighs. I've got to get away from this atmosphere.
And so, next day, we leave.

Ireland of the welcomes

Tasha runs in the gate of 36 Monkstown Road. A toddler now, she
ignores the outstretched arms of my mother and runs onto the
grass, then stops. She is surrounded by hundreds of white and
yellow flowers. Daisies. She plonks down, picks one, looks up, and
smiles for her audience. The audience falls in love.

My family spoils Nicky. The house is half the size of the one in
Ealing, but the warmth of the welcome is not in dispute. Nicky
gets on well with them all. Jem, as we are now calling my father,
always loves the girlfriends of his sons. Some more than others. This
one, Nicky, he loves for the way she talks, walks, laughs, and tells
stories of West Africa. Nicky has a great sense of humour, and so
does Dada when he gets going. This is the daughter he never had.

I feel proud of my English wife. Dermot and Thomas both like this
exotic creature.

I watch my mother talking to her animatedly about how the
postmistress always asks after 'the Africans': How are they all, Mrs
Ryan?

Why are you still called Ryan and Bearnárd is not? Nicky asks.

Well, he changed his name a long time ago. We can in Ireland,

you know. We have two official languages, Mama smiles at her.
And you have – or I should say had – a lovely surname yourself:
Du Valois.

Oh, that was from the French Revolution, they say. My ancestors
would have been guillotined if they hadn't fled to England.
I watch them chatting away, and I remember the fear of my
mother about Protestant girls. But that was *Irish* Protestants. She
has accepted this English girl. I think that she will have done so
even if Nicky had stayed Anglican. They like each other in the way
women do. With nods, nudges, smiles and whispers. There is a real
warmth between them. It takes the tension out of me.
We leave Tasha, who is revelling in all the attention, with the
doting grandparents and travel in Dermot's cramped Volkswagen
beetle down to the West. Dermot's friend has a cottage
overlooking the Atlantic.
It takes us twelve hours to do the hundred miles across the
breadth of the island. Dermot does most of the driving, though at
times Fiona, his girlfriend, takes over. We stop at hotels and eat
and drink. Dermot drives slowly and well. We take a couple of last
pints in the pub in Tullycross and arrive at the cottage in the dark.
I stand outside and let Dermot introduce Nicky to George, the
owner, who is also down from Dublin for the long weekend. They
go inside in a noisy bunch. I feel suddenly intimidated by them all.
The night is still and silent up here on the hillside. Wind, gorse,
heather, bracken and briars mute the roar of the Atlantic. There is no
moon, and only a few stars. There's cloud up there, I think. It's like
the nights out training in the Wicklow mountains, looking out for
rain. What do these people here know about my leaving the Army?
Leave that alone, I say to myself. Get on with your feckin' life.
I sniff the cold air, then take in lungfuls. I can hear the laughter
coming from inside, and pluck up courage to go in. Nicky is a
better mixer than I am.

The light and hot air hit me in the face. The laughter, music and turf-smoky mood is all mixed up with the aroma of curry. Faces turn towards me, and I am confused as usual by the sudden attention. George comes across the room, smiling in welcome, and we shake hands.

What will you have to drink, Bernard? I hear you lot have drained a few pubs on the way.

He holds out a bottle of Guinness. I do not want more but I say, Thank you George, and pour it into the glass that he gives me. Nicky looks flushed and happy. She loves company, a party. Dermot is stirring a giant saucepan and holds out a wooden spoon to Nicky. Taste this curry, he says. It's marvellous. He says it like it is a mystical experience.

That's brilliant, says Nicky. She holds up her wineglass.

To the cook, she says.

George bows gracefully and they raise raucous glasses to the 60-watt globe with wisps of blue turf smoke coiling around it. I stand back in a corner and watch the party take off, staying out of the limelight – like a cripple. We get to bed at 4 am.

In the morning, I climb out of the lumpy bed first, leaving my exhausted wife asleep. In the kitchen, I take a mug of sweet tea from Fiona.

First time here? she asks.

Yes. I'll go outside for a look, I say.

Mind the mud, she laughs.

I step on stones strategically placed and walk round a bramble bush. The sky is huge and blue. The waves roll in long lines, white-topped and thunderous in an unending roar that neither rises nor falls. Islands are crouched low on the near horizon, green with grass and streaked with grey rock. A conical mountain stands on the far side of the bay looking like it is in charge of all it surveys. A brown hawk slides sideways in the wind, its yellow beak caught by the sun. A kestrel. Swallows too, and martins sweep past with screeches of excitement as they catch their breakfast on the wing. Beautiful. So beautiful. This is my country. This is Ireland of the Sorrows, as the poets describe her. But to me, there is nothing sorrowful about this scene. I could be happy here, I think. Away from other people who will always be strangers.

But the sounds of other people burst out the door. Nicky arrives arm-in-arm with Fiona, Dermot, George and Thomas.

What do you think of this then? Dermot demands of me. Hey?

Very beautiful. What is that mountain called?

That's Maoilrea, Bald Mountain.

I've got an ordinance survey map, says George, I'll show you where we are.

The table inside is a mess of bottles and glasses. So he spreads it out on his bed.

Here we are, he shows us and we pore over the map. George is an accomplished sailor and mountaineer – and, as he proved to us all, he cooks the best curry in Ireland.

The noise of breakfast and the smells of rashers and black and white pudding frying seduces our ears and nostrils. More tea is poured from the huge cast-iron kettle that lives on the hob next to the turf fire.

Did you know, says George to Nicky, that some of the turf fires in the cottages of Connemara, never go out? They've been burning for over two hundred years. The ashes are banked up at night, and in the morning they are stirred gently and fresh dry turf – or peat, as you would call it in England – is put on and it lights up again for the first tea of the day.

That's amazing, says Nicky.

And then the soda bread is made, he adds. Would you like some? Great slabs of butter are spread on the bread. I can see Nicky is happy here with these people. They are kind, interesting, clever and funny.

251

After the 'heart attack' breakfast, as George calls it, Dermot – or Dermo, as his friends are calling him – pours the first wine of the day.

Soon we are all at it and Dermot makes some sort of smart remark to me. I feel the hot flush I got as a boy at home. It's like the time we were eleven or twelve and I tried to strangle him on Christmas day. I can't give him an answer quickly enough and feel myself going red in the face. Relax, I say to myself, but the tug of old wars bends my brain.

Tension rises between us. It feels like my mental feet are dragging in mud. Dermot is confident with his clever friends. He regards me as a man of action and few words, unable to express myself, a lesser being. But doesn't he know that this so-called action man failed when he had the chance? Nobody mentions the IRA. It is never in the news now and is assumed to be dead. I know better, though. Yet the knowledge that lads like Éamonn, Tony Hayden and Séamus are still involved, makes me want to leave Ireland and be with people who know nothing of my past.

Nicky can't feel the undercurrents. I don't discuss any of this with her. How can she understand Irish politics? Not even the Irish do. I am still a prickly, uptight eejit. Or just a prick.

13

Running aground

NIGERIA IS NOT AS hot, not as humid as Sierra Leone. The local
people here work harder, are sharper, better educated – and more
corrupt. I set up home in a modern flat and await my girls'
arrival. I miss them. Our letters are intense with our love and
how much we want to see each other.

The Lagos Kingsway Supermarket in comparison to PZ in
Freetown is like Sainsburys to the corner grocery shop.

So you love it, do you? says Bert Crouch, my boss.

Well, you've missed the best times. The good days are gone. Forever

What was it like then? I ask.

Before Independence in 1960, we went home every day at four
o'clock, he says. Everything was cheaper, and the blacks did what
they were told.

This is the nostalgic theme whenever whites, the expats, meet.

What is the policy now in the new Nigeria? I ask the MD at our
first business meeting.

We will have to work harder, he says, because they are letting in
all kinds of competition. The old comfy arrangement of a majority
of British companies is no more. They are letting in the French,
Germans and Japanese. Even the Italians. And there are rumours

of trade unions. He raises his eyes heavenwards.

Exciting stuff, I think. I'm twenty-eight, in love, fighting fit, and people have great expectations of me.

Nicky and Tasha arrive after eight long weeks, and we are like squirrels making a nest. Nicky is pregnant and happy. Tasha runs around the balcony chasing her hamster. The servant, Clement, dotes on her. He is an Ibo. From the east. Most of my best supermarket staff are Ibo.

I ask Bert about the Ibos in the store.

Well, O'Riain, you'll be glad to know that we call them the Irish of West Africa, he says.

Why's that, Bert? I ask, suspecting an English trap.

Because they are the troublemakers, that's why, he laughs. But I sense no snide malice from him.

Up go the Ibos again in my books.

They drive out the Yorubas and the Hausas by doing their jobs better, he says. And they love politics – like you lot.

Ah, Bert, we don't love politics. It's forced on us.

He frowns an embarrassed frown, and I change the subject. The little tin god is on his colonial throne, no matter that it's obsolete. But I like him. What do we wear for the GM's cocktail party? I ask.

Your tropical rig – and behave yourself! I'm an old Coaster, he smiles, I can get pissed. But you can't until you've been here a few years, do you hear?

Mike Rendon loves playing Scrabble. What I don't know is that he has a crush on Nicky. More than that. He's in love with Nicky. He blinks through his glasses at the Scrabble board, frowns at his tiles, and looks at her. She smiles encouragingly and re-crosses her legs. The ceiling fan thump-thumps and stirs the soupy air. Why is he taking so long to make a word?

Come on, Mike, Nicky says, I'm beating the lot of you, anyway. Would you like to stay for supper? She gets up and goes to the kitchen.

He gazes after her. Mike is a typical Coast bachelor. English, public school educated, represents several big British importers. Lonely, and young.

Clement is off for the evening, so Nicky prepares the supper. She puts the tray on the dining table and stands, hand on hip, as she says, Do you chaps concede defeat, then?

Yes, we chorus.

Mike is not our only Scrabble partner, but he seems to be our most reliable. He is always available.

One day when I come home for lunch, Nicky sits down, picks up her knife and fork and looks at me. I hope that you are not becoming one of those guys that abandons their wives, she says. You're spending too much time drinking. Don't you think?

Why? I say. You have plenty to do — with your coffee mornings and mahjong and afternoon tea parties at the Club.

She looks hurt and defiant all at once as she gets up to arrange scarlet flowers in a bowl. Huge, vivid things.

Mike was saying today that the reason for the high divorce rate out here is the neglect, she says.

Did he now? Where did you see him?

He just popped in to say goodbye as he's going upcountry for a few days.

Didn't pop in on me.

Well, how could he? With all that traffic in town. He sends his love anyway.

He does not, I say. That is for you only.

She has that grin, behind the flowers, and my stomach panics.

Oh, don't be silly, she says. But the idea pleases her – I can see that.

This isn't supposed to happen, I think. Nicky is expecting our second child. She's happy and I'm doing well in my job. Why isn't everything fine between us, then?

But all I say is, I can't find anything good at the library, Nicky, so I'm going down to the bookshop. Want anything?

No, thanks.

As I leave, I look at her books on the hallstand. Romances. She must be happy.

MacManus Justin arrives!

At last Nicky is admitted to the Lagos Maternity Hospital. She pleads and I plead with black and white staff that I be allowed to watch the birth.

The nuns in Sierra Leone allowed it – they encouraged it, I say.

If something goes wrong, we don't want you in the way, I'm firmly told. Final word. Nicky is induced again, as she is over her time. At about seven o'clock, the beginning of the 'happy hour', Manus Justin is born. They let me in when the cleaning up has been done. He looks like all newborns look, pink and vulnerable. But he's fine, and so is Nicky.

You still want to call him that Irish name, then? says Nicky.

Yes, we agreed. Manus. You picked Tasha.

After your IRA friend who was killed? Something MacManus? But I'll pick his second name, OK?

I want our son to have the heart, the humour, and the courage of that man, I say, and I kiss her on the cheek.

His second name will be Justin, she says. Justin is puce and yelling.

He can only improve, I grin.

He's gorgeous, says Nicky. And I really want to call him Justin, yes?

She gives me her sweetest smile, and henceforth Manus is known to everyone as Justin.

I'm going home now, I tell her. I'm banjaxed.

Nicky looks beautiful in the bed, relaxed and happy with her son beside her.

Why don't you go to that party in Apapa? she asks me.

I don't want to go, I say. It'll just be the usual crowd, drinking and messing.

Well, I think you should relax a bit and then go home. She is being kind and loving.

What I do next is stupid and brainless. I drive across the bridge to Apapa and walk in the door, greet the usual crowd, and tell them of the birth. A glass of whiskey is put in my hand.

You can't drink Heineken on a night like this, somebody shouts, and glasses clink and clash. Bottoms up, and all the usual stuff, and another drink is in my hand, and my head is lighter. Through the throng of smiling drunken faces I see the brown one. Black hair shining, a half-smile, and eyes that say, I like you.

She edges closer. She is tall and bends slightly back and forth to the rhythm of 'Guantanamera'. Her eyes are locked on mine. The whiskey makes me focus on her, and the other faces become a blur. Surely a woman like this is with a man? But I am in her arms, dancing slowly, when the music changes to another slow number. Somebody lowers the lights, and I'm relaxing – as Nicky told me to do. I am tired and happy. The woman is bumped from behind and is up against me now. Her perfume is like the scent of Nicky's soap, sandalwood – but then she is taken from me. A guy is leading her out into the garden. Must be her husband.

Two grinning faces loom, and one says, If you get in there with Maria Stoppard you're made, Bearnárd.

Is she a goer? someone asks.

If she isn't, she's certainly a tease then. Have another, he says to me.

No, no. Give me a beer, I say, wanting to be able to focus. What if this Maria comes back? I want to be able to see her properly. Then suddenly, she sort of shimmers in front of me and says, Where were we?

The lads leer, and I am dancing again. Maria tells me that her maiden name is O'Meara, her father was in the Indian army and her mother an Indian princess. I am bowled over. She is the best-looking woman in the room. In all Lagos. She keeps looking at me with brown eyes that look like they might have tears in them but are smiling all the same.

On the way home, I float, not just from alcohol. I am flattered out of my head. I feel suddenly guilty about Nicky. Then I remember Mike Rendon. Tit for tat, I think.

Nicky and Justin come home and Tasha is fascinated with her little brother. People are in and out all the time. During one such visit, Tasha puts her hamster in the cot with Justin. He is gurgling up at the visitor, when the animal's head appears on the pillow beside his head. Nicky squeals, but our son doesn't mind. Happy times. During the next week, I see Maria Stoppard from my elevated office in the supermarket. She is wandering slowly along the aisles and looks up to catch my eye. My eyes are taking in the long brown legs and the swaying black hair, which she tosses about. For the next weeks and months we meet like this. There is nowhere else, apart from the interminable parties. Here, all discretion goes out the window with alcohol.

Everybody knows by now that we have a crush on each other. Nicky asks me about her, if I am having an affair. Because I'm not,

Bearnárd, Tasha, Justin, London

I pooh-pooh the idea. But because it looks like an affair, nobody believes this.

Fury and fear

Richard and Marjorie come out for three weeks. We take Nicky's parents to a nightclub on the Ikorudu Road. Mike Rendon is there – alone, surprisingly. He asks Nicky to dance, and I see them dancing in the way I do with Maria Stoppard. I am unnerved now. I stand up and walk to the edge of the dance floor. My stomach is in a knot. Now they are smooching. I never smooch with Maria. Although we dance close, we talk non-stop. About everything. But with Nicky and Mike it's different, I can see.

I go back and order more drinks. But Richard says no, he has had enough. His face is frowning and he wants to go. When Nicky and Mike come off the floor there is the grin on her face that she cannot help. My stomach contracts and I down a few more.

Time to go, says Richard, and Marjorie is already on her feet. Mike's glasses glint on and off with the strobe lighting. He looks like a guilty schoolboy. I know we both are.

That night we have our first violent row. I accuse Nicky of being unfaithful with Mike. She accuses me and Maria. I say, You started it first with the Scrabble. She says that was all innocent. I say that Mike is in love with her and she is encouraging him. She says I am a fool. And I slap her.

Justin stirs in his cot. Tasha and Nicky's parents are at the other end of the house. Nicky is crying. I am both furious and frightened. My anger dies and fear and regret grow.

But neither of us wants to give way.

The weekend parties gyrate with wild music, beer flowing and egos dancing to the latest hit records from the UK and America. Colonialism is a bogus way of life. We order people around who are often much older than we are. We live in a luxury that we know we cannot afford at 'home'. And we suffer the frustrations of commanding a workforce that is often unschooled, untrained and unwilling. We come home at night and the bottle is the easiest way to relax. Tennis and golf work for a while, but the 19th hole wins the last battle. Add to this the West African humidity, with the heat of the night just one or two degrees lower than at midday. It's a trap.

I go to see Father Hanratty. He's an old Coaster.

I've been out here thirty years now, and do you know what my greatest fear is, Bearnárd?

What, Father?

Being sent home to Ireland, boy. That's what. I'd die there in a few months.

He takes up his frosted glass, looks at the beer, and downs it. Another? he asks.

We pour the next two and I tell him a bit about Nicky and me.

I'm too ashamed to tell him that I slapped her.

But I'm jealous, Father, and frightened that I'll lose her.

Would you go back to Europe? he asks.

I've no job there. And you know yourself, Father, that if we do ten years with Unilever, we can retire and never have to work again.

He looks at the bats swooping in under the eaves of his verandah and at the orange-red sky beyond it.

If you can hang on in this beautiful place, and both of you stay away from these other two, you'll be OK. He pauses. Can you get a transfer?

They want me to stay at least eighteen months longer, Father, to sort out the Apapa store.

We listen to the bats and the night birds.

Do you want me to hear your confession then?

No, Father. You've heard it already.

Well, not quite.

Things fall apart

The parties go on, we go on, the jealousy grows, and one night I lose my temper again in fear and rage. I scream at Nicky in the bedroom, and when she denies flirting I slap her again. And again. The more she denies it, the more I am sure that she is lying. My own guilt at flirting with Maria is mixed up with all this. But I am convinced that I am only retaliating.

The children wake up and Tasha comes out onto the landing to see her mother crying. I tell Nicky to shut up and she tells me to shut up.

Did you tell me to shut up?

Yes I did, she yells back.

I slap her again and push her halfway down the stairs, then drag her the rest of the way down. A cut on her forehead is bleeding.

Now get out of here, I snarl, and go and see if Mike Rendon or one of the other lads that fancies you will have you. She holds onto the banisters with both hands, sobbing.

I look up, and there is Tasha pleading with me. I can see her face in the half-light. It is red from crying.

I look at my little girl's face, eyes squeezed shut with pain. Please, Daddy, stop! Stop!

I want to stop, but at the same time my anger has not run its course. My heart pumps with hatred for Nicky for causing this, but I go and take Tasha in my arms. As soon as I feel her body, the anger drains out of me like dirty water down a drain. I put her in her bed and hear Nicky in Justin's room doing the same thing.

We do not talk for days.

The weeks that follow are blurred. I go to work, smile at the customers, my colleagues, bosses and staff, as if nothing is wrong. The Ibo province in the east is threatening to secede. Northern Hausa Muslims are killing Ibos, who are mostly Catholic. A mob comes down our road one Sunday morning, armed with pangas. Father Hanratty has warned his parishioners. Nicky and I put our Ibo gardener in an upstairs room. He stays under the bed for three days. He leaves on a lorry one night for Biafra. We never hear what happens to him. Life for us whites goes on, unchanged. Nicky takes the kids to parties, plays mahjong, and goes shopping as if all is well. Still, we barely talk. I am ashamed, defiant, and frightened at the same time. There is nobody to turn to. Everybody must know about us, I think. But nobody says anything. It's as though everybody is in the same boat and no one wants to upset it. A Dutch couple living next door come round the day after our next big fight. They look embarrassed. Is there anything that we can do? she asks.

262

Nicky says yes, she is tired, could her friend take the kids for the afternoon, and then disappears. When she comes home after a few hours I ask her where she has been. With Amy, she says. And goes to fetch the kids, next door.

That night I explode in the car on the way home from the Club. I slap that nervous smile again. And again. At home, I drink till I collapse.

The phone rings in the morning. It is Nicky's friend, Amy.

Can you come over here? Your wife and children are here.

Nicky is sitting in Amy's living room with blood on her collar and a cut over her eye. I start to apologise. I look at my kids and sink in shame. Where is Joe? I ask Amy.

He's gone out to play tennis, she says. Are you all right to take them home?

I'll never be all right, I think. I am mad.

Next Sunday morning, a friend of Nicky's arrives with some magazines for her. I take an Alka-Seltzer to clear last night's fumes from my head and go upstairs. The kids are staying with friends. There is no sign of Nicky. I phone Amy. She is not there. I know where she is.

I drive to the block of flats where Mike Rendon lives, knock on his door and push my way in. His glasses are lopsided and I feel sorry for him at that moment. He is shaking. The bedclothes are rumpled. I am calm, almost serene.

Is Nicky here, Mike?

No, of course not, he says, and tries to stand between the wardrobe and me.

I give a gentle push past him and open the door. Nicky is curled up, fully-clothed, among the shoes and hanging trouser bottoms. She climbs out and grins that nervous grin. I am still calm. Calm.

It's almost as if it is a relief to get confirmation, to know at last. Mike starts to gabble something and I say that it doesn't matter, I have been a bad husband and I just want to take my wife home. This is like a movie, I say, looking around. We all smile and move towards the door.

Nothing happened, Nicky says softly, reassuringly.
Mike shakes his head so that his glasses go skew again. I smile. I start to laugh. They stare at me. It's your glasses, Mike, straighten them, I say.
I walk out of there and down the stairs. I feel free. I believe Nicky. Nothing serious happened.

We just talked, she says on the way home.
I am in a sort of daze.

Mike told me that he wants to see you once before we go on leave, I say to Nicky.

And you don't mind? she asks.

No, I don't, I say, still calm. I'm going to stop flirting with Maria Stoppard, and I hope that you will stop with Mike.
She stares at me. She is not sure of something. Maybe it's me and my calm – or maybe she's not sure she can stop seeing Mike. I do not know.
We live in a cocoon of stillness, as though nothing strange has happened. It all looks normal, sounds normal.
A week later, after meeting him for coffee, she comes back and says she will not be seeing him again. I feel weak, confused, but still calm. I know that we are on the brink. I will make it up to her in London, maybe take her for a week to Spain.

The red letters
Nicky tells her parents about the violence when we arrive in London. We decide that I should spend a week away, and I arrange to stay with Andrew's mother in Wimbledon.

Four little monkeys, London Zoo

Nicky's father is sad and serious, and just looks at me.

I ask, What are we to do? and tell him that I am desperate. I must stop all this, I don't know where it is coming from, and I am very frightened of losing my family.

He can offer nothing. He seems at a loss. No words come.

You've been married for a long time, I say to him. What do you do when there are problems?

I never struck my wife, he says.

But she found out a few years ago that you were having an affair, I say. How did you solve that?

That's none of your business, he says, and I am sorry that Nicky told you about it. He gets up to leave.

But what do *we* do? I ask.

I don't know, he says. I'll have to see what Nicky wants. And he leaves.

Next day, when I empty the suitcase that Richard has brought to Andrew's mother's house, a letter falls out of a pouch. It is from Amy's husband, Joe, to Nicky. Pages of passionate words. So my instincts about Mike were right. He did not sleep with her. Joe is the one.

I phone Richard and tell him, I ask him for help. He says that I can tear the letter up. His daughter has decided to give me one more chance. His voice is cold. As mine would be towards anybody who beat Tasha. But what does 'one more chance' mean? Catholics can't get divorced, so what does that mean? Nicky tells me that it isn't an affair, that he is just a passionate writer. I want to believe that because I have never slept with Maria. Never. Maybe I could have, but it never seemed the right time or place. Just flirting. So maybe Nicky and Joe are the same. But deep down, I do not really believe that.

Back in Nigeria, we are sent to Jos, a town in the north. Maybe the powers-that-be think that Nicky and I will be better off in a new town with a new crowd. There are no secrets in the small expatriate community. Least of all about affairs. But nobody says anything.

We live on tenterhooks. A tin miner called George gives Nicky the eye at the Club. After a few drinks she forgets about me and dances with abandon. She loves male attention.

In Freetown I was proud of her popularity. Because I knew that she loved me. But now it is different. The lads smirk, and say that George is a card. I know that what Nicky and I had is almost gone – our love, our fascination with each other. There is a deep-down desperation in me now. When I come home from work, we do not make eye contact. No connection. It's gone.

On the night that Manchester United wins the European Cup final, I go upstairs after the lads with their short-wave radio have left, and go into the bathroom. In the toilet bowl are half-flushed pages in red ink. I dry them in a towel. It is a letter to Mike

Rendon in Lagos saying how desperately unhappy my wife is.

I go into the bedroom. Why? I ask, holding the damp pages up.

I am so unhappy, she says, but I don't want to involve him again. That's why I tore it up. She is starting to cry.

Only George, then? I ask.

Oh, don't talk rubbish, she says, he's like that with everyone. I am half-blind with tears, and walk out and sleep in the spare room.

A week later, after another evening session at the Club, the Kingsway personnel manager who has been drinking with us comes to supper and to stay the night. He is doing his rounds of the north.

In the middle of dinner, calm on the surface, I open a third bottle of wine. I do not know what Nicky is saying to the manager, but I can see George's face leering at me. Next moment, I am appealing to this mild little man sitting there, oblivious of the tensions, for his opinion on George and his bullshit. And my wife and her bullshit.

He is horrified. Nicky tries to calm me.

Then I get up and say, You deserve this, and slap her face. And again, and again.

Our visitor drags me off, and I remember nothing more.

The next days are a nothingness. Nicky and the children fly to Lagos. I receive another visit from the personnel manager. This time he hands me my notice. He keeps shaking his head and saying that in his entire career he has never... that I had a great future... that everybody is sorry...

Nicky's farewell

The weight is crushing, my mouth is dry as dust, there's a pain in my chest, and my eyes will not open. This must be what people feel when lying beneath a collapsed building.

Nigerian staff party, Jos

She is leaving me, that is what she said. Who is leaving? Nicky?
Someone else?

This crushing, hopeless weight tells me that my world has
collapsed. Nicky's face, running with tears, appears from among
the milling bodies in the aisle of the plane. She is kissing me,
kissing me goodbye. I can't see the two kids, hidden behind the
seats. It is her first friendly gesture of any kind in days, and I
know that it is the last, the absolute last forever. I move my lips,
try to swallow. This is the death of a love.

London gloom

The days pass in London, with Nicky at one end of the city and
me at the other. Paradoxically, the idea of getting together seems
increasingly likely to me, even though the evidence points the
other way.

The smell of the hot London Underground dust, shot through
with a million volts of electricity, is the smell of sadness and
desperation, the loss of my children. I mount the escalator as it

carries me up – as it does each weekend – into the sunshine or grey clouds or rain of Hampstead tube station and a rendezvous with my soon-to-be ex-wife and my forever children, Tasha and Justin.

They are sitting in her father's car, that blue Cortina, beneath some chestnut trees. I will gather some chestnut flowers, I think, and tell them about conkers-to-be in the autumn as I try to loosen my throat to talk to Nicky.

She is stiff, embarrassed as always, and gives a nervous smile a she says a tense Hello, how are you?

I am fine, I lie. Then Tasha hugs me and Justin stares at this almost-stranger.

We agree on the time for the handing back, and Nicky drives away. Is she looking in the rear-view mirror? At me? No, she's looking at her kids.

Justin is already examining some insect in the grass, while Tasha is holding my hand and looking up into my face. Daddy, do you still love Mummy? she asks.

 Yes, of course I do, I say, and try to smile. This is the truth. Then she looks at Justin who is trying to free a beetle from its carapace. And do you still love us, Daddy?

My throat tightens so I cannot speak. Look, I say, pointing at nothing in particular. They turn to look, I snuffle in my hanky and dread the next three hours with the ones I love.

Divorce proceedings have begun, her parents are implacable. Why do I still have hope? Because I know I am sorry. I know what I did is wrong and she will understand. It has to be like that.

Days are desperate, nights are impossible. How to sleep? I talk for hours with unfortunate friends who have to listen to my interminable analysis. How sympathetic they are – and how fed up too.

Divorce and Big Tim

I go to see 'The Thomas Crown Affair' on the day of the divorce. It is still unreal. There is no divorce in Ireland. It is just a word that you might use in Scrabble. In the last minutes of the film, Faye Dunaway is looking up at the jet that is carrying Steve McQueen to Brazil with the loot. You know, or hope, that she will follow him.

Out on the street, I look at my watch. I am a free man. This is not what I want. I hear a jet and look up into the blue summer sky. Where can a fresh start be made? I will get a job here for say, six months, and try to win Nicky back. If that doesn't work I'll follow McQueen.

Hard physical labour helps me sleep at night. Down the bottom of the hill from my bed-sit in Hampstead is another world called Camden Town. I start as a labourer on a building site and volunteer to join Big Tim and two other Irishmen on a concrete gang. Our job is to pour concrete to make the floors and pillars of blocks of council houses. I love the lads and the *craic*, the jokes and the laughs. Big Tim tells us the story about the Dubliner who'd applied for roofing job a few weeks before.

That English foreman over yonder, says Big Tim, asked him if he knew the difference between a girder and a joist. The lad scratched his head and said, Sure, didn't Goethe write *Faust* and Joyce wrote *Ulysses*?

There's some great ideas flowing around this great planet of ours, says Big Tim, our leader, but a strike this minute is not one of them.

Big Tim is saving for his annual holiday in Tipperary. And we could all be fired for starting a branch of the Union. Us four, who make up the concrete gang, are resting on our shovels.

The shop steward joins us. All right, he says, we need more members before we do it – but for God's sake, lads, not a feckin' word about the strike or the college boys will have us out on the street.

The 'college boys' are the managers, surveyors and assorted Englishmen who walk around the building site in suits and hard hats. They suspect that we are about to make demands. One of our grievances is that the workers have no hard hats. Nor do we have protective gloves for handling bricks, or a single first aid kit on a building site with a hundred and twenty men. Up the road at Taylor Woodrow, the men have these basics. But not at our Dickensian, family-owned business.

Now, Bearnárd, says Big Tim, me and Donal here want you to be the second shop steward. He can't organise this site on his own. And organise we must – or we've lost our jobs.

He shifts his bulk on the scaffold plank above the wet concrete.

You sign on with the Union tonight, and ye two can draw up the list of demands in the pub.

Why me, Tim? The only experience I have was on the other side of the table in Nigeria.

He squints at me. Well, now. When we do listen to you talk, we do almost think you're a bit of a college boy yourself. His eyes twinkle. And that'll give them buckos in the hut beyond a bit of a surprise.

I'm elected.

Next day, the sun is splitting the trees in Camden Town and tar is melting on the street. Donal and I knock on the door of the site manager's hut.

Good afternoon, Mr Brown. We represent the Transport and General Workers Union on this site. My hands are shaking. We would like a meeting with you at your earliest convenience.

His mouth falls open. So does Donal's.

Here is our list of demands. Nothing onerous, as you will see, I say.

The manager stares at the paper, and then back at me. There's no union on this site. The owner doesn't allow unions, he says.

Well, there is now, Mr Brown, and if you try to fire us or anybody else, we'll lead everybody off the site. Is that clear? I think he is going to burst, his face turns so red.

We look forward to hearing from you within twenty-four hours, I say. Good day.

I nudge Donal, who is standing with his mouth open. Neither he nor the Englishman has heard an Irish navvy talk like this before. I feel elated and a bit light-headed too.

What the fuck is 'onerous', Bearnárd? says Donal.

A pain in the hole, I say.

The lads on the third-floor scaffolding report the black Jaguar when it arrives the next day. A junior surveyor calls up to us where we are laying a slab on the second floor. I shout down, Come up, please, we cannot hear you. The lads nudge each other. The surveyor arrives panting and angry. Will you report to the management hut right away, he glares.

And?

And what?

Please, I smile.

He pauses just a moment. Please, he says.

Well now, isn't that a well-brought up young man, says Big Tim, and winks.

Donal and I pull on our singlets and wipe our concrete-encrusted boots on the mat. A grey-haired man in a dark pinstripe suit sits at the head of the table.

In the next half-hour they try cajoling, bullying and threats of arrest and bribery.

Is all this, I say, because you do not wish a) to obey the labour laws of your own country, and b) to give your workers what your competition gives?

Pinstripe is apoplectic. This meeting is over, your demands are refused!

I nudge Donal and we both stand up. You are hereby served with strike notice, says Donal, who has rehearsed this line.

And our solicitors will be informed, I say, and we walk out.

The word flashes around the site, every man downs shovels, and instructions are given on how to behave tomorrow.

Next morning, about twenty coppers stand around the entrance. Who's in charge here then? the head cop asks.

We are, say Donal and I. I point at our armbands.

See that your lads behave themselves and there'll be no trouble, Paddy, he warns.

His name is Donal and mine is Bearnárd, I say.

He gives me a sideways look and nods.

Two days later, all our demands are met.

This is a grand day for the great and noble worker, says Big Tim in the pub that evening. Well done, all here!

As luck will have it, Nicky, Tasha and Justin arrive the next day. I have asked her to visit me at the site. I want her to see what I'm doing. For them.

Can't you get a job in an office? she asks.

No, because I need to do physical work to tire myself and sleep well at nights.

Daddy, what do you do in there? Tasha points at the corrugated iron fence.

Come inside, and I'll show you.

We stand on a catwalk and they stare at the cranes and the four-storey buildings going up. One of the Irish lads walks past. He salutes this fashionably dressed, good-looking young woman and her children, almost trips over his boots, and disappears in a blush of embarrassment.

Nicky laughs.

May I take you out to dinner? I ask.

In a Spanish restaurant, she tells me that she cannot stand living at home or in England. She loves Africa. If I go to Africa and set up a home again, she thinks that I may have learned my lesson. She might try again.

Andrew is in South Africa, I say.

Well go, she says.

I meet the lads at our Union meeting a couple of nights later.

South feckin' Africa? says Donal.

Big Tim says nothing.

You can't go there, says another. Apartheid. We're all protesting next week, sure. They are horrified.

Then Big Tim speaks. No man can stand in the way of another and his family. Sure, didn't the Irish fight for centuries to gain the right to live together without let or hindrance? Let the man go. He wants to regain his family.

Their faces are confused, angry and sad.

Big Tim grips my hand and says, God speed. May the road rise gently for you, boy.

My eyes fill with tears and I blunder out into the darkness.

My friend Bob Quinn rides the tube and the bus with me to the airport. We have spent many an hour pondering the mysteries of life in general, and women in particular.

We can't live with them, he says, and we can't live without them. Send me a postcard.

Back to Africa

It's October 1969. A South African girl offers me a boiled sweet on the packed plane from Luxembourg. We talk all night long as we fly over the Dark Continent.

Would you like to come to lunch at my sister's house in Johannesburg tomorrow?

274

Love to, Laura, I say.

I find a bed at the YMCA in the centre of the city. Laura picks me up at midday and takes me to meet her married sister and family for lunch. They live in a sprawling ranch-style mansion with a pool and tennis court. Are you impressed? Laura asks. Not everybody lives like this, but many do. She points at the other huge properties around.

Where do the blacks live? I ask.

Oh, we talked enough about that on the plane, she says. Come in for lunch.

Apartheid is working, Laura's brother-in-law Bruce tells me at the lunch table. How come you know so much about Helen Suzman? And Mandela? He's a terrorist, you know.

Well, so was I, I laugh, in Ireland – and we have read all about Mandela.

He interrupts. The blacks are like children, and we love them, don't we, darling? he says to his wife, Verne, who grimaces, clearly embarrassed. She is putting macaroni cheese on the table as four small kids play around her ankles. He takes a mouthful.

I lived for six years in West Africa, and we… I begin.

He interrupts again. We are giving them the best education, hospitals – everything. Their own. Do you know what the word apartheid means? Apartness, he says. We are developing their places separately from us. They will have their own states, and we will have the rest of the country.

But isn't 'the rest' about eighty-something per cent of the land? I ask him.

That's rubbish, he says. Communist propaganda. You've been in England too long. Have another beer?

I am glad to escape from there.

In the next two days I meet only friendly people. The whites all want to know what I think of their country but I realise the question is just an excuse to tell me what they think of it. They are unsure of themselves, eager for approval. Anxious, almost – like me.

I catch the train and head for Durban and Andrew. Children and nappies surround him in a small flat. But he is still his usual self.

You will not believe the crumpet in this town, he says. His wife smiles, a shadow over her face. For you, not me, he adds. You are free again.

No, I'm not, I tell them. Nicky is coming out from England. I hope soon. If she does, I'm going to make it work this time. Got to get my kids back, I say.

Andrew shakes his head. Forget it, he says. That was a mixed marriage from day one. And you know it. Forget her.

But what about my mixed-up kids? I've learnt from what happened, I say. And I still love her… well, I think of her a great deal.

You see, he says. You're not sure.

I *am* sure that I want to prove that we can do it, I say.

I lease a rent-controlled, two-bedroomed flat on the seventeenth floor of a block overlooking the harbour. Yachts bob about below and cargo vessels ride at anchor in the bay – happy memories of my days at sea. The kids will love this view. Will Nicky?

Fear closes in on me whenever I think of her. What if this, and what if that?

I get a job on the strength of my West African experience. Kingsway has given me a decent reference, with no mention of why I left. So the socks, ties, and sweets counters are my new domains in a department store called the OK Bazaars. Bottom of the ladder, just about, but working with good people. Fergie is an older man, ex-French Foreign Legion and a Prod from Belfast. He is in charge of the Wimpy Bar. After work, we buy two-litre jugs of Tassies wine – all we can afford – and drink the nights away. We have adventures. We pull the field-gun off its plinth outside the Town Hall, roll it into the middle of the main drag, and exact a toll from the motorists who stop.

There's no such a love as the wonderful love of one drunken slob for another, we say. Fergie sings Legion songs and I sing 'The Old Triangle' and we both have happy tears in our red-rimmed eyes. I tell him all about Nicky and what happened. He listens. And then shakes his head. It's not reconciliation that you want, he says. What you really want is to prove that you can undo the damage.
I have not heard Fergie speak like this before.

You know deep down that you are not suited. Then he reaches for his glass and says no more.
I am also silent, tired at last. Maybe he's right.

Help the drinking man, we say sincerely. Some do, and when the blue flashing lights arrive we run down a back alley off West Street to while away the small hours in a strictly illegal nightclub called the Casino. It's illegal because black and coloured musicians are playing for a mixed audience. But the Security Police drink there in mufti, and blind eyes are turned to it all. The music is jazz and soul. The dancing is slow and moody. The cops get quietly drunk in the shadows until dawn.

The South African security cops are slack, for all their fearsome reputation. They do not turn up my 'criminal' record in Ireland or my trade union and Communist Party activities in London. My application for permanent residence does not mention these goings-on. It includes the names of Nicky and the kids. Residence has been granted to the lot of us – apartheid South Africa needs whites.

Crossing the colour line

A coloured musician, Roy, introduces me to his trade union friends.

This is Paddy, he says, from Ireland. One night we go to a warehouse in the docks to attend a strictly forbidden mixed cast and mixed audience play. It is put on by an embryonic trade union that I want to join. But unions for non-whites are banned by law. And with the family due, I have to be careful.

Amid the smoke and chatter, the place is jammed with Indians, coloureds, blacks and a sprinkling of whites.

A little salt and lots of pepper, says Roy, looking around grinning. Halfway through the first act, the lights go on. Plainclothes cops burst in and tell us all to stay seated, then take our names and send us home. I am petrified that now they'll check my past. I hear later that they arrested and charged the players under the Suppression of Communism Act. Roy is threatened with jail.

Two nights later, two Afrikaans-speaking security policemen visit me in my flat.

If you want to stay in this country, then do not mix with those sorts of people, one says. He checks my passport. Any family?

They are arriving soon, I say.

They look at my books and records. All my political and historical stuff is in storage in London. As they are leaving, they look at the iconic picture of Ché Guevara on the wall.

Who's he? They ask.

Oh, some American pop star, I say.

OK then. Remember what we've told you. Behave – or you will get forty-eight hours to leave this country. And your family too. *Verstaan?*

I understand, I say.

Totsiens, then, he says. And they leave.

Totsiens, I say. See you.

I cannot be thrown out now. I can't allow it. Nicky and the kids are arriving next week.

Hate me or love me

The atmosphere is as heavy as the coastal humidity when Nicky and the kids arrive. She is not at all sure of things, and hedges her bets. She sleeps in the main bedroom with the children. She tells me about a South African who'd fallen in love with her on the Union Castle ship that they came out on.

Nothing happened between us, she says, but he wants me to live with him.

And the kids? I ask, trying to disguise my fear.

Oh, yes. They get on very well.

She looks at my son. Especially Justin, she says.

The pang is like a stab in the stomach. Can I trust myself to stay cool? I've been promising myself this since the divorce and the weeks here waiting for them to arrive? The weeks and months of remorse in London cannot be wasted. I'm a different person now. We go to Lourenço Marques, capital of Mozambique. Driving through the bright-green sugar cane fields of Swaziland in my Volkswagen hatchback, the January heat is fierce. The hotel that I can afford is not the best. The kids are hot and bored. The holiday is first cousin to a disaster. We celebrate New Year in 1970 with Gatao *vinho verde* and go to bed early.

Next day, I am sad and defeated.

What's the matter? Nicky says.

I want you to hate me or love me, I say. It's the nothingness that I cannot stand.

A few days later, back in Durban, I find a letter from Nicky. She thanks me for all I have done in the fortnight that we have been living together but does not believe it can work again. She wishes me well.

I am relieved, and I grieve at the same time. I realise that it is the kids I am going to miss. Too much spilt milk has flowed under the bridge, as Big Tim used to say, for Nicky and me to love each other again. She goes to East London, further down the coast, where her Union Castle friend lives. She says that I must not worry about seeing the kids, that she will arrange for me to see them. I believe her. She has never before kept them from me. She's the stable one. It's me that needs to slow down, calm down – otherwise my kids will never get to know their father.

14

The rear-view mirror

I GET A LETTER FROM Laura. She is coming down from
Johannesburg in April for a few days with her married sister – the
one who'd made the macaroni cheese. Would I like to show them
the sights?

I park the car outside the Lonsdale Hotel but I don't get out. The
doorman is looking at me sideways. No waiting, he is saying. Just
then, the passenger door opens, Laura says hello and gets in. I hear
the back door open too, and slam shut. I look in the rear-view
mirror. A smile, lovely eyes, oval face and dark hair. Not bad.

We have a few drinks at a favourite pub and walk on the
esplanade. Laura's sister, Verne, is having trouble with her
marriage. We compare notes. She talks openly about herself, her
kids, and her life. She is easy to talk to and good company.
Nothing seems to get her down.

Then it's time for the Casino. It's ten o'clock, and things will be
hotting up there.

The lads on the door wink at the new talent. The piano tinkles softly
in the smoky atmosphere as I raise my glass to Verne. I fancy this.
The cabaret and Roy Petersen are on form, and the mood and the
illegal drinks are going to our heads.

Smart chicks, Paddy, Roy winks at me. The girls have never before been in a mixed-race place. The exuberance of it all knocks them out. Laura can see what is happening between her sister and me on the dance floor, gives me a nod, says look after my sis and tactfully leaves in a taxi. At about four o'clock I invite Verne to watch the sun come up over the harbour from my seventeenth-floor balcony. We don't see much of the sun, but we do see a good deal of each other.

When I awake, I turn my head and leap out of bed with a yell. There is a big black spider on my pillow. Verne wakes and says, What's the matter?

Look, I say, look, in a panicky voice, pointing at the black legs. You'd better get up in case there are more of them.

She picks up the 'spider' and smiles her big smile.

That's one of my false eyelashes. Did it give you a fright?

Over bacon and eggs I tell her of my childhood fear of the spiders that lived behind the wardrobe.

Well, I won't wear them again. Then she smiles, When I'm with you.

That night, Roy and his multiracial band play jazz at the Blue Note, an illegal club in the Durban docks.

I introduce Verne.

As in Jules, Roy, I say.

Would you like a drink, Jules? He asks. We're taking a break. We climb down the iron stairs and into a kombi. A bottle of Klippies and some Cokes appear. Eight of us are crammed in to the light of a solitary street lamp. Voices are muted as the lads watch for police patrols.

There is only one glass. Roy drinks first and passes it on. One by one, they drink and refill that glass.

Verne watches it getting closer. Drinking utensils are not shared in 1970 apartheid South Africa. The Zulu guitar player is next to Verne. He wipes his lips, drinks and passes the glass to her. Her eyes shine, she gives him her biggest smile and says thank you and drinks. I nudge Roy.

Time to play some happy music, he says. The guys guide Verne up the dark stairs.

This must be the girl for me, Roy, I say.

Who, Jules? Probably too good for you, Paddy, he says.

A week or so later, I get a long chatty letter from her. It's as if I've known her for years. She's a friendly sort and heading for a divorce, it seems. I write back and keep her contact number. Then the bombshell arrives: 'My youngest, Warwick, drowned last week.' I stare at the blue paper. Her tone is matter-of-fact. Her husband blames her for the death. A quiet courage comes through in the lines. I write and tell her when I can next come up to Joburg. I find myself thinking of her happy smile – but will she be smiling after this tragedy? In my letter I also tell Verne that Nicky is still hinting that she might come back to me. So I cannot commit to anybody else. But whatever happens, I tell her, she and I will still be friends.

All the time, I remember, too, those long brown legs.

I arrange to meet Verne in Joburg. Her divorce is underway. I am struck again by her good looks and her open, honest face as I listen to her talking about her life and her kids. And the dead one, too. Reading between the lines, she is so busy looking after the other three children that she has had no time to grieve.

Still running

I am offered a post in the OK Bazaars training department in Joburg. Fergie, the lads and I spend the last of our salaries and many late hours saying a four-week farewell.

As I drive on the highway listening to the Moody Blues' 'Days of Future Passed,' I have time to consider what is happening in my life.

I spend the nearly six-hundred kilometers trying to count the number of beds that I've slept in in my life so far. After a hundred, I give up. I love the road. A young man at the side of the highway signals. I'd prefer to be him, the guy with the rucksack, hitching. It's the best freedom. Not knowing where you'll sleep that night. But I can't give lifts today, as the seats are chock-a-block with my small possessions.

Leaving Durban is the break that I need to stop thinking about Nicky. I know she's keeping a line open to me for the sake of the kids. She's good like that. I must stop misinterpreting her motive. Maybe this girl in Joburg is the one – Verne. But she'll want to marry again – for her kids' sake too. No ways. We'll have fun while it lasts, but no more than that. And maybe she won't want to hop from one marital bed to another so quickly. She probably needs a bit of freedom too.

I signal that I'm full to a hitch-hiker with a Canadian flag stitched to his rucksack. Yes, that's the freedom I crave. Forget about marriage. I'll work hard, make money and get back on the road, I decide. The world is waiting and so is Joburg. Egoli, my Zulu staff called it. The City of Gold.

I meet Verne immediately and introduce her to Andrew, who I stay with while I find a place of my own. Andrew has tired of babies, nappies and also his wife, and is living in Joburg with a new girl, Kerry.

I did the honourable thing and married Gerda – but look where it got me. Anyway, she's better off without me, he says, eyeing Verne.

This hoor hasn't changed at all, I think to myself.

My new boss asks me to share a desk with Rob Banks, a training

Justin and Tasha, Rhodesia

consultant. We get on right away and spend the day talking about everything under the sun except work. No objectives are set by our boss, who spends his time politicking. Another Rob, Rob Kamp, sits in a little box of an office with the door always closed, so we call him Kapsule. He does actually work. The three of us meet the boss once a week to play liar dice. Nothing else.

I introduce Verne to Banks, Kapsule and their wives. They take to her immediately and invite us to their homes as a couple.

Verne and I go to movies, parties, restaurants and pubs with the lads. They enjoy her company. I take out other girls too, but Verne is the regular. She is settled now in Parktown North, on the other side of town to her marital home. Her divorce was messy.

I'm starting a new life, she says cheerfully. I'm really enjoying my new job.

A modelling agency has seen her potential – slim figure and elegant walk. Of course, I'd noticed it all myself.

We speak of relationships, lasting or otherwise, and whenever we do I say that I don't wish to be married again, that it's not necessary if one has a good friendship. I say that marriage could ruin things. She says nothing – but I can see that she doesn't agree. These days in Joburg, I run when a girl starts making setting-up-house noises. Ten minutes into a conversation and I've brought up Spain or South America or going back to sea. The walls of my various abodes – all temporary – are hung with pictures and posters of faraway places.

I concentrate on the job at hand but I know exactly where my passport is.

Nicky's shadow

I spend a lot of time now at weekends with Banks and Kapsule and their circle of friends. It's restful, after the riotous commune I live in. I'm enjoying my freewheeling life, but the thought of Verne with another man does not sit well with me. Yet I know that I can't expect to play the field and expect her to be celibate.

She'll be snapped up, says my friend Banks.

No, she won't, I say. She's got three kids. And they're not the easiest.

How do you mean? he asks.

Well, they're a bit wild, you know, undisciplined.

You mean they have high spirits, Banks says.

I look at him hard. I like this guy. And I admire his straight talk. No badness in him, as Mama used to say. But he's irritating me now.

So what are you saying then?

That you should marry her, he says.

He's dead serious.

I'm not marrying again, we've been through all this before, Banks, I say.

Now I'm exasperated. Friends are supposed to agree with you.

I explain, Verne is a fine woman, but if Nicky gets fed up with her chap in East London, she might come to live in Joburg. Then I'd woo her all over again.

No, you wouldn't, says my friend with a knowing grin. You just want your kids back. You wouldn't want to live with their mother again. He pauses to see how this is going down. And you can't have your kids without her. Move on, O'Riain. Your ex-wife is just an excuse.

I know he's right. I am in love with the memory of the love I had for Nicky. Now, because I might be falling for someone else, it may be easier to let Nicky go.

But Nicky will not say it's all over. There is a 'maybe' in her voice that I hang on to, a knee-jerk reaction of hope. The guy in her life, Charles, is crazy about her, but he's a Catholic and won't live with her unless they're married. He goes one step further. He cannot marry her, he says, unless her first marriage is annulled.

Are there still Catholics like that? I ask her on the phone. You converted. Isn't that good enough for him?

He's a good man, she says, and I'm considering whether to marry him or not.

It's like a hot knife in my throat. She is not coming back. She talks about her parents. They say that she should have nothing more to do with me. When she asks me to contribute maintenance to the kids, I refuse. I know that her well-off parents are sending her money. I resent her now. All the efforts to win her back are in vain. Within weeks, a court order arrives and I am humiliated and ashamed. Fuck her parents. They are 'I told you so' merchants and never tried to save the marriage. But I send money to Nicky now. I don't want trouble with the law. She is trying to stand on her own feet and to bring up the kids on her own. So I should support that. And I must forget her. Time to move on.

Some months later, she and my kids move to Salisbury in Rhodesia. Things seem to have come apart for her and Charles.

Rome sets asunder

Nicky phones me from Rhodesia.

Will you agree to an annulment of our marriage? she asks.

But we are divorced, I say, a little mystified.

The problem, she says, is that Charles has to have my first marriage annulled before he can marry me in a Catholic Church. He's staunch, you know.

I think about this for seconds only. If it will get you and Tasha and Justin out of that war-zone up there and give you all stability, I'll do whatever I have to.

It could be painful, she says. I've been in touch with the Church authorities in London. They want us to say, maybe, that we never loved each other.

I can feel the anger rising in my throat as I say, But we were happy for years.

I know that, but this is the only way that he'll marry me.

After that phone call I grab my hiking stick and storm out onto the street. I smash the tops off weeds along the pavement. That's the Cardinal, smash; that's the fucking Archbishop, slash; that's the bastard bureaucrat who is telling my ex-wife and lover and mother of my children what she has to say, to pretend that our union, blessed by Holy Mother Church, never existed, was never valid.

When I come back, Verne sits me down. This is what you want, she says. Your kids will have a safe home. Go through with it. What do you have to do?

A priest is going to phone, I say, to tell me.

The call comes through to my office. Is that Mr O'Riain, a soft Irish voice asks.

It is, I say.

This is Father Gerard. Can I see you about the request for the annulment?

I go to the Cathedral in Joburg. Father Gerard, a Franciscan, has been charged with the investigation.

Gerard is my father's name, I tell him. He would be offended and saddened by what you are asking us to do, Father.

Ah well, it's something we have to go through with. And Bearnárd, the laws of the Church don't always accord with logic. He sounds a bit sad himself. His heart's not in this, I can hear. He pulls a bible down off a shelf and places it on a side-table. Sunlight from a stained glass window is angling down onto the book. Pointing to it, I say, The spotlight is on us, Father. Do you want me to swear on that?

I do, he says. He starts looking for something among his papers. I want to smash the Church, the Church that taught us all the truths about obedience, rules and laws. And threatened with hellfire if we transgressed and died in a state of mortal sin. The Church that frightened Mama and Dada, told them that they would suffer damnation if they didn't make us go to Mass, confession and communion.

The priest reads out the rules of the annulment process. More feckin' rules. I draw a deep breath and control myself.

Will you tell the truth then, my son? He slips into confessional mode.

Father, I say, my objective here today is to make sure that my ex-wife can marry the man who loves her and who is going to give my two children a home.

He looks at me. And will you swear to this?

I will if that's what it takes, Father.

Now I can see that he's troubled.

I've told you my purpose in being here, Father. We must do whatever the Church wants to annul the marriage. Can we get started?

For the next twenty minutes we go through the charade of truths, half-truths and plain lies. He asks me if the marriage was consummated, his face an unhappy mask.

We have two children, I say quietly.

I have here an affidavit, he says, from a witness that indicates that you were not in love at the time of the marriage. He looks up.

Is that what the tribunal in London wants to hear? I raise my voice.

He shuffles his papers.

I will not contradict what they have been told, I say.

He takes a deep breath, and we finish the rest of the questions in the next five minutes. He says the annulment will take about a year to finalise.

Will my children be bastards in the eyes of the Church, I ask him.

Ah, that's beyond my competence, he says.

If I weren't already a pagan, Father, and hoping that my children will be free of all this hypocrisy, my question would be very serious. What if they ask their mother, or me this question?

I cannot say, Bearnárd.

Is your faith in the Church not a bit damaged by all this, Father? Not your faith in God, but the Church?

I pray for guidance and that God will enlighten me, he says. I have faith that He will.

The old cop-out.

I shake his mottled old hand and say, Remember our objectives, Father. It's the future we want to take care of.

He smiles and turns away, his back bent – in sadness.

Luigi in and out again

Verne and her kids are sharing a house with another model friend of hers. I will not commit to going steady. Don't pin your hopes on me, I say one day when we're talking about the future. I don't want to bind myself.

Then one evening, an attractive journalist friend rebuffs me. She'd written an article about my learning to fly light aircraft. In response to my advances, she says she just wants to be friends, and that's all. So I up and drive to Verne's house where I expect a better reception. The house is in darkness – but there's an Alpha Romeo in the driveway. I feel the bonnet. It's warm.

My stomach does a loop. It's only ten o'clock on a Friday evening. Her kids are with their father. I walk quietly around to the back. Her bedroom light is on. I listen. A male voice. I feel instant alarm and resentment. Verne has given the impression that she will always be there for me.

I rap on the window. Silence. I bang again.

I know you are in there, I shout.

Who's there? Verne calls out.

It's me, I shout back.

I hear whispering.

Go around to the front door, Verne's voice calls, and I'll let you in.

She is wearing a dressing gown. I brush past her and into her bedroom and look all about. I'm not thinking straight. I come out and see a dark-haired guy, good-looking, sitting on a couch in the lounge. He's the Italian who has fancied her for ages.

This is Luigi, Verne says. I've told you about him. He was Bruce's and my friend.

She is nervous and jumpy.

I think you'd better leave, I say to him.

He gets up and says that he knows who I am, and that he'll go. He says goodnight to Verne and she walks him to his car. She comes back in.

What does this mean? I ask. I didn't know you were seeing him.

How dare you come knocking on my bedroom window!

I've never seen her this angry. I apologise and say I didn't know that she was involved with someone else.

I'm not involved, she says. He's an old friend, and I can go out with him if I want to.

I hoped I could stay tonight – but now I can't, I say. I can't possibly.

No, but we need to talk, she says. I don't know where I stand with you. I'm not 'involved' with Luigi, as you put it, but I could easily be.

She glares at me. I'm not at all sure of myself, so I say nothing. I'm afraid to ask her if she was having sex with him. What if she was? She's entitled to. But I don't ask.

You have to make up your mind, she says. I know that you are seeing other women. Like tonight. Where were you?

I was discussing the article on flying with Jenny. Nothing else.

I don't believe you, she says. Now what are you going to do?

You, if you will let me, I say, foolishly.

She gives me a scornful glance and ignores me.

Are you still going to call for me in the morning to go to that meeting? she asks.

Yes, I say.

That night, before I leave, I promise to stop playing the field and she says she will tell Luigi that she has made her choice. This is a close call. Is this dog in the manger, I ask myself, or do I want this woman on a permanent basis?

For now, it's yes. We'll see what happens next.

No room for kids

Bruce has been nagging at Verne to send the kids to a boarding school. He went to one, so his kids must, too. Every weekend that he has them staying with him, they come back wailing and crying that they want to go to boarding school, that Daddy says it will be exciting, there'll be swimming pools and tennis, and so on.

You don't even have a pool, Bearnárd, says Roger, her eldest.

So she gives in to Bruce and agrees to let them go. But she doesn't like it. She drives down to Natal and hands them over to two prep schools. The kids are upset, but they are also eager.

I'm not in any mood to invite them all to live in the new place that I've bought and am renovating at weekends, the first home I've ever owned. I want my freedom and I don't want to commit. It's a male thing – as old as the species. No doubt our ancestors, roaming these hills around the Transvaal highveld, slept in one cave with one woman and shacked up with another when they were far from home. It was either that or risk being eaten by a lion.

I run these arguments past Verne. She doesn't buy them. She makes no bones about being a one-man woman.

The atmosphere is strained as I quietly rebuff all attempts by Verne to establish a long-term basis for this relationship. She is a mother first and last, and wants security.

Kapsule tells me I'll destroy my friendship if I get married. Banks says this is the woman for me.

Marry her, O'Riain, he says. You will not find another one like this.

We don't have enough in common, I say. She reads Mills & Boon, for God's sake.

So, lots of people do, he says. But you told me that she had read Dervla Murphy?

OK, I forgot that.

Conveniently, he says. Are you saying she's not your mental equal?

Yes, I suppose so. She is not interested in politics or history. I can't have a conversation with her about what's happening in the world. Or more important, *why* things are happening.
I am intolerant of her, and bully rather than persuade. I get irritated and critical. She withdraws and is so hurt that she will not read the *Geographic* if it is the last printed thing on earth.
But the inevitable happens. She spends most of her time at my place, and the travelling back and forth soon becomes a pain.
So I invite her to move in to my house in Westdene. She gives notice in Parktown North and arrives with Sipho Dick Mbuye, her nineteen-year-old domestic who comes from Botswana. He's a pleasant, shy guy, and shows immediate interest in the building work. Verne is happy and so am I. For the moment.

Marriage trashed

I fly up to Rhodesia to see my children, to meet Nicky's latest man friend, and to see Tasha and Justin's school. They love it. It's set in beautiful countryside, there are good teachers and it has a high standard.
But the war in Rhodesia is hotting up. The two liberation armies, the 'terrorists', are gaining the upper hand. Nicky tells me that Ian Smith's government is coping, with South African help.

Are the kids safe? I ask.

I wouldn't be here if they were in any danger, Nicky says.

And what about Charles in East London?

Sipho Dick Mbuye, 1980

He had his chance, she says, and he didn't take it.

A week or so later she calls me in Joburg. The annulment document from the Archdiocese of Westminster has come through. Nicky reads me phrases over the phone: 'Since the Catholic Church is only concerned with arriving at the truth…' and 'a Declaration of Nullity has been given in respect of your marriage…' It has taken a year for the bureaucrats to complete the job.

So Charles in East London can marry her now. Or she can marry any Holy Roman, for that matter.

I phone her back to ask if this means she will marry Charles. But Nicky is enjoying the good life in Salisbury, and my kids are doing well at school. There is no sign of them returning to South Africa.

Hot and cold and hot again

Verne is working as a model and enjoying it. But all is not well. The kids will soon be home on holiday. She wants them to have the security of marriage and a permanent home. I fear that I won't handle it well, that I will not get along with her kids. They are being pulled every-which-way by Bruce, and I can't blame them for seeing me as a rival to their father. I don't help things by showing impatience with their mother, criticising her, and sometimes shouting at her when they are on holiday with us. I see the frowns on their faces when this happens. Angie, her daughter, in particular. Her loyalty to her Ma is deep.

One evening after work, Verne says that unless I marry her she will have to end things. She says it in a quiet voice with no drama. She knows what I'm like if she raises her voice or gets emotional. So we sit quietly on the white flokati rug in the living room. Soon we are both crying. She sobs and sobs. It's the end of us. I know she loves me. I believe that I love her too.

But I will not marry her. Or anybody, I say. It's not you, I explain. It's simply that I am not the kind of person who should be married. I damage the thing that I love. I'm self-absorbed, arrogant, always upsetting people with my political arguments. You deserve something better.

The more I speak, the more Verne cries. I look at this lovely person who has done so much for me, gone along with all my plans and my wild friends, enjoyed trekking with me in the mountains, doing all sorts of things that she has never done before.

She leaves that night and goes to stay with her mother.

My friends are aghast. Banks says I am a fucking idiot.

'Eejit' is the word, I say. But it's the right decision. For both of us.

He shakes his head in disbelief. You'll never find…

I interrupt him. We've had this conversation before, Banks, I say. My mind is made up.

I go out partying and drink till I'm drunk. I am happy with my friends. I feel free.

But the fact is I miss Verne around the house, not being there when I come home.

Sipho goes around like someone in his family has died. He is wondering what is going to happen to him now.

You can stay here till Verne has found a new place, I say. But I'll miss you, Seep.

I get out my Atlas and make plans to go off travelling for six months. I decide to rent out number 26. No problem.

But *we* are going to see Verne again, say Banks and Kapsule's wives. She's our friend too.

This is something I do not expect.

You'll see her at our next party, O'Riain, they say.

Up the drainpipe

I hear rumours that Verne has been seen out and about. Someone said she is dating an Israeli pilot. Pilot? Romantic and ruthless, love them and leave them. I imagine her in bed with a dark, curly-haired Sabra who can't say his 'r's. I lie awake at night and my imagination runs away. Missing sex, that is all it is, I say to myself. But I don't want anybody else to have her.

A few evenings later, a friend who seems to know Verne's every move tells me that she is staying for a few nights with Andrew and Kerry. I know that house well, and where the guest bedroom is. It's only fifteen-minutes drive away.

A light is burning in the spare room. A creeper-covered drainpipe is attached to the wall beside the window. From it, I can reach her window sill. I know Verne is a romantic. But will she tell me to get lost? Half the thrill is not knowing what reception I'll get.

I tug the downpipe. Tight and solid. At the top, I reach across to the window sill, and, standing on a narrow ledge, I look inside. It's a warm evening and Verne has left the curtains open. She is reading. A candle is burning on a bedside table. All I can think about is what a looker she is – and sex.

Psst, I hiss.

She looks up as if I'm the tenth person to call tonight.

It's me, I say, without any originality. Can I come in?

She frowns. What do you want?

I'm about to say 'you', but tell a lie instead.

To talk to you, that's all, I say.

She swings her legs out of the bed, those long legs, and walks across the room. Her nightie is transparent against the light of the bedside lamp. My fingers are tired from holding onto the window frame and my arms and feet are taking strain, but I still manage to get a hard-on. If you rush this, I say to myself, you'll get nowhere.

You'd better come in before you fall, says Verne, looking at my pained expression. But to talk only.

She has not smiled once. This is going to be tough. She gets back into bed and pulls the duvet up to her chin.

So, what do you want to talk about?

It's the 'so' that gets me.

I've missed you, I say in a low voice. No sounds come from the rest of the house.

She just looks at me, her face impassive. Maybe that pilot has made inroads, I think, and I feel a pang in my stomach.

Is there anything to talk about? she asks.

Yes. How are you, what have you been up to?

Are you here to check up on me?

No, no, no, I say.

The conversation is stilted and awkward and she gives nothing away. Her eyes say that she is still interested, but her voice says she couldn't care less. It takes me ten minutes to realise that unless I am prepared to invite her back to Westdene and make some kind of long-term commitment, she is not going to even begin to thaw.

OK, so I had better go then, I say, hoping that this will break the icy atmosphere.

Wasted your time then, haven't you, she says with a smile. Don't break your neck as you leave.

I look hard at her. One of the greatest things going for us is sex. We both love it. And here she is in bed. Just these thoughts, and I'm aroused again. Jaysus, I say to myself, am I in charge here? And I stand up and take the edge of the duvet and begin to turn it back. She sits bolt upright.

If you go any further, I'll call Kerry and Andrew.

She means it. She feckin' means it. This is a Verne I do not know. I frown at her, not sure what to do next.

Go home, she says, and think about what I said. She goes over to the door, opens it and listens.

I'll let you out the back door, she says, or you might break your neck.

I wasn't looking forward to the drainpipe, and follow her down the stairs. As she opens the outside door I peck her on the cheek. She holds still for three seconds and then whispers goodnight. That three seconds sustains me on the way home. She'll only come back on her terms. She's made up her mind. And so have I. I love her and need her. And not just for sex.

The ghost of her face

A week later, after a heavy day running a workshop for the company executives in the Carlton Hotel in the CBD, I get drunk with some of the participants. I think I see Verne in the bar, but it's a look-alike. I keep seeing her face. In my hotel room at two o'clock in the morning, I ring her mother's house in Edenvale. After an age, Verne answers. I thought it could only be you. You'll wake my mother.

Can I come over? I try to say.

Are you pissed? she asks.

A little, but I know that I love you and want you back.

Well, what are you going to do about it?

Can I come over and tell you in person? I say

What will you tell me?

That I love you and want to marry you.

There is silence. I try to imagine her in that nightie.

What's your room number? she asks. You can tell me there.

It takes her twenty minutes or so to arrive. I jump the gun.

Stop it, she says. Tell me again what you said on the phone.

I do this, after I get down on one knee to say it. I need you for a whole lot of reasons. I respect you, I trust you, I say. You look after me – and you, you are just right for me. For each other. She smiles at this, and from my kneeling position the best lovemaking in a long while begins.

The sparrows are coughing outside the window as she leaves. She asks me all about last night again to see if my words have evaporated. But they have not. This is the woman I want, and she knows it.

Will you marry me? I ask.

Yes, she smiles. Are you sure? Are you sober?

Sure I'm sure, I say.

15

An unfrocked wedding

NEITHER OF US WANTS anything to do with organised religion. Nor
do we want a fancy wedding that will be like our first ones. This is
to be a break with the past. So we go to a church in Yeoville and
fulfil the requirements of the law. Then back home where a
defrocked Methodist minister friend agrees to perform a
ceremony.

The fact that your Church kicked you out for speaking your
mind makes you right for us, says Verne.
She chooses the track 'Urubamba' from Los Incas, for our
wedding music. I call my parents in Dublin and they speak to
Verne for a long time. I am not very sure of what my mother must
think. Divorce – and now a new wife that she has never met.

Are all the children there? she asks.

Hey, Ma, I say, 'course they are. Verne's three. My two couldn't
come. I'll call them one by one to talk to you.

I feel as if I know Verne, she says. Her letters are lovely. So
warm. And she loves you, I'm sure. Everything will be fine, please
God, and we look forward to seeing you both soon. Dada
stammers his long-distance blessings.

It's a mighty party. Verne's kids, her parents and cousins and aunts, and our drinking friends and companions are all there, and the little house is bursting. Looking at the children playing in the garden, somebody asks the obvious.

Now that you're married, how many more are you going to have?

Five kids between us are enough, don't you think? I say. This isn't so much a marriage as a merger!

<hr/>

We pitch our two-man honeymoon tent in the Maluti Mountains in the Kingdom of Lesotho. Next day, we hire ponies and their owner to be our guide. For two weeks we are peaceful and happy. The Basuto horsemen salute us with the dignity of free men, straight-backed astride their ponies.

Their blankets are beautiful, says Verne, I'd like one for tonight. She buys one from a trader – without bargaining.
I criticise the purchase, spoiling the happy scene. Later, as we sit outside our tent in the last rays of the sun, I tell Verne that I hated my father for doing exactly this sort of thing to Mama. The wine bottle gleams and we touch glasses.
We draw up a list of the good things our parents taught us, and then the bad habits. The first list is way longer. But some of my bad ones are like time bombs.
Here's to our parents, I say, and the clink of our glasses mingles with the bleating of the goats on the mountain above us.

A violent comeback
The first time I hit Verne is in our bedroom six weeks after the wedding.
She accuses me of flirting with a girl at work. It's true. Then she says there is more to it. But there isn't, and she won't listen to me. We've been drinking wine – me far too much. She is so upset

that I know she won't sleep with me tonight. I admit to flirting but tell her there is nothing more. She carries on accusing me. Her voice is half-crying, she is so upset. And then I slap her. Across the face. She collapses on the bed.

What have you done? she says. What do you think you are doing?

Well, stop going on and on at me, I shout at her. I've told you there's nothing to it, and you rattle on.

I storm out of the room. I'm shaking. I see the room in Nigeria, Nicky's shock, the tears falling down her face. I think, this is not possible. Verne is not Nicky. There is no infidelity. But there is. I have been flirting, and as far as Verne knows, it could have gone further. So my guilty conscience reacted and I lashed out. I go back inside and apologise and apologise. I tell her that it will never happen again. I mean it.

We sleep apart that night.

Turned inside out

Up to now, Verne has turned herself inside out, as she puts it, to be like I want her to be. That's an impossible task, I admit to myself, because if I'm in a cantankerous mood, nothing will satisfy. The more Verne tries, the more awkward I can get. But now, she is standing up for herself. I think she realises that she doesn't need me that much, nor does she have to bend over backwards any more. Her refusal to accommodate my moods raises the tension between us. One evening when I come home after a stressful day, she does something with the food that annoys me. I bang out of the kitchen, shouting about waste or whatever. Verne says something under her breath. I hear the voice but not the words.

What did you say? What did you say?

I said that just because your parents made you eat every little thing is no reason why I should change the way I cook. If I want to throw something away, I will if it's no good. She turns her back on me.

Don't speak about my parents, I roar at her, what right have you to speak about them? I grab her hair and swing her around. Her face twists.

Let me go, she yells, and I shove her across the little kitchen then bang out the door and onto the street. This is not the first time that we have a shouting match, but it is the second case of physical violence to go along with it.

Halfway down the road under a street lamp, I sit down on the grass verge. I have a sense of desolation. Verne is not a bad person, so why do I go berserk with her?

What is the real reason?

Why was I violent with Nicky in Nigeria? Is Verne the wrong person too? Will the fact that I think she is daft sometimes lead to more stupid violence? It's me that's the stupid one. I am destroying not just our friendship but myself as well.

I go back inside. She is in the bedroom with the door closed. My supper, cold by now, is on the kitchen table. I eat it and knock on the bedroom door. No reply. I look inside and she is asleep. She has this ability to sleep off our rows, to switch off. I do some office work. Later she comes out to make tea.

I am sorry, I say.

You are always sorry, she says. It's no good. We have to do something about this.

What?

See somebody, a psychiatrist or somebody, she says.

I remember the advice that I gave her about her husband. I remember my regret at not going to a counsellor with Nicky.

OK, I say. I'll go.

But we don't go. Deep down, I still believe it's her fault – well, mostly. This will pass, I think.

The incident is quietly forgotten.

Five friends

When Tasha and Justin come to spend school holidays with us, all the kids get on well. There is only five years between the eldest and the youngest – Tasha and Graeme. Verne takes to my two and gives them real affection. She does not favour any of them. But I can't help favouring Tasha, and I treat her in a special way.

She was cold-shouldered in London by her English grandmother at the age of five, I explain to Verne. She was the 'Irish' child. I felt that Nicky was infected with that prejudice too. And, I say, Tasha still believes that her mother loves Justin and not her.

All seven of us enjoy curry dinners at the Perfumed Garden restaurant, and hikes and camping soon become family events that we all look forward to.

The two girls put on plays for us, using the bay window in the lounge as their stage, and they take many curtain calls. The three boys spy on them during costume changes amid hysterics of budding sexuality.

In spring and summer they dive off the wall at the end of the pool that we built with the volunteer labour of Banks and Kapsule and friends.

Now that Bruce is begetting more offspring, he is less interested in criticising Verne and me to her kids. They stop comparing the contents of our fridges, our wardrobes, and the size of our little *pondok* with his mansion.

Somewhere to call home

After two and a half years, the teachers say that boarding school is not for Verne's children. As the end of term approaches, a confab is called between us and Bruce and his new wife. She wants nothing to do with Roger, Angie or little Graeme. She wants kids of her own. He is insisting they stay at boarding school. Verne keeps quoting the advice of the teachers. The tension rises. There is only one logical thing to do. They need somewhere to call home.

They can come and live with us at the end of term, I say. Nobody says a word. I look at Verne's face. She loves me at that moment. I feel like I've done something good and unselfish for once. But logic dictated it. And I did not feel the fear at what I had done till much later. Only when they came to live with us.

One Saturday evening, it's already dark, and there is a loud knocking on the door. I open it, and Graeme is standing there with a strange woman.

I found him walking on the highway, she says. He said he wanted to walk all the way here, but I gave him a lift.

Graeme runs to his Ma beside me. He doesn't cry, although his lip is trembling. He has run away from his stepmother and walked several miles in the dark.

From now on we'll call you Tiger, I say. He is eight years old.

No food in this fridge

I want a family life. Verne and her children offer one – but I fight against it. I am too niggardly to give myself over to it and to give them a chance to get to know me. And, who knows, even to love me.

Verne's kids are home for Christmas and for good. We organise their schools in Joburg. Two traditional Anglo prep schools are selected with Bruce's full approval. He's paying.

There is trauma when they come back from weekends with him. The pot is stirred in silly and unthinking ways. Our habits are criticised. We do not feed them enough. Bruce's second litter are fatties – and so our lot are malnourished.

One Sunday evening Bruce drops them off. Roger stomps in and pulls the fridge door open. Why is there never enough food for us in this house? he demands.

Tell Roger to shut up, I say to Verne.

She cuddles him instead and says she will make him a sandwich to go on with till suppertime.

I see red.

You are spoiling these children rotten, I say. They have no gratitude. They can go and live with their father and see how they like it.

All my resentment at the invasion of my home by these kids comes to the surface. I forget the reasons why they are here. I hate the noise, the squabbling and all the normal things that kids do. I didn't have my own to bring up, and deep down I don't want anybody else's.

Of course, I know that all I need to do is go to Roger myself and speak to him about food, about our way of doing things, persuade him in a quiet way that each home is different, not better or worse than another. This is the kind of thing I teach at work in management programmes. But here at home, I'm a different person. Especially after a few beers.

Verne is distraught with the noise and whinging from her tired and irritable children.

Do not give Roger a sandwich, I say. He must wait like the rest of us for his supper.

Don't tell me how to bring up my children, she snaps back, I'll do what I like.

I grab her hair and pull her round till she is facing me. I yell in her face. I call her names, I call her kids and her ex names. The kids' eyes are like saucers, too petrified to cry. I phone Bruce and tell him to come back here and collect his brats and his ex-wife as well. I want none of them in my house ever again.

Verne and Angie are crying now. Bruce arrives and I march the kids out to him.

Take them back to your full fridges and keep them there, I say.

Can Mummy come as well? cries Angie.

No, I say. Now go with your father.

That is the first big fight in front of the children. In front of Bruce too. Now he will hear all about our disagreements and the rows. I hate Verne for hours afterwards. In my mind, I go over every little step leading up to the explosion. If she did not spoil them it would not have happened. If she didn't feel guilty over the divorce it wouldn't have happened. If, if, if.

I am so tired that I just want to give up.

Marrying Verne was a mistake. That mantra is back. She hasn't taken in what Bruce is doing. He, me and the kids are pulling her three ways. And she doesn't back me up. Even if I'm in the wrong, parents must be united in front of their children. All is lost otherwise. In Ireland, my father criticised my mother forever over the way she was bringing us up – me in particular. I hated him for that. And now I'm doing it.

We go to bed that night without talking to each other.

Next day we call a psychologist.

Just walk away

Dr Chris Nicolides is recommended by a friend. He is a Doctor of Clinical Psychology. He is easygoing, bespectacled, and his gentle manner puts us at ease as he sizes us up. He allows us to choose our positions around the low table in the middle of a circle of armchairs. His staff have already put us through psychometric tests. The results lie on the table in front of him. He makes small talk. He laughs easily. We eventually relax.

Verne tells him why we are here. I listen to her account of what happened on all those occasions we fought. I listen to her perceptions of why it happened.

I can hear my voice describing what I did, what I felt like when I was shouting at Verne, and what I thought it did to her. Dr Chris is attentive, watches us carefully, does not interrupt, takes no notes.

I can see he is taking in every nasty detail, every hurt, wince, tear and sigh that he observes. I look at Verne. She is opening up. She likes him. This is what we both need – an intelligent, empathetic and experienced counsellor.

We see him three times. Verne gets things off her chest. It allows me to hear for the first time how she is affected, the hurt, the feelings of rejection at the wasted efforts to please me, and the damage to her love. I listen, mostly.

Can I say something? says Verne on our third visit. All these years I have believed that these rows were my fault, that I was letting him down.

She turns to me. I've turned myself inside out to change, to be like you wanted me to be.

Dr Chris looks at me, an eyebrow raised. I want to argue that it's not as simple as that. But I know that it is true for the most part.

True, I say. Now I know that the problem is me, within me. Verne sees that I am shaken by all this and am taking her words to heart.

We ask for and get Dr Chris's advice. It amounts to walking away before the anger wells up. He advises Verne to leave the room also when the temperature rises.

Walk away, he says. Get up and just walk away. Both of you. It works. The next time we meet we'll explore the causes, the triggers. His eyes tell us to be patient.

On the way home after the first session, we almost start again. But no postmortems, we decide. It is humiliating to reveal our private thoughts in front of each other. It provides us both with ammunition to hit back in an argument. We decide to keep our thoughts to ourselves after each session, and only to bring them up when we've slept on it and are a bit calmer.

So we talk about the whole thing next night, sitting out under the willow tree at the pool, looking out over the dam after sunset with a glass of wine. We can see Egyptian geese land on the water.

I am determined to stop this, I say. And to cut down the drink.

Well, I appreciate you telling Dr Chris all you did. That's why I left my first marriage, because Bruce wouldn't go for counselling about Warwick or us or anything.

I think going to a psychologist is like going to a medical doctor, I say. I have a sickness in my head. So I must fix it. I can't go on denying it. If only I'd done this in Nigeria.

Now I will have to tell Verne everything that happened in West Africa. Up till now I have skated over it. I've refused to believe that it is recurring. Because Verne is not Nicky. And neither of us is fooling around with anybody else. I tell her what happened. She is shocked.

Why did you not tell me before?

I was ashamed, I say.

Tails, we win

Verne's love is unconditional. That's hard to deal with. It is even a burden. Her love is a hundred per cent. I don't know what mine is. I have a discussion with Banks and Kapsule about percentages. Verne won't join in the polemic, and prefers to talk to the other women about other things.

Like an old sneak thief sliding in at the back door of my mind, comes the thought: I've married the wrong person. I take off my shoe and bang the heel on the floor.

What are you doing? asks Banks.

I'm getting rid of a feckin' stone in my shoe, I say.

It's hard not to take someone like Verne for granted. She has no guile. No plotting behind backs for her. What I see and hear, I get. Yet suspicions are sparked off by a phone call, by a piece of paper with a telephone number on it, by her being out for hours and no shopping to show for it. Pure feckin' fear of shadows. But with me, the history of deceit runs deep.

My behaviour damages us both. What if, the nasty little voice says, she decides that there's been one fight, one slap, one foul barrage of abuse too many, and at that moment meets another man?

What if that has already happened?

The first voice says, See? You are right to be suspicious.

How stupid, says the other voice. You'd know immediately with a girl like Verne. Your trouble is that you want to control her like you control your business and everything else you do.

Yes, I want that, says first voice.

When Verne reacts emotionally to something you do or say, discuss it with her, don't get emotional, says second voice. If you treated your staff like you do Verne, they'd resign en masse.

First voice is silent.

The rows happen in a three-month cycle. For the moment though, all is peaceful. On the surface. I'm aware of Verne and the kids treading carefully around me if I'm in a bad mood. Or if I'm drinking. I hate myself for that, for having that effect. These days it's three steps forward and one or two backward.

Are we making progress? I ask Verne.

You mean us?

Yes, I mean with us not having rows. Is Dr Chris helping? Am I any better?

Oh yes, she says.

She smiles in that always-optimistic way of hers. She is throwing me a rope for the hundredth time, showing faith in her efforts and mine.

You are not denying any more. I wouldn't be here if I didn't believe that you are trying. I'd have left you.

You are great procrastinator, I say, laughing. You always put off what you can do to another time. *Mañana*. That's how I've survived with you.

She frowns. What are you getting at?

I think that you would have left me long ago if you were a do-it-now sort of person, I say.

Are you criticising me again, she asks?

No, no, no. I'm making a joke of it, I say, a sliver of exasperation creeping in.

Oh, that's all right then. Do you fancy a movie this evening?

Oh yes, I do, I say. Yes, I do.

I change my clothes to go out. A coin falls on the carpet. If it's the coat of arms, our marriage will survive, I say to myself. I pick it up. It's not.

Best of three, I mutter to myself. And so, spinning again on the third toss, we survive. It has to be that. Nothing else will do. I'd have tossed that feckin' coin forever, otherwise.

Triggers and red buttons

On my next solo visit, I tell Dr Chris about Nigeria. I hear the scratch of his fountain pen on his pad. He asks what the triggers are for an outburst, what sorts of words are used, when is it most likely to happen, and so on.

I tell him that being told to shut up is a trigger. I don't want your opinion, it is saying. I don't even want to hear you. So shut up.

Tell me what happens when Verne tells you to shut up, he says.

I can feel the blood rising to my face, I say. I feel like attacking her, slapping her.

You say slapping. Do you only slap?

I have never used my fist, I say. That is for men.

And what is for women?

I am silent. I know that my father never ever raised his hand to my mother. And he rarely did to us kids – except when we were small. I never saw a relative or friend doing it either. And if I did, I don't remember.

I've only seen men strike women in the movies, I say to Chris, never in real life.

Then I remember seeing a man strike a woman in Cross Avenue in Dún Laoghaire.

How did you feel when you saw that man hitting the woman? he asks.

I felt sorry for her. And for the little children who were crying, I say.

So why do you do it?

Because I'm angry. And often because I've drink taken. Because I'm angry with myself. I think that I've made a mistake by marrying Verne. It's a mistake for her too, Chris. We don't have enough in common. I did not love her passionately when I married her. It was a quiet sort of love. I didn't want to lose her. I pause.

He says nothing.

I have to learn that this quiet sort of love is what I need, I say.

Give me one more example, he says.

I'll come home in the evening and there'll be small talk, I say. Then she'll say something that I think is silly. I've lived with criticism so I condemn easily, too easily. I'm arrogant, judgmental, I know, but I also know when something is plain silly. I may dispute the point or I may keep quiet. Half an hour later, something else will crop up where she'll express an opinion and I'll ask her where she gets it from. She'll say a magazine, and I'll suggest that mags are superficial and that it would be better if she'd finish the book that's been lying half-read for ages. She'll say that she likes magazines and I'm too arrogant by far. I'll ask her again if she can't see the other side of the issue, and she'll say she is not interested.

Then it comes, the thought that always comes sooner or later. The fear that I've married a person that I can't talk to, have a decent conversation with. I feel the frustration rising. And fear. More words are bandied about, voices rising in unison. No, not in unison. In conflict.

Then she gets up to leave the room, I say. She walks past me. I reach out. I grab her shoulder and shout at her that she's the stupidest woman I've ever met. She shouts back that I am a dictator. I see her hair, her lovely hair, her features, her body, the body that I love – and I shake it in fury. I have married the wrong person, I shout.

And then I hate myself, I hate the awful stupid thing that I have done, trapped myself with this lovely, awful, stupid, loving idiot.

When Verne comes in from her session with Dr Chris the next day, I'm dying to know what happened. Real regret has set in with me, and fear that she may have changed towards me in some way.

How did it go? I ask her.

He says that I have made it my mission to get this relationship to work. *My* mission. He says that he can see that you love me, she says. I told him that I thought that I was the problem. But he says that it lies in your past, in your childhood.

I immediately recall my mother being silly about the Scouts or my friends, my wanting to talk to her and her inability to discuss – her closing herself off.

He said that we need to listen to each other, to stay calm and not interrupt, Verne says. And you must respect my opinions.

I do and I will, I say. I promise.

Some of her opinions drive me mad. Like not reading newspapers because they only have bad news. So I can't discuss with her what's going on in the world. But I don't say that now. Now I have to make peace and find a way to make it last.

I am an intolerant person – of politics that I don't agree with, of people who piss me off. At work and among casual friends I manage to be sweet reason itself. But my intolerance is loosed from its moorings by alcohol, then sails out, guns blazing. Some people will not invite us back to dinner parties. Vietnam is a colossal war crime, I say after the third drink. The Yanks are terrorists. Our South African police are a private security force to protect us whites. And so on.

I stop going to see Dr Nicolides.

Underneath the lamplight

It is six months later.

I am in the middle of a street, bathed in the light of a lamp, kicking a woman on the ground. I am yelling in manic rage. I am drunk. Two men are standing nearby, asking me to stop. Someone else appears and shouts at me. Loud party music comes from an open front door. The third man comes up and threatens me – the kicker, the yeller, the foaming-at-the-mouth drunkard – and demands that I stop. I do, and stagger away.

The man who has kicked the woman on the ground is me. It is I. Bearnárd. And that woman is my wife.

Verne moves out with the kids and goes to stay with her cousin, Ursula. Alone, I go to Chris Nicolides. I tell him everything, what led up to it, what happened, as best as I can remember. We talk for over an hour.

Leave Verne alone for a week or so, he says. Then try to get her to come and see me – with you or without you.

Meanwhile, I go to work, and nobody knows, or at least seems to know. My friends and staff behave normally, as if nothing has

315

happened. If someone well known had done this, it would be in the papers. Or maybe not.

Verne and I do not communicate for a week. Then I call and tell her that I've seen Chris and that he wants to see us both — together, if possible.

So we see Dr Chris again. He listens. His eyes are deep and dark. He looks away. But then he turns and looks at me again.

Are you OK? he asks.

Yes. No. Why? I say.

Because you look very pale, he explains.

Verne looks sideways at me and away again.

I am sick with what I've done, I say, physically sick.

He shakes his head. Yes, it is very bad. But you'd be surprised at how much of this I deal with. It's widespread, he says.

I am revolted to hear him say this. It makes the world an even worse place to be in.

There were other people watching, Chris, I say. There were two friends, men friends. Why didn't they stop me?

People are afraid to interfere, he says. And there's a belief that it will make matters worse.

Verne listens, her face expressionless.

Fear. Always the word fear. It is at the root of so much of what we do – or don't do.

If one of my friends had pulled me back from Verne I would have stopped, I say. Verne could have been badly injured.

I know, says Chris.

I recall my anger at Verne not wanting to stay at the party. All our house friends had been there. It was four o'clock in the morning. Many of us were drunk – the men, anyway.

Please can we go home now? Verne had asked.

I hate leaving parties. Mama always made me leave before my pals. And that night I hated the sound of Verne's voice, pleading.

Dr Chris nods. Go on, he says.

But the kids are on their own, Verne had said.

You always want to leave. They'll be fine. Sipho is there, I said.

He won't hear if something happens in the house, she said.

Then I remember drinking a whiskey, I say. On top of the wine.

Then I see myself on the street under that light, Verne lying on the tarmac, staring up at me. Her face is still.

I remember kicking, yelling. I hated her.

Who did you hate? Chris asks.

I hated the person on the ground, I say.

And who was that person? he asks.

But he knows who it was. What is he getting at?

Do you mean it's me? I ask.

Maybe, he says.

After a long silence, Verne asks Chris if she can see him on her own too.

Sure, says Chris, we're getting somewhere with this.

It is only years later that his question is answered – long after Verne forgives me, once again.

A time of violence

This has been a year of violence, and shortly after Verne moves in with me again, Soweto explodes. It is 1976.

On the day after June 16, pictures of burning buildings in Soweto are all over the front pages. I drive to the township to see for myself what is going on and am stopped by a police roadblock. A beerhall is burning a few streets away. Ten cops are aiming their rifles at distant figures that look like school kids. A cop in a flak jacket comes over to me.

What's going on? I ask.

We're potting them like rabbits, he says. You better go.

As I drive away, I smell the rubber of burning tyres, taste the acrid smoke, and hear shots like firecrackers. Only a few people are around, and they do not look at me.

That night I tell Verne what I've seen and heard.

There's going to be war, I say. We speak of leaving South Africa. She remembers friends of her parents leaving after the Sharpeville shootings in 1960.

Where would we go? she asks.

Canada? My brother is always at us to come and live in Ontario, I say.

The seeds of disquiet are sown.

A taste of Europe

Verne is packing for her first overseas trip. There's great excitement. Paddy O'Rourke, the Irish Consul, hands her the new Irish passport.

Now you are an Irish girl, he says, and shakes her hand. He looks at his watch and says, It's almost lunchtime. Shall we celebrate with a drink?

He takes out a bottle of the best Irish whiskey and recommends his favourite hostelries in Dublin, then wishes us God speed.

―⊶―

We cross London by tube. Verne sits down and gives her trademark smile to the woman next to her. She's ignored. She smiles at the guy opposite, and he looks away. She looks at me as if to ask has her make-up come adrift. I shake my head and say, It's not you. On the escalator up out of the Underground, I tell her of my two happy years in London. They are a private people. If you smile at them in public they think that you are a pervert.

We hire a camper-van in London, cross the Channel and arrive to Paris where Verne falls in love with the boulevards, shops, bars and bistros. She wants to buy all the Monets in the museum of the

Impressionists. She loves the French, and the more I tell her how rude they have always been to me, the more charming they are to her. Perverse bastards.

Across the border in Spain, the smoky smell of grilled sardines draws us to the fishermen's wharf in San Sebastian, and we poke periwinkles out of paper packets at a dockside bar. I promise her that we'll return to Spain one day.

In Dublin, the welcome is huge. I watch Mama and Dada's faces. Instant affection.

And here is one of the prodigal sons, Mama says, turning to me. Patrick is the other one.

Ah, says Dermot, the fatted calf will be killed all over again. Verne's smile, her open face, and my parent's desire that she be made to feel welcome ensure a wonderful first day together. Within the hour, she is in the kitchen, chatting away and helping Mama prepare one of her famous homecoming meals. Dada, who misses a daughter-in-law as always, fusses around Verne, offering her a cigarette, putting an ashtray next to her third cup of tea, and asking her about Africa.

My grandfather was an O'Neill, she tells him.

Go 'way, he says with a smile.

She looks at him, then at me, and grins. She's heard his first Irish-ism.

My father looks really Irish, she says. He has a red face – and a temper.

Dada, who still has his jet-black hair, smiles back at her with his brown eyes.

And I'm w-w-what they call black Irish, he says. We come from the original inhabitants, a small, dark people from the Mediterranean. These so-called Celts, and he points at Mama and me, are runners in.

What's that? she asks.

Oh, they only arrived yesterday, he says.

Verne looks puzzled and looks at my Ma.

But I thought..., she begins.

Don't mind him, Mama smiles, he means that we've only been here in Ireland for a couple of thousand years. He's an original inhabitant. And how long has your family lived in Africa?

Four generations, says Verne. We are Africans.

You can expect to get a bit of flak here, says Dermot. The anti-apartheid movement is strong.

On Christmas Eve, the Dublin streets are thronged. As we jostle our way towards the next pub, a tall black man with a woolly hat appears out of the crowd in front of us. Verne's face lights up.

Where are you from? she cries.

Swaziland, he says with a keyboard smile. And you?

Johannesburg, she says.

They embrace on the spot.

My sister, he says.

My brother, she laughs.

She has been away from Africa for three weeks.

He made me feel so homesick, says Verne. I surprised myself. I've hugged my nanny, but never hugged a black man before.

Within minutes of arriving in a pub, someone says, Excuse me, but where is that accent from? And the conversation flows.

They are so friendly, Verne smiles, and they know all about Mandela and Robben Island, and all.

My brothers look proud of her.

No one attacks us for living in South Africa. The pubs are alive with good humour and laughter. We are happy that night.

Bearnárd, Dermot, Patrick, Thomas

Losing our footing

The old fear, the insecurity soon resurfaces. With Verne, though, this is not tied to jealousy. There is a different source. My deepest fear is that she is not good enough, not bright enough for my family and friends. When Dermot asks her if she has read Orwell's *1984* she says yes. I feel annoyed straight away because I know she did not finish it. She often loses interest halfway through the books I give her to read. So, when I show my irritation with her, the others are mystified. And Verne is upset and goes quiet. I succeed in placing a pall over the day. And over myself. My dissatisfaction gnaws deeper. But I am also ashamed of myself for feeling ashamed of her.

Come for a walk, I say to her. I'll show you an old ruin where people used to live till the famine took them.

Do we have to? she says.

OK, then we'll just go for a walk.

Not too difficult, please, she says. It's very wet and slippery. So we walk on the shiny tar road. It's beginning to steam a bit from the sun that breaks through the rain clouds. I suspect that this girl is not that adventurous, either mentally or physically. Then I think of the others here with us. I know that some of them wouldn't even come out for a walk, never mind climb down a slippery path to the beach. Like we're doing now.

Help me, help me! Verne cries.

She is stuck above a rock that is sticking out of the tussock grass. I want her to just jump as I did. Shut the fuck up, I say to myself. You'd be complaining even worse if she didn't want you to help her, if she was independent of you. You just don't know what you want. What did you say? asks Verne frowning. You look angry.

I'm sorry for being crotchety, I say, and I take her hand. I'm not a nice person to be with.

Are you happy to be here? she asks.

Yes, I am. It's just that Ireland unsettles me a bit. The past is never far away.

Do you mean your past, or history?

No, my own past.

But didn't your brother tell you last night not to be daft about that? That nationalism is a curse?

Yep, I know. He's right.

We are walking along a deserted beach with Atlantic rollers collapsing on the sands. Sandpipers and long-legged curlews scurry away from us, their thin cries carried on the incessant wind. Verne's hair blows back from her oval face, showing her fine features. I love this girl. She is as uncomplicated as I am screwed

Much in common, Connemara

up with my crossed happy/sad wires causing short circuits in my head. From this moment, I resolve to myself, I'll make this holiday special for her. And show my family that I have married the right person. And show myself too.

I like that girl, Dermot says. Do you? He looks at me, questioning.

Dermot the wise one. I took more than my ration of the emotional space as we were growing up and left him in the lee of the storms to wonder and work out what it was all about.

I love her, Dermo, I say.

Voices in the night

Back in Dublin, we meet Éamonn my old O/C for a few jars. Over the pints, he tells us of current Republican politics and the fierce uprising in the North, with all his old verve.

Afterwards Verne says, I've heard of dancing eyes. Now I've seen them.

That night, I pause at the door to the dining room late one evening. I hear their voices, just like years ago. I go in.

It's lovely and warm in here, I say, closing the door.

My parents look up and smile. This nightly double act of arguing is life-sustaining now. They couldn't live without it.

What were you two talking about? I ask.

Well, Dada was just saying that Thomas always comes in very late, says Mama. And I was saying that he is thirty now and Dada shouldn't be grumpy about it.

I take the old bull by his horns. I smile at him. You are not worried, Dada, are you? It's just something to complain about, isn't it?

Ah no, he says. Thomas comes in at night, and if he makes a noise he wakens Mama up, you see. He looks at me with the mildness of approaching old age. They are both pushing seventy now.

But Dada, Mama says, looking at him again. Thomas is very good and rarely makes a sound. Leave him alone now.

They are back facing each other across the flickering coal fire, in the roles of protagonist and antagonist. But these two love each other. It's a romantic comedy with a tinge of the tragedy of sadness and strife that it used to cause when the cast of the play had four boys in it too.

The bottle was never a stranger to his hand

Is Thomas in yet? he asks.

No, I say.

I'll just go and put something on for him, says Mama rising. It's half-past midnight.

My father looks up. You see, she's still spoiling him, he says. But he smiles, unlike in the past. I can see he wants to talk.

Thomas contributes to the home, doesn't he? I ask.

Yes, and about time, he says, but he should show more consideration for Mama.

You complain – criticise a lot, Dada. Why?

He picks up the tongs and rearranges the coals. He is about to answer, but I interrupt.

You did that all the time with me. Do you remember?

He looks up and his expression is clear, with no hint of a desire to defend himself.

Did I? he asks. And he waits.

This is not the man I'd once hated.

You used to go on at Mama *about* me but never *to* me, I say. Do you remember? Mainly at the table. That table.

We both look round at it, brown glowing oak, a wedding present.
My heart tightens a bit when I remember overturning it.

I didn't know how to b-bring you up, he says.

Silence. I do not expect this candour. He's nervous now.

You used to say that it was Mama's job to bring us up, I say. Was
that wrong?

Yes, it was, because I should have b-been involved too. He
pauses. I ignored you. These days it has all ch-changed, you see. I
was reading only the other day about how Ireland is changing –
the whole world, in fact.

He looks at the fire in his usual way. No stuttering now. He's onto
something.

I hated you, I say.

He looks up with that mild look again.

Really? he says. Yes, I suppose so.

The tension goes out of me. I love this man.

What changed you, Dada?

When you went to jail, he says. I saw what I'd missed. You had
your own ideas and I never really listened to them. *And* you didn't
like de Valera, he smiles now. I hated that man too.

Mama comes into the room with a plate of sandwiches for all of
us. It is after one o'clock in the morning.

You must have Spanish blood, I say to him. Look at the hour.

Well, they say my hair is Spanish, he says, touching its blackness.
As he gets up to go to bed I walk over to him. He is standing, a
bemused expression on his face. I put my arms around him. His
shoulders are stooped from forty years at a desk. He doesn't know
where to put his hands. I pull back and hold him at arms length.

Verne has taught me to hug, I say, like this.

I embrace him again and catch the look in his eyes. Like a child.
My eyes fill with tears and I am too embarrassed now to look at
him. Instead, I hug Mama, who is smiling all over her face.

She breaks the silence. You know, Dada, Verne asked me a question when she arrived.

He looks at her, his eyes glistening.

She asked me why is it that Bernard doesn't hug. And I said that we are not a demonstrative family.

Well, that's changing, isn't it, he says. She's a grand girl. Goodnight.

And don't stay up too late with Thomas, says Mama.

Oidhche mhait, I say. Good night.

Codhlagh sámh, she replies. Sleep well.

Canada – via South America

Back in Africa, Patrick sends us the latest Canadian government policy on immigration. He has worked out that I qualify, but that the window will close in twelve months.

Apply now, he says, and don't lose out. Will Verne and her kids leave? And what about yours in Rhodesia?

That night, I take Verne out to supper and we discuss leaving South Africa.

We can see the political scene worsening. The blacks – and even the Indians and coloureds – are more militant. The world is pointing a finger. But John Vorster, the Justice Minister, is not relenting. He is digging in. There is a breakaway movement in the governing party. This pulls white politics even further to the right. English-speakers are frightened into the *laager* and vote for the apartheid government again. We decide it's now or never. We can make a new life in Canada. And we can come back to South Africa when and if a democratic government replaces this one.

The kids are at an age where changing schools will not be too disruptive. I can only hope that Charles is successful in persuading Nicky to leave Rhodesia. They must get out, that's my worry. He phones one evening and we discuss what strategy he should adopt to get her back and marry him. I suspect that the worsening war will tip the scales. Charles, armed with the annulment and a home, is ready and waiting for Nicky.

—◆—

I've been boss of my department for almost four years now. I'm in a fur-lined rut. And some of the younger bloods are jostling for my job. The odd knife flashes. All this and more we discuss over a second bottle of cabernet.

How will we get there, asks Verne, via London or what?

I sketch a map of the north and south Atlantic seaboards on the paper tablecloth. We talk about options – going via Madrid, Paris or Dublin. We discuss how much money we'll get for the house, how much is in my pension fund, and a thousand things besides. Then Verne points at the map.

I know, she says. Look. Why don't we go via South America? I am stunned. What?

You are always saying how you want to go back some day, she says. Can we go across here? she asks me, pointing to the south Atlantic.

And so the great idea is born. I embrace it – and Verne too. That's feckin brilliant, I say. Lateral thinking sideways across the Atlantic. We apply to the Canadian Embassy in Pretoria and start the long, secret process. Nobody must know. We buy two 'how to' books on travel in South America. We spend hours and hours planning the route through Brazil, Argentina, Chile, Bolivia, Peru and the Amazon basin, to Manaus. From there, we plan to fly to Toronto. It does not occur to either of us to buy a book on Canada.

—◆—

When the time comes, we go to the kids' schools.

Will taking our kids out of school for three months have a bad

328

effect on them? we ask the headmaster and headmistress.

On the contrary, both say. Travel in South America? Excellent. Can only do them good. If you survive, that is.

The news of our emigration is bad news for Tasha and Justin, Sipho, our friends and family.

Bruce is in two minds. He complains that he will only see his kids once a year. But his new wife is openly delighted. She wants him for herself.

I'll fly over to Canada once a year, he says, or I'll fly you out to South Africa, OK?

His kids look sad and say nothing.

My two have just arrived back in East London from Rhodesia. I think it was the rifle training at school for twelve-year-old Justin that tipped the scales for Nicky. All whites in Rhodesia are now on a war footing. She dusts off Charles's seven-year-old proposal and marries him.

Tasha and Justin are not happy with our decision.

You have been asking Mummy to bring us back to South Africa, and now you are going far away to Canada, says Tasha.

I will fly you out there every year, I say. Canada will be exciting for you to visit, won't it? At Christmas they have snow there.

They look at me with serious, sad faces.

We don't know what it's going to be like living with Charles, Tasha says.

He's a good man, I say. I've met him. He will look after you all.

Can we not come with you? she asks.

Mummy needs you with her, I say.

Justin looks hard at me. What is going on in his mind?

I'm going to Grey College, he says. I'll miss my school in Rhodesia.

My mind is made up, so I miss all the subtleties.

As I leave them, I think back to the pain my parents felt when

Patrick and I left Ireland. It's always worse for those who stay behind. The ones leaving are full of plans – excitement and apprehension all mixed up. They have little room for regrets.

We prepare ourselves for hitch-hiking in South America by taking a train to Welverdiend in the western Transvaal. Our new ex-army rucksacks are filled with bread, tins of corned beef, baked beans, and a brick each.

We set off walking back to Joburg.

Why do we have to walk, Mom? asks Angie.

To get used to the road, Verne explains. Then she says, Can we stop here, hey? It looks like a nice spot.

The boys collect sticks and we get a fire going under a tree.

The last time we cooked on a fire, Tasha and Justin were with us, says Roger. We'll miss them in South America. I put the pang away – at the back of my mind.

Verne ladles out the beans and bully beef and passes round the bread rolls, and I make tea in the little black kettle.

Will we eat in restaurants in South America? asks Graeme.

You bet, says Verne. They say that the food is great there. And we'll eat like this too.

Back on the road, the three kids stick out their thumbs at the passing traffic. After only fifteen minutes, we are picked up by a kombi. When we tell him what we are doing, the driver cannot believe it.

I am going to take you all the way home, he says.

But then we won't be practising hitch-hiking, says Graeme.

That's fine by me, says Verne, smiling at the driver. Thank you very much. We place an ad in the paper for a position for Sipho. He sits in the lounge while we interview three or four prospective employers. Good domestics are in demand. A friend finds a home for Chosnik, our pavement-special dog. The house is sold, and the furniture consigned to storage in Toronto.

A grand party is thrown by our friends in a Melville restaurant, with a cabaret, presents and speeches. It's overwhelming, and we both cry. Banks makes a speech and says with conviction that we will be back.

Bruce comes to the airport, and so do three of our friends. When Bruce walks away, he doesn't look back. Perhaps he is crying.

I am anxious. I tell the kids that from here on they must watch their rucksacks, as there will be thieves in South America who live off tourists and travellers.

Which are we? asks Roger. Are we tourists?

No, I say. We are travellers.

16

South American shoestring

THIS JOURNEY DESERVES a separate telling, another book. But
something of it must be told here. We initially plan on three
months, travelling the 9 000 kilometres from Rio de Janeiro to
Manaus on the Amazon, but stretch the shoestring to four.

Dos Coca Colas con tres vasos, por favor. This sums up how we do it.
The 'two Cokes and three glasses, please' is a lesson in sharing, in
conserving our dollars, in discipline – and most of all in one of the
kids pouring three exactly equal shares while the other two watch
with narrow eyes.

The trip begins in Rio with us having a terrible row over the kids'
discipline. I want to give up, turn back. But we pull ourselves
from the brink. Our sun shines again as we watch the two boys
tussling for a ball on the sands of Ipanema beach with a ragged
team of bronzed Brazilian soccer fanatics. Angie insists on
wrapping her mother's scarf around her non-existent breasts –
such is the attention she gets from the local lads.

In Buenos Aires, Uncle Jack's widow, Maria, and her grown sons
give us a grand welcome. The night train across the pampas is
freezing, so the kids sleep in the luggage racks. They throw

snowballs in Bariloche in the Andes, and we marvel at the beauty of the lakes that we cross to Chile.

No meat from Argentina allowed, says the customs officer. So in one meal we feast on our entire supply of biltong from home. Our hitch-hiking practice pays off. Five lifts take us from the deep south to Santiago, a distance of nine hundred kilometers. Then, on a northbound Chilean bus, Graeme announces, ¡Tengo diez años! I am ten!

Are you truly Africans? our fellow passengers ask with incredulous eyes as Graeme distributes his sweets.

Angie's hill

I wonder, can we walk up that hill there? Angie asks me in Antofagasta.

Sure, I say, I'll go up with you.
A path leads from the back of our pension around some shacks and up overlooking the Pacific Ocean.

This is lovely, says my stepdaughter. Can we sit down here?
We sit on a long flat rock.

Angie is silent, and I fall into a stocktaking mood. How many days is it since we crossed the Andes? How long have we been on the road? Five weeks. Are we still within our budget for the three months? And none of us have been sick. Verne has a bag of medicines, tablets, sticking plaster, and so on. She is the medic.
I look sideways at Angie. She seems to be in a serious mood.

A penny for them, I ask.

I was thinking about Dad, she says.

Do you miss him?

If we see him just once in a year in Canada, he won't know us any more. And we won't know him.
It hits me. The realisation of what this means, this simple fact.

Say that again, Angie, I say. How do you mean?

Well, after a few years of him visiting us for only two weeks or us visiting him, he won't know what we are doing. He won't know us. She looks at me. She is only ten, nearly eleven, and she has hit on something so simple and true. I remember my two kids querying the idea of us emigrating – but at the time my mind was on other things.

Tasha and Justin and I will become like strangers. I saw them two or three times a year when they were in Rhodesia, and that wasn't enough. This will be far worse.

It is as though this same thought has been lying just beneath the surface of my mind. Now that it's out in the open, it is clamouring for attention like a newly hatched chick. And crowding in on top of the images of my two kids are all our friends. There's Verne's father, brother, sister, and Ursula too. Banks, Kapsule and their wives who are close to Verne. And Sipho. Their faces are in a crowd looking up at Angie and me on the hill.

We have made a mistake. A big one.

She took me by surprise, I say to Verne. It has never seriously occurred to me to turn back

Verne is calm. It's important that this is coming from her daughter.

What about the furniture, all our stuff? she asks.

We'll send a telegram, and they can send it back.

She takes it well at first. Then the enormity of what we've done sinks in. That night both she and the kids are angry. We can't go back. Our friends will laugh at us, they complain.

Let's sleep on it, I say.

That night, I look out the wide-open window at the desert stars. I feel at peace, with that instinctive sense of certainty that comes of making a right decision. It's been a narrow escape.

Next day over our fried eggs at the crack of dawn, Verne says, Pack your rucksacks. We have to be at the station soon.

Bleary-eyed, we climb aboard the train for La Paz, to continue and finish our journey before going back to South Africa. The railway officials have stuck pieces of paper with the word *Reservado* onto our seats and beds. I try to tip them.

No, *señor*. How can a family travel in any other way? It is our pleasure.

The power of the family unit has had the same effect throughout our journey.

The Atacama Desert is a wonder of pale grey, blue, copper, red, ochre and gold. Dormant volcanoes watch us as we clank-clank up winding mountainsides. The next night, twinkling yellow lights are spread out below us as if we are looking down at the stars. Have they fallen? Are we upside down? We are looking down at La Paz in its bowl from a mountain ridge.

We explore the ruins of the pre-Inca city of Tihuanaco, then on to the little town of Copacabana on the shores of Lake Titicaca.

¡Ay gringo! the coarse, hoarse voice rasps across the bar. Two police officers are sitting at a table, one beckoning imperiously. He takes my passport and orders me to report to the police barracks next morning for a shave and a haircut. Bearded long-haired males are synonymous with communists in many South American countries. Much cajoling, several beers later, and playing the 'Irish card' I soon get my passport back.

Another train, another birthday. An Irish village priest plays 'Happy Birthday' on the pan-pipes. A cake is put on the table, Roger sparkles, Angie and Graeme lick their lips with pleasure, and Verne glows in the candlelight.

I am thirteen, Roger says. And then it dawns on him. I'm a teenager, he yells. See, Graeme, I'm a teenager!

One-up in the sibling rivalry stakes. Happy nights are back again.

On to Cusco, and the newly rediscovered Inca Trail. Armed with an incomplete map, hired sleeping bags and iron rations, we climb to 4 200 metres and down again over six days and nights before reaching Machu Picchu. Then over wild roads with even wilder drivers, we descend to Lima. We abandon our children for the first and only time to the care of a bar- and brothel-owner and her vast family. Margaretha is black. Verne and I have our first night out alone in over two months.

Can we stay a few more days, please, Mom? That's the kids' verdict.

<hr/>

Crossing the Andes for the fourth time, we search for and find a riverboat, the *Sinchi Roca*, in the Peruvian Amazon. The five-day trip down a tributary of the Amazon takes twelve days. The crew runs out of food, Roger catches fish, and we survive.

In Iquitos I put the stub of a yellow candle into a wedge of cake in front of Angie at a local restaurant. We sing her the birthday song and the locals join in. She is twelve now. A sudden cloudburst drowns our voices and we run out into a warm torrent gushing from the roof.

It's my wettest birthday ever, Angie grins.

At Leticia on the Brazilian border, Graeme goes fishing with a local lad in his canoe and comes back with piraña for supper. He points to his fisher-friend's feet. Look, Mom, three toes missing. Pirañas, he says.

What if the canoe had capsized? is the unspoken question. It is only months afterwards that we learn all the details of the kids' escapades.

<hr/>

A large white ferry takes us down the Amazon itself for five days

*Fully fledged travellers — Angie, Graeme, Roger, La Paz,
Bolivia*

and nights. Most of the time we cannot see the far bank. On our
last evening in Manaus, we try to sum up our journey over supper.

A big thank you to Mom for keeping us alive and well, I say.
None of us has been sick in almost four months. Our South
African bacteria, battle-hardened after four months of travel, have
defeated their notorious Amazonian cousins.

Three cheers for Mom, they yell.

As always, the locals stare and smile at the sight of these children.
I take Verne in my arms at the table and thank her.

You have had a lot of shit to put up with, I say.

Yes, says Roger, we caused you lots of worries, Mom.

337

She smiles her famous smile.

You were all great, she says. I nearly died of fright a few times, but we all survived.

Stories are told and retold that evening. We head for the airport. We 'borrow' a bus, left idling by its driver, joy-ride around the airport, and with our last dollars, buy three large Cokes for each of the kids, two litres of beer for ourselves, and kiss and hug one other goodbye.

I'll be home with you soon, I say to them.

My family takes off into the night over the jungle for Rio and South Africa. I head for Canada, Patrick and Eva – and also for Ireland.

'I think she's mad'

As my plane takes off from Manaus to Bogotá and Toronto, I stare at the disappearing jungle with a feeling of almost dreamlike achievement. Was it irresponsible, did we put the kids' lives in danger, our own? I have never felt like this before. Is it the feeling that a marathon runner experiences when he wins? Silent, floating, the sweet scent of success. We have stayed the course. Together.

Patrick and Eva have a son and a daughter and understand the worries Angie expressed on the hillside overlooking the Pacific. When I finish telling them of the journey, many pints of Guinness later, I realise how much I miss my Irish family. But Verne and her children would have been cut off here in Canada from their families in South Africa. We have made the right decision.

I go for walks deep in the Canadian woods, with Patrick and on my own. I think long and hard about Verne and me.

What other woman would have done what Verne has done?

Back to Africa – Mama and Dada saying goodbye

demands Eva. I think she's mad. But she's a great woman, as well. Eva looks at me long and hard.

But... I start to say.

Don't be an eejit, she says. What are you running away from? I only met Verne once. Where will you find another one like that?

A rhetorical question, I believe, says Patrick, grinning. Then they want to know what I'll be doing back in South Africa. I tell them that I have to make a fresh start now.

Verne and I discussed it sitting high up on a mountainside in Peru one day, I say. We'll start our own business. Something that provides a service. That's in short supply in South Africa. Big business is for the birds. You can't live on what they pay you and you end up with a paltry pension. I'll end up like Dada, turning the heaters off in winter and then having a row with Mama who is freezing.

That's terrible, isn't it, Patrick says, suddenly serious.

And he was still doing it last time we were over there, says Eva.

I don't want to end up like him, I say. He's a good man, but lack of money has twisted his life, all our lives.

339

Depends on how you handle it, says Eva. Wise Eva.

Yes, but Dada is bitter, I say. They had to give up going out, give up seeing their friends, because they couldn't reciprocate.

Do you resent him? asks Patrick.

I resent that he was so bitter, I say, that he criticised me, Mama – and now Thomas. He was judgmental – and I learned this from him. Dada didn't thrive in his marriage like you two. And I don't want to risk living with Verne and having the same undercurrents of dissatisfaction.

Are you prepared for another divorce, Eva asks?

No, I say. I'm scared shitless of that. I can't fail a second time. But I'm afraid, at the same time, that I've married the wrong person. Again.

You use the word 'afraid' a lot, says Patrick. Why?

Well, I am afraid, I say. Dada never did more than gripe, complain and give out about everything. I lose my temper. I can be violent with words – and also with my hands.
There is a silence.

Dada suppressed his rage at the world all his life, I say. Dada loves Mama like I love Verne, but he also never stops criticising her and the price of tomatoes and Thomas. I don't want to be like that.

The difference is that I explode with Verne, I slap her about. Is it to do with the old battles at home? I've been going to a shrink – and must stop it.

We didn't know that, says Patrick.

Well, it's true, I say. I fear the future with Verne unless we get it right.
I tell them about the counselling and the efforts that we have both made.
Out of the blue, Patrick asks me if I ever felt close to Dada.

Yes, I say. When I was about four, he used to take me out into the fields and help me collect buttercups and cowslips. We'd take them home and I'd put them in front of the statue of Our Lady in their bedroom. Dada said that was to keep us out of the War so those German bombers wouldn't bomb our house. Dada was my friend then. And when all us kids were out playing in the fields and it was teatime, Dada would come out and yodel. Yodel-ay-ee-tea! Yodel-ay-ee-tea! That's what he did. No other father could do that. All the other kids were told that when they heard Dada they were to come in for their tea too.

Your father can't yodel, I remember saying to the other boys.

My father doesn't stutter, one yelled back.

Patrick and Eva are smiling at all this stuff. I am rested, calmed and warmed by my Irish Canadian family.

From Toronto, I fly to Dublin.

Home is Africa

I am sorry to leave my brother and his family, but not sorry to leave Canada. I think that many people must emigrate for the wrong reasons. Either things are not going well in their jobs or in the home, and they think that starting somewhere else will be the answer. Like having another baby to save the marriage.

I'm going back home to work on my marriage, I tell my parents in Dublin.

I notice you call South Africa 'home', says Dermot.

It is now. All six of my family are Africans.

I spend a week in Dublin, and they are enthralled at our experiences as a family as we journeyed through South America.

You should write about it all, says Thomas.

I lost my notebook on a mud bank trying to catch a turtle for our supper, I say.

Serves you right, he grimaces. Poor turtle.

A letter from Verne arrives in Dublin. She describes landing at Johannesburg airport in the early morning: 'Businessmen stood staring at us. Roger told Angie and Graeme to be sure that they wrapped the rucksack straps around their legs so that they won't be stolen by *bandidos*. Their South American habits are alive and well. I'm so proud of them.'

She tells me too that Banks, Andrew and her ex-boss Val have clubbed together to put down a deposit of R200 on an old house in Rosebank for us to rent. We have no money. The pension money from the OK Bazaars, the money from the house, as well as our savings, are all gone. It will be a fresh start. Completely uncluttered. It's a strange thing. I've never felt more relaxed in my life. The freedom of the road, of living as we did for four months, has given me a confidence that was not there before.

Handbags and houses

I come back home to Africa. My wife, her kids and my own two children were all born in Africa. It is their only home. I resolve to bring my parents out here to show them my adopted country.

I phone Tasha and Justin. I realise that they are upset at not being part of 'the adventure' to South America. And now they're trying to understand the turnaround. I put Angie on the phone to them. They understand when she explains it.

Verne's kids are welcomed back at their schools.

Angie comes running in the gate one afternoon, blonde hair swinging. I have to do a project for school on the Incas, she says, out of breath. Can you help me, Bearnárd?

No problem, I say.

So she spends hours with maps, photos, pictures, pens and paint. Angie is a good artist. I go with her to Auckland Park Prep School.

Several teachers come in. Angie does the talking and describes the slides. Her project is a success. Rather than being teased at school because they came back, all three kids are admired because of what they have done. Graeme tells them that the toe he lost in an accident two years before was bitten off by a *piraña*. All three bask in their fame and find many projects to do based on everything they've seen, heard, tasted, smelled and experienced.

Verne gets a job selling handbags door-to-office-door and I find myself selling houses by mistake. One day I go to pay the rent. The elderly estate agent convinces me against all the evidence that the market is buoyant. Ten weeks pass before I sell my first house and receive my first commission. It's Verne's handbag sales that save us. For six months we struggle. I join a big real estate company, and in a few months I open a branch in Greenside. Then on May 1 1980 – Labour Day everywhere else in the world – Verne and I open our own company. But success comes slowly. In due course we buy a house.

And we fight. One fight is about my father.

Again, I criticise Verne for allowing Roger to eat something just before the evening meal. It's like a re-run of a bad movie.

She snaps back. You are so critical. Just like your father, she says.

Of course I'm like him, I shout. He is the best in the business, a great teacher. I hated him for it then. And Mama with her silly voice asked for it. It's like a merry-go-round. You and your inanities are just like her. That's why I'm like him.

I can see that Verne doesn't know what I'm talking about.

I'm not interested in your parents' hang-ups, she says. I'm interested in my children, and that's all. I can't do anything right according to you, so I just want you to leave me alone.

A huge weight falls on me. I cannot get through to this person. I

Would you buy a house from this man?

suspect she feels guilty about her youngest that drowned. So she overdoes it with these three.

You've learnt nothing from South America, I bellow. We were getting some discipline then. And the kids said they liked it. You are so guilt-ridden about them, the divorce, Bruce, and all that. You think they'll love you less if you are strict or have rules.

You are a dictator, she shouts back, you don't care for my kids.

Who took them in, then? Who?

Only because you had to, she says.

Then I grab Verne by her hair and shoulder and shake her.

That's a fucking lie, I shout, and you know it. She is crying now. The screaming of an airplane engine in free fall is the screaming of my out-of-control voice. Say it's not true, you bitch. I am almost crying with rage, and throw her on the floor. I took these kids in when they were unhappy at school. I didn't have to, I yell down at her.

You took them in because you didn't want to lose me, she says, lying at my feet.

Angie is crying. Roger and Graeme stay in their room.

I should have let you all go, I say. I knew I was wrong. I should never have married you. Get out now! Go and stay with your cousin and take your spoilt brats with you.

I walk out of the house and away.

Halfway round the block, the heat gone, I regret it all. I search inside myself, outside, for the trigger that sets off these mad rages.

Next morning I tell Verne that I feel dirty, damaged and less than a man for what I have done and said. I am like a spent firecracker, burnt and ragged.

It's no good, she says. You're not going to change. I was wrong to think you could.

Fear wells up. She mustn't leave. I can't have another failure, another failed marriage. All my recent success in our new business is nothing compared to this marriage. Do I love her or hate her? I love her goodness, her loyalty. I hate her silliness. And her stubbornness. SAS. Stubborn and silly, stupid. She can't have a conversation without getting emotional. Like Mama.

I am rational with bankers, lawyers, difficult agents and clients, all day long. But with Verne it's a conflict between not wanting to lose her and being convinced that I have made a mistake marrying her. Two fears fighting each other. It's a no-win thing. Lose-lose. I'm trapped.

When those twin jaws close in on me I lash out, like a drowning man Her hair is like swirling seaweed that I can cling to to save myself, and my anger is the current that sucks me down into the darkness.

Square one

Verne and I sit in Dr Chris's reception, not looking at each other.
Her face is tense, drawn. I am still in shock. I have been since
Saturday night. It is now Tuesday, the first time that he can see us.
Dr Chris looks carefully at me. Looking for the horns, I think. My
mouth is dry.

In the next hour he asks Verne and me questions about South
America. He does not condemn. He has no need to. I will go to
the executioner's block if asked. I have lost all respect for myself.
What is there to live for now?

You have everything to live for, he says.

He has heard from Verne what happened. He has heard everything
I can remember. No holds barred, nothing held back.

I don't know what to do, Doctor. I thought that this couldn't
happen again, I say.

We'll see what we can do, he says. It is clear to me that you
still care about Verne. You do not hate her. We'll get to the bottom
of this.

In the silent car on the way home, I can barely believe that Verne is
sitting beside me. She went to her cousin Ursula's place on
Saturday with the kids, and said she was not coming back. But
now, for the moment at least, she is here next to me.

How can I make this up to you? I ask.

You can't, she says in a voice that is dead. She collects some
clothes and drives away. Her face is stiff.

I live in an empty house with a subdued and silent Sipho who
moves like a person in a house where someone has died. I think it
will be better if I die.

I call Verne next day and she agrees to talk.

I destroy a piece of myself every time there is violence, I say to her.

She says nothing.

I feel dirty, demeaned, I say. I barely have enough confidence to go to work. I do not know how to say sorry, how to let you know how bad this is.

She looks at me.

And me? How do you think it affects me? I am totally down, my confidence gone. I thought this had stopped. You really do think that you've married the wrong person, don't you?

I do think that sometimes, I say, but deep down I know that you are the right person for me. I love you. I do. We've done so much, been through so much.

We talk for over an hour. It is clear to me that she does not want to kick me out. But she should. What if it happens again?

I have drawn up a list of all the positives I see in our marriage and I give it to her. She studies this, we argue a bit over the wording, but she accepts that my feelings are real, genuine.

If you were not seeing Dr Chris I'd leave you. If you had *ever* abused me sexually, *or* ill-treated the kids, I would not be talking to you. I'd be talking to a lawyer, she says.

I know, I say. May I talk to Urs? I ask.

If she'll agree.

I call her. I have to talk to somebody who's on Verne's side. Ursula is not only Verne's cousin, she is her best friend.

She's agreed to see me. I sit on the edge of my chair, frozen, as Ursula fixes me with cold eyes.

I remember that somebody saw you not too long ago, Bearnárd, with your foot on Verne's head, she says. That was under the street lamp in Melville. I've seen the state that you are in after a violent row. It is terrifying. Your eyes are wild, your voice is ferocious, and if words could kill, Verne would be dead. When I see you and Verne together, I can see how she angers you. She does it by the way she disagrees with you, or by not taking your point of view.

347

Best of friends – Ursula and Verne

I have no words, my head is in my hands.

Do you know how I really feel about you? You are a scumball.
You are Jekyll and Hyde. Since knowing you, I look at every other
Irishman and wonder about them. But of course it's not just one
nationality. And every class of person behaves as you do. And you
know what, Bearnárd, I don't think it's finished. It's happened so
many times before.

My heart is a ball of lead.

I think that Verne should fuck off. I realise now that she doesn't

because she loves you. It's as simple as that. She is very
determined to work at it, to rectify the situation between you.
Ursula sips her coffee. Verne should lay a charge every time it
happens – I've told her that puts pressure on the abuser. And me? I
wanted to tell your friends, but I didn't. Once Verne wanted to hit
you with the frying pan when you were asleep. Do you know what
I said to her? I said, Do it.
Then I hear her say, She stays with you because of love. And she
was, and is, stimulated by you. You have opened her up to ideas,
interested her in things that never appealed to her before. Love.
You have to learn that kind of love. Before it's too late.
She looks away from me.
I sit in silence, and fragments of her words are like shrapnel in my
skull. Scumball. Frying pan. Lay a charge. Tell everybody.

Kikuyu grass

I go to Chris again and tell him a story about a guy I know who
was not afraid. Verne and I were fighting in our kitchen, I say.
Ernie heard a smack and Verne crying. I passed him as I went
through to the lounge while I opened another bottle of wine. His
girlfriend Jane was sitting in a chair. I lurched across the room,
holding up my finger, looking for sympathy. I said, Look, she bit
me, and held out my bleeding finger to Jane. At that moment,
Ernie, a little guy, came into the room. He saw my raised hand.
He leapt across the room and beat me to the floor, sat on my chest
and thumped me. I thought it was because of what I had done to
Verne. I lay back and said, You are right, you are right. But Ernie
was not defending Verne – he was defending his girlfriend. You
see, he'd witnessed abuse as a kid and, although he was afraid of
me, his disgust was greater.

   Good for him, says Chris.

I see Chris two or three more times. I remind him about the time I had kicked Verne on the tarmac.

I don't believe we ever got to the bottom of that, Chris, I say.

Have some more coffee, he says. And we'll explore.

Our arguments have lessened in frequency and intensity, I tell him. It used to be peace for three months, and then a row. But the intervals have got longer. We both avoid the triggers, walking away when we feel the temperature rising.

And love? Yes, it is always there, hidden like strong kikuyu grass under a compost heap, sometimes unable to see the light of day, but still alive, fed by the goodness of the soil, waiting for air, for the sunlight.

Chris and I spend many sessions just talking about what it is that makes men and women tick. We pick apart my mind like a ball of knotted string.

Can there ever be certainty that it won't happen again, Chris? He hesitates, loath to disappoint.

You have answered my question, I say. Am I like an alcoholic, I ask?

Yes, he says.

Well, I have a theory, I say. A leopard cannot change his spots, but he can rearrange them. Isn't that what the alky does? He joins AA, he stops going out with his drinking pals, he stops going past his favourite drinking holes. He takes another route home. He changes his behaviour.

Yes, says, Chris, I can buy that analogy.

So that is me. I'll call Verne, I say, and convince her.

A boyhood incident

Verne has come home. But her three kids are nervous, perplexed. I tell her that I'm going for hypnosis therapy. She says that because I am being honest with Dr Chris she thinks there may be hope for me.

A week later, Chris hypnotises me. He says that he is going to take me back to an incident in my childhood. He holds a pencil in front of my eyes and says, You are going to relax. You are going to remember a time when your mother would not let you have something, thwarted you, when she was being silly, and spoke to you in the voice that you hate.

I was fourteen, I begin. I am sitting in the kitchen talking to my mother. She is washing clothes in the sink. It is Saturday. I want ninepence to go to the pictures with my friends from school. I don't have ninepence, she says. You don't have to do everything that your friends do. Can't you open a book or play or do something else, Bernard?

Give me fourpence then, Mama, I say, and I can bunk back to the ninepennys when it's dark.

Oh no, I won't have you doing that, she says, that's dishonest – and the children from Cross Avenue go there. And somebody might see you.

Why do you care who sees me, Mama? I'm going to miss the beginning, I say.

You are annoying the heart and soul out of me, she says, rinsing soapsuds off her hands, please leave me alone.

I want the money, Mama, I yell, Give it to me or I'll …
I see her purse on the kitchen table.
She looks round as I grab it.

Please don't do that! She is crying now.
I run through the house. My brothers come out to see what the yelling is about. I push Dermot out of the way, run down the hall,

351

then down the front path, with Mama's voice behind me. I don't stop for the gate but vault over it. As I run down the road I stuff the purse in my pocket.

I hear Dr Chris's voice. What do you think of your mother?

I hate her, I say.

Why?

She made me do something terrible.

She made you?

Now I feel the tears running down my face into my beard.

I love my mother. I know why she worries about us, about me. She never has enough money. She is doing her best.

So why do you hate her?

Because she's silly, she won't listen to reason. Fourpence? Afraid of someone seeing me? Who, for God's sake?

My chest is heaving, tears are running down my face.

He tells me to wake up. I can remember what I said. I can also see my mother in her kitchen, as clearly as if it had just happened.

Dr Chris puts me under several times in the next few weeks.

Am I a sick person, Doctor? Was I mad even then, as a kid?

No, he says. You rebelled against a mother who was herself frightened for your future, frightened of making the wrong decisions. Your father was frightened that he couldn't support his family, afraid of not being able to make decisions. He was frightened of the Church. And you have inherited the fear. In your case it leads to anger. But you have to come to terms with yourself now.

He opens my file.

Let's look again at the psychometric tests that you did when you first came here, he says, holding out his copy. He points. 'He tends to need to dominate and control others...'

And here, he says. 'His inability to express himself emotionally

352

may lead to a build-up of emotions and a tendency towards "explosiveness" or aggression. This is especially evident if he feels "blocked off" by female authority figures.'

Your mother was dominating and forceful? asks Chris.

I always saw her as being loving, not dominating, I say. But now...

Who made the decisions in the home, the big ones? he asks.
I think back to the arguments at the dining table. Mama's voice pleading with Dada to agree to something so that he would appear to be the head of the household, as she called it.

Yes, she did frustrate me, I say. Her voice. So is that what I hear when Verne complains or won't do what I ask? Or worse, won't listen?

Maybe, he says. She says that she bends over backwards to please you. Is that your perception?

It is. She has always done that.

So, why are you not satisfied?

Her efforts to please me don't work because I get the feeling that she is giving way to me too easily. And I know this isn't fair on her because she is trying. But it's as though she is not a whole person any more, and I don't respect that.

And it goes beyond that, I continue. I have this thing that she is stubborn and silly. And therefore the wrong person for me. That makes me uneasy, unhappy.

But you told me about your first marriage, he says. Was that the wrong person too?

Definitely, I say. That was a mixed marriage of class, and of culture. I have more in common with Verne. I identify better with South Africans somehow – white and black.

But it wasn't Nicky's fault, she was just as much a victim as me.

It's just that I fear having made the same mistake again.

You fear? He says. Fear is the dominant factor?

Yes, it is. And my fears lead to anger. I'm convinced of that. I want to lash out at them.

⸺

Over the next few months, we address my fears one by one. Peace returns to the home and love creeps to the surface, into the sunlight again. I have begun to understand that I abuse Verne verbally when I want to connect with her but can't. The violent words and deeds emerge out of hopelessness – and fear – when logic, my logic, fails.

A woman takes over

A friend tells Verne about a woman psychologist who deals with domestic violence. Dr Chris encourages this change. After the first visit to Gill Scott, Verne is positive, as she feels very comfortable with Gill's female perspective. Yet I feel this woman's disapproval – strongly. And all I want is for her to see that I'm determined. In one of my first sessions with Mrs Scott I tell her that I do not abuse Verne because of hatred. But because of fear and anger. Because I want to connect with her – or rather, I want her to connect with *me*.

You may also be a misogynist, she says, looking coldly at me. After my fourth or fifth visit, Gill says I do not seem to be a misogynist after all, that I in fact appear to like women. You get on well with them in a working environment, she says. But you are intolerant of Verne because you are emotionally involved with her.

Can I change, I mean permanently?

Yes, it's possible, though unusual. If I did not think that you love each other and that you are both trying to stop what has been happening, I would advise Verne to call it a day. I hate violence. But you seem to have a basic respect for her. You are not trying to get at your mother through Verne as much as before. You are facing yourself now. You are out of denial. That is the first step. Facing myself? During one of our fights Verne's wardrobe door swung open, I tell Gill. I saw this face in the mirror – red, eyes popping, distorted, ugly. It was my face.

Gill says nothing.

I see myself as a controller, I say, like my mother.

Yes, you are. But you're aware of it, she says. Violence is an expression of trapped feelings. When your mother was not hearing you, you erupted.

And she dominated at home – I realise this now, I say. None of us did then, although Jem, my father, must have known. He was subjugated because she had to make the decisions, she had to make things happen. She tried to disguise it, but he must have felt humiliated anyway, I say. And I saw this.

What effect did it have on you? Gill asks.

I despised him, I think. But in a funny way I must have hated Mama for doing it to him. Remember, I wanted him to notice me again like when I was four or five years old. So I hated him more and said so when I was in my teens. I hated him. I suppose he suffered doubly. His wife was dominating him and his eldest boy despised him.

I pause and look outside at the weavers flitting around their nests, grass bubbles suspended from the stripped tree branches. The female weaver rejects the nests that she doesn't like. And the male builds another and another, until she is satisfied. Was this what my father was doing all his life? His best? But never satisfying his family? He did not have the bright yellow and black plumage, the cheeky confidence, of the weaver male. Tears come unbidden to my eyes.

Gill crosses and uncrosses her legs. She remains silent.

So when I hear Verne speaking like my mother, I say, I hate her

Airport welcome — Angie, Justin, Tasha, Sipho, Tiger, Verne, Roger

for it. But what I'm really hating is my mother, for unwittingly putting Jem – my father – down.

And Verne does not know that she is doing this? says Gill.

Of course not, I say.

I tell her about Jem and my thoughts on the weavers. She smiles. It's not often she does that during our sessions. There's not much cause to, with me.

We'll work on this, she says. With both of you.

And we do, over the years that follow. Gill tells Verne what to say when I verbally abuse her. 'I'm sorry you feel this way.' She repeats it. The effect is immediate. I am defused. Just those six words. They work. I go to Gill when my seismograph picks up rumblings that foretell an eruption. I hear myself whinging one day to her about some petty thing. In a low-speed flash photo I expose to myself how childish I am. I accuse my wife of being inane. But my own brand is top-quality stupidity. Gill and I laugh about it. The sessions become more relaxed, the incidents at home fewer.

Abusive men can be cured, she says to me one day, but they first have to come out of denial, as you have done. If you give up smoking, she says, you get rid of the ashtrays, don't you? Well, you two can start getting rid of yours now, I think.

Each member of the family goes to see Gill at some stage. She could write our entire family history.

⁂

Mama writes to us once a month, and Dada adds notes. 'Did you know that tomatoes have gone up to… And the bloomin' things come from Tunisia now, I ask you.'

Verne replies, but says nothing about our troubles.

We arrange for them to come out to South Africa, and Orla, Dermot's wife who is a trained nurse, comes with them.

The day Banks comes around to the house, he turns to me and asks, Who is that little man over there?

It's my father, I say.

He gapes at me, mouth open. You've never mentioned your father in all the years I've known you, O'Riain.

I don't think I have, I realise.

Jem does not want to go back to Europe. Too bloomin' cold and wet, he says. If Mama goes first, may I come and live with you? he asks Verne. She hugs him and says, Yes, yes.

Letters of thanks arrive almost daily after they go back.

⁂

A year or so later, Orla writes to say that my parents are getting frail. It's time to travel to Ireland again, the third time in four years.

What other countries can we include this time? I ask Verne, looking at the world map on the wall.

Isn't Ireland going to be enough? she asks.

She sees the little-boy face crumple and smiles, OK, let's go somewhere we haven't been before.

357

17

Unfinished business

MAMA AND DADA ARE now in their seventies. They listen to our stories, to our versions of what went on in our childhood, in the comfort of Goggins's Lounge, their local pub in Monkstown. Three brothers run it. Gorgons, we call it. One brother even looks a bit Medusa-like, with curls and all. But Mama says that they look like the three Kennedys. Well.

Irish pubs are far more than just drinking dens, even though many devote a great deal of time, effort and money to proving the contrary. Talk, laughter, gossip, arguments, music, singing, political discussion and rows are all facilitated by drink. *Craic,* we call it.

We go to Goggins for our unfinished business. It usually starts at home, then slows down until someone will say, Let's go down to Gorgons.

Jem, as we all call my father these days, will start off by telling us exiles – Patrick and myself – about the price of tomatoes. It is the benchmark for him of whether the world is stable or not. Once his Jameson Crested Ten whiskey is before him and our pints are in hand, one of us will start. I tell them about Elizabeth Kübler-Ross and the issue of unfinished business. Particularly between children and their parents. In my case and in Thomas's, it is necessary to talk about it. But we all join in.

It becomes a healing family tale. We offer our memories, and the laughter is great. In one of these general confabs, Mama confesses that they moved from our first house because they thought Protestant kids would corrupt four-year-old me and soon-to-arrive Dermot.

But you know now, Mama, that all kids play with their willies – Muslims, Jews, and Buddhists – the lot – one of us says.

Ah now, the Jews haven't that much to play with, says Dada with a straight face.

Yes, Mama says, ignoring him. I know now that all children do it, but we didn't know it then.

We wink at one another but don't interrupt. The Church taught us that Catholic Irish people were different, superior, she says. Even English Catholics were suspect. As for the French and Italians, one priest wondered out loud whether they would ever make it to heaven!

Don't start me off! exclaims Patrick, my ex-Christian Brothers brother.

On these occasions, when Mama goes to the 'Ladies', Dada tells us more stories.

Don't breathe a word of this now, will you?

No, Jem, of course not.

There was a young lady who used to write notes to me at the office.

Yes? we say in anticipation.

She was very lovely, and she had a voice like the singer Deanna Durbin.

He has a faraway look.

How did you know? Thomas shoots in smartly.

We sang together once on a staff picnic.

Mama and Dada — Determination and Fortitude

We gaze spellbound. Here is our father, almost in heaven, telling tales verging on infidelity.

One day Lily [his name for our mother] found one of her notes.

Were you married?

Oh no. But we were engaged.

What did Mama do?

She said I was to go and see her — we had no telephones in those days — and tell her never to write to me again. She said I could not love two people at once.

But could you, Dada? we ask, licking our lips and keeping our eyes open for the returning *materfamilias*.

He does not answer that. Maybe he has not heard. Out of respect, no one pushes it. But a confab follows, on relationships.

Did you tell the girl to send no more notes, Jem?

I did, he says. I was in love with your mother.

And you still are, says Patrick, putting his glass down emphatically. Look at his face, he says to us. And he sweeps his arm outwards, putting it around Dada's bent shoulders. We raise our glasses to him and his love.

There is the lesson, I realise. If you have the love of a good woman, do nothing that will damage it. Be aware of how lucky you are to have it. And so we deal with our unfinished business. Like the morning of the over-turned breakfast table. It stays in all our minds like the stain on a carpet that we will never throw out. The stain is ugly but softens with time. We get down on our mental knees to read its faded message.

It is early January, and the crocuses start poking their purple and yellow heads above the frozen ground. A cold wind comes in from Lapland and sends the last of the leaves skittering across the pavement as we wave them all goodbye.

Six weeks later, Jem dies. I have a quiet drink at home that night when Verne goes to bed. I play the Three Tenors in his memory. I write him a telegram. 'Where are you, Dada? We were so different. You so quiet. And yet so bitter. So intense, and yet so kind. You could always smile, even when you were unhappy. How did you manage, with so much inside and outside you to overcome? You've given me strength, you and your lover, Mama. Thank you, Jem. I have loved you.'

Two weeks later, Orla phones.

Howarya? Mama wants to speak to you, she says.

I'm so lonely without Gerry, she says in a whispery, sad, broken voice. The voice that used to call so strongly when the food was on the table, getting cold.

You are the eldest, Bernard, she says. I want to go and be with Dada. Will you mind if I go now?

She is asking my permission as the eldest. I know that she is suffering now.

Didn't you just hold on for Dada, Mama?

Yes, I did. I couldn't leave him on his own now, could I?

Antarctica — Verne in her spiritual home

This last with a bit of the old strength.

You have done your bit, Mama. By all of us, and many times over. You must go to him now, I say. Sure he'll be waiting for you.

Oh, I know he will, she says.

God bless, Mama.

God bless, Bernard. A pause. And Verne and Tasha and Justin. A pause. And Verne's three lovely children.

There is a silence and a crackling on the line.

She's exhausted, says Orla's voice. She'll go quickly now.

Barbeque on Russian icebreaker, 1997

A few weeks later, my brothers and I carry Mama's coffin into the packed Church in Monkstown where she married my father. I speak from the altar steps. I shall remember her for her unconditional love, I say. For all of us. And she always had some to spare for anyone else who needed it.

Two days later, we four brothers bought black-market tickets and watched Ireland beat England 13–10, to lift the Triple Crown.

They did this for us, says Patrick. Mama knew that we'd all be here for the funeral!

Travels in strange places

Down all these years, during them and ever since, we have travelled whenever we could afford the time and the money, to out-of-the-way places. Verne loves the simplicity and easy-goingness of the poorer countries. We like staying in pensions – as long as they are clean; we like trains and boats, even buses if we have to. Verne is brave. Courage is going up the less-travelled

Last gift from Mama and Dada: Ireland wins Rugby
Triple Crown, 1985

pathway when you are quaking inside. I love looking after her,
looking sideways at her amazement on seeing Machu Picchu for
the first time, or when a Tibetan nomad holding out the reins of
his yak says, She is yours, just seeing Verne's face when a steaming
plate of chickens' feet arrives on the table with chopsticks, her
delight in trying new food, her spirit being moved by the
magnificent Antarctic wilderness. All of these experiences and
more unite us, and we don't fight 'on the road'. If we do argue, it
is soon resolved.

So this story will not be complete unless it tells something of
these travels.

Black Sash fund-raising, late '80s

In China we disconnected the loudspeakers playing loud martial music in the railway carriages, played hide-and-seek with the female conductor who decided to lock the lavatories while the train stood still for ages in the snow-covered Gobi Desert.

In Tibet, Verne showed a Chinese army officer how to dig the back wheels of twenty-eight trucks – full of soldiers – out of deep sand, South African style, with branches and rocks. She offered her copy of the Dalai Lama's banned autobiography to a Security Police officer when he asked politely if he could read it.

If the Dalai Lama were here, she said, he would give it to you.

In Muslim Indonesia on a ferry, we visited our strictly segregated cabins when they emptied at lunchtime, to make hot, humid love.

Why are you always late for your food? demanded the head waiter.

Because we were dreaming, said Verne.

In Java she told me to go ahead of her when climbing Mount Merapi volcano to see the sunrise from the summit. Coming down, I found her spooning with the fortunate teenage guide in the shelter of a bush. There they slumbered, he with his shivering arms about her.

What is this? I inquired as politely as possible.

He'd have died with the cold if I hadn't let him, she said smiling. The guide's gratitude was touching.

In Thailand on a river trip, Verne's bamboo raft stayed submerged beneath the smooth-flowing waters of a river, but Verne straddled it for five kilometres, looking like a mermaid.

In the Morrocan Sahara, an English girl challenged her about living in apartheid South Africa. Verne tore into her and gave her some serious facts about her activities in the anti-apartheid Black Sash women's organisation. In any case, she went on, I'm a fourth generation mother of three. Where do you expect me to go?

In Istanbul, Verne wanted a Turkish bath. We entered a men-only bathhouse when it closed for the evening. A lithe, curly-haired Adonis pummelled me almost to death on a white marble slab in the steamy half-light of the vaulted bathhouse that was like a scene from a Fellini film. When he judged that I was *hors de combat,* he arranged Verne on her slab and provoked me by soaping her gently in a most suggestive manner.

I won't let him go any lower, she shouted above the splashing fountains of steaming water.

I'll kill him if him if he does, I shouted back, wondering how I'd even manage to stand up.

Best massage I've ever had, she purred afterwards.

In the far north of Quebec, she agreed to my quest to build an igloo. So, with two Inuit and my brother Patrick, we built one out in the wilds. In the middle of the Arctic night, Verne and I crawled outside to pee in -30° C.

It's easy for you men, I had to take my pants down, she said next morning.

Never mind, Patrick reassured her, this brother of mine likes life-threatening experiences.

Well, she said, as long as he knows that from now on he is married to one!

At peace — Verne and Bearnárd, Dún Laoghaire harbour

The only country we disagreed on was Fidel's Cuba. I can't buy anything to read, she said. The censorship is disgusting. And even our friends are afraid to speak out.

But I continued to look at the country through my still-rosy spectacles.

The only activity we have not agreed on is the bullfight.

I know it is an art, a ritual, she says. But I just do not enjoy what happens to the bull. But she took a picture of my running feet in Pamplona. You'll never grow up, she says.

Travel satisfies my longing to be moving, to be distracted from looking too closely at myself. And I have found the companion I need in Verne.

He travels safest in the dark night who travels lightest, said Cortéz, the conqueror of Mexico. My wife survived four months in South America with a small army rucksack. These days she carries a

Tasha, Verne and Bearnárd, Dún Laoghaire

small additional case, her magic bag. It is almost as precious as our passport pouch. For it contains the medicines, lotions, vitamins and creams that enable her to keep that spring in her step.

We have hung photos of our travels on the walls of our house – peaceful times, affirmations of what we can be. We keep mementos of places where we have felt inspired, hoping perhaps that someday the positive energy of these times will become the norm rather than the exception. So that we can also hang pictures of ourselves together – us happy, in ordinary circumstances – on the same walls.

18

Losing our hearts to Ronda

Apart from the fiesta, why do you want to go to Ronda? Verne asks me.

Because it's got a famous old bullring, and it's right off the beaten track.

We are on our way from Morocco to Granada to see the Alhambra. But this is not to be.

Forty-nine kilometres from Marbella and the glitz of the Costa del Sol, in the mountains, Ronda perches on a clifftop. Moorish battlements rise above us as we approach, and the horseshoe-shaped gateway heightens the impression of driving into a north-African medina.

I love this vibe, says Verne, as we mingle with the locals and peer into the cafés and bars full of shouting Andalusians – regarded by the rest of Spain as being *loco*, crazy. The smells of garlic, frying olive oil, cigars and wine, waft along the streets.

There is a buzz as the annual *feria*, or fiesta, is about to begin. Serendipity.

The noise of flamenco blaring from loudspeakers, and shouting children and laughing voices, gets us out of bed the next day. Street parties are in full swing. Two laughing women in the crowd grab Verne and they dance the *sevillana,* all twirls and hand-clapping. We stagger out of the throng and on to the next group, for there is no escape at a *feria.*

At times we are overwhelmed – the noise, the music and the difficulty in understanding the local dialect. But they love us for trying, ply us with drinks, and will under no circumstances allow us to buy a round. The barmen simply ignore us.

It's noisy but we stay. A bar in Spain can crackle into overdrive with a suddenness that takes your breath away. This gypsy will sing, that one will dance, hands clap like castanets, and someone is yelling in your ear at the same time.

Why don't we buy a place here? asks Verne.

But it is more a statement than a question. Within days, a local agent finds us an apartment built on ruined battlements and looking out over a valley at distant mountains. Verne has fallen in love. I am right behind her.

In a darkened bar we see the bullfighter Antonio Ordóñez. My hero of past years. Born in Ronda, he is one of the greatest matadors of all time. I dither like a schoolboy going for his first autograph. I stand up. I sit down. This is the great man, the national hero. *If* it is he.

I step inside and stare at him. He turns, cigar in hand, and smiles.

Are you *el Maestro*, Antonio Ordóñez?

I am, he says grinning, and who are you?

And that's it. I tell him that I'd seen him fighting in Alicante in '59, in Pamplona, that I've read Hemingway's book about him. He laughs with surprise, puts out his hand, and welcomes us in rapid-fire Spanish, intrigued that a foreigner knows about him. He introduces us to his wife and friend, Juan Bosco.

¿Te gusta los toros? You like the bulls? he asks.

I like them.

Would you like to be with us at the barrier during the next fight? he asks.

It would be an honour, I say, in complete disbelief.

I walk away in a daze that is Ordóñez-induced as much as by the wine.

Some months later, *el Maestro* dies. His ashes are strewn on the sand of the arena.

In the years that follow, we return to Ronda several times and go to Spanish classes. We love the flowers in the springtime fields, the haunting Easter ceremonies of the Semana Santa, the horsemen clattering up our narrow street, the evening *paseo* in Calle la Bola, mingling with the crowds, eating *tapas* with our wine.

It's four o'clock, B. I'm tired and we have school in the morning, says Verne one night.

We won't ever hear flamenco like this again, I say through the smoke and noise.

I'm walking home, then.

I let her, and stay till dawn.

When Verne doesn't agree with my enthusiasm for all things Hispanic, I feel resentment. But peace between us prevails. At least it does, until that morning.

Heartbreak

I am typing a story for a newspaper in South Africa. I can't get it right. A flutter of fear whispers that I've lost my touch. Ronda is in the mountains, and my feet are cold on the tiles. I am frustrated at my loss of language. I look at the screen of the laptop. The story will not come. The words are hidden.

Verne is sweeping the flat. She appears at the door, waving a white rug. I want to throw this out, she says in an irritable voice. It's shedding bits all over the floor. We can buy a new one.

Why can't we fix it? Use it in here? My voice rises. Why do you always want to buy new things?

I told you – this rug is falling apart, she shouts. Her face is angry now.

I get up, grab the rug from her, and shake it. Bits fly out. I snap, and my eyes go blind. I yell, my voice rising to an ugly crescendo. For thirty years you have wasted food, thrown things out that could be mended – you just want to spend, spend, spend.

She sneers, Oh shut up.

I pick up a chair and smash it on the floor. I see the white glue on the bits that I repaired yesterday. Don't you tell me to shut up, I roar.

Calm down, she says, shying away now. I'm sorry.

Don't tell me to shut up, don't you tell me to shut up when you are in the wrong.

Smash. I hit another chair off the floor. I hear the words, the horrible words, the roaring in my head.

Her face is terrified now. The anger that we thought was locked up forever is back. I don't care. I hate her wastefulness, her thoughtlessness, her stupidity. She'll never change. She is begging me now to stop.

A broom is lying on the floor. I pick it up and threaten her. How dare you tell me to shut up, I shout. I am choking with rage, almost crying now. I swing the broom and catch her upraised arm. She clutches herself, sobbing with fear and hurt, and runs out on to the terrace.

Then the rage subsides like a burst balloon. I stare at the chaos in the room, bits of chair so carefully mended yesterday, the broom in my hand.

I start to pick up the pieces. I try to put a chair together again. It

Juan Bosco, a journo, el Maestro, Bearnárd, Plaza de Toros of Ronda

doesn't work. I put the pieces aside and start to sweep the floor.
I am useless.
Verne is on the terrace, staring out over the fields and the mountains.
Will she leave? Fear returns to its natural home in the pit of my being.

For two weeks we live with a cloud over us, like the dark smoke of a bush fire.
One night I go to watch Manchester United on a friend's TV.
Walking back home alone at midnight, the pain starts. My chest tightens in a steep, narrow street. I lean on a wall. I've never experienced this. My breathing is difficult. I walk five metres and

stop. I sit on a doorstep. I walk another few metres, sit down, and take another few steps. Around the corner at the top of the hill is the only Irish bar in Ronda. I'll go in there and have a glass of water and a rest, I think. It takes me ten minutes to walk-gasp-stop-walk twenty metres.

I go in the door. Brian the owner is serving a bunch of Spaniards. I don't want to make a fuss, so I walk slowly past them to the end of the bar where I'm alone. The pain tightens. I raise my hand to catch his eye. At that moment, he puts a pint glass under the Guinness tap and starts the pull. I watch him as he puts the first glass up on the tray to settle. Then he starts to pull a second pint. The pain squeezes like wire around my chest. I don't think my voice will carry over the shouting of the locals. Please look down here at me, Brian, for jaysus sake. He judges the pints to be ready for the final pull. I won't interrupt this. It's a ritual not to be disturbed. Irish people know this.

Then he serves the pints and turns and walks towards me.

Howareye, he says.

I think I'm having a heart attack, I say.

In a second, he has me out on the street, sitting on a chair on the cobblestones. Somebody bawls from the bar.

Help yourself, shouts Brian. You stay there now and drink this, he says. He holds a glass of water to my lips.

I don't remember much after that. A light is flashing. Guys in uniforms and caps are around me. One smiles and says *No te preocupes*, don't worry. I feel no pain. I pass out.

Then there are bright lights in my face and three or four white coats around me. One is smiling. At that moment I know that I am

374

not going to die. He wouldn't have smiley eyes if he thinks he's
going to lose me.

¿Cómo estas? the white coat asks.

Good, I say, very good. Where are we?

The hospital of Ronda, he says.

Juan Bosco – the same Juan we'd met with *el Maestro,* now a good
friend, works here. I ask them to phone him as we've no phone.
He'll tell Verne.

The doctor says he is giving me an injection because the road to
Málaga might 'molest' me. I love it when they say things like that.
I say thank you and the lights go out.

Fernando, the head nurse of the Intensive Care Unit at the
University Hospital in Málaga, leans over the trolley as he rolls me
out of the operating theatre. How is it? he asks.

I have had a *cataclismo,* I croak.

No, Bernardo! You have had a *cateterismo!*

An attack, though mild, is a near cataclysm, of course, but I am
confusing the two words. The heart surgeons had shoved a catheter
up my femoral artery and placed two stents, little springs, in the
almost-blocked arteries to keep them open. Angioplasty.

A hundred years later, the surgeon had smiled and told me to stop
smoking cigars and eating tripe and *chorizos.*

Verne arrives on the second day with Juan Bosco. I am glad to see
her. She looks beautiful and tired. She smiles. But her smile is
forced. On her second visit, this time alone, Verne asks me if I
know what brought on the attack. I tell her that my cholesterol is
too high at 7.4, and the cigars have to stop. I explain that two
arteries were almost completely blocked.

Anything else? she asks, fixing her eyes on mine. Then she says,
You have major stress. Self-inflicted.

What do you mean? I ask.

Verne does not allow me escape. I mean your anger, she says. All these years. Your mad temper.

I am trapped in her stare, my mind not focusing at all.

The doctor told me that anger will – no, *has* – damaged your arteries over the years, she says. But you already knew that. And you choose to ignore it?

I have lain in the ICU for two days, light-headed at my near-miss. The fact of the row has hardly crossed my mind.

Now it lies between my wife and me like a meal that has gone cold. Think about it, Verne says, then rises and leaves the ward. She turns at the door and waves. A small, sad wave. No kiss. And she always kisses goodbye.

After supper, the lights dim and I can no longer read. My wife's words are knocking on the gates. Now they break in and overrun my defences. For decades I have led my family and myself on a mad dance of fear, joy, adventure, violence – and failure. Failure to hold my evil temper, failure to control my guilt. Failure to stand still for long enough to see, not just look.

My lawyer friend Louis asked me the question one day in Joburg when I was complaining about my life.

Is *Verne* happy?

Yes, I said.

Well, he said, for the same price you can be happy too. Jewish wisdom.

Instead, I have almost killed myself. And maybe the most precious thing I possess has finally, finally died. Verne's love for me.

———

In the half-light of the ICU, I write this phrase on every second page of my diary: 'For the same price I can be happy.' Am I too late to use this insight?

Lying in the dim light of the ICU, grey machines beeping like tree frogs, I hear whispers of soft Spanish prayers.

In the never-dark of this place, shadows mirror my mind.

Thoughts pass imperceptibly from the now to another and former time. I must stop, stop running.

⚺

In the morning, after the bedpan is removed and I've eaten breakfast, I notice that Verne has left her diary and sunglasses on the bedside table. I lean over and pick up the little blue book. Will she have written about the row, the fight? Will she have written about what she feels for me now?

I see the word 'FEAR' written four times on three pages of my wife's diary. Four letters gone over and over again, the pen almost penetrating the paper.

Four capital letters. They are hypnotic. Verne has used three of the tiny pages to write down what happened. I read them, over and over.

They do not describe the event itself, but her reaction to it, her dread.

On the fifth day, Verne comes to take me back to Ronda. She drives Juan Bosco's car out of the city through dusty roadworks and diversions. She looks ahead of her, concentrating on the driving. Soon we are out on the mountain roads. Grey cumulus cover the sun.

A flock of sheep is blocking the road. We are silent. The *pastor* is calling to his animals and waving an apology to us. The sheep pass by, bleating, and we drive on.

What are you going to do? she asks after what seems an unending silence.

I have had time to think, I say. And I have had a fright. A bad one. I do not want to die. Or to kill myself.

Verne does not reply to this. And she says little more on the way back to Ronda.

Friends come to visit us. On the outside, we are our usual selves. But there is a quietness in Verne that is not normal.

What can I say or do that has not all been said before?

Juan Bosco comes to see us. He had a serious heart attack five years before. Verne asks him about it.

He tells her, then says, Your conduct changes after it. There is a realisation that life will never be the same again. It is a mental and a physical thing.

Give us an example, I say.

I used to drink too much – everything too much, he laughs.

Like a normal Spaniard, I laugh.

¡No me vaciles! he says, demanding I take him seriously.

And, he says, raising a finger, my *infarto* changed my head as well as my heart. I have never once felt like returning to the old ways.

Verne looks at me. She smiles as of old for the first time since the incident with the smashed chairs.

There is hope for you then, she says, if Bosco can change.

Hope for *us*, I say.

Bosco grins and looks at us quizzically, but says nothing.

Have you changed, Bernardo? Verne asks, looking at me hard – but I see the hope in her lovely eyes.

Forever, I say, and reach for her hand.

Bypassing an iceberg

What happened? asks Gill Scott. You look like you've seen a ghost.

I have, I say. My own.

She is our first appointment on returning from Spain. We tell her the story of Ronda, everything.

It is like the Titanic, she says. They were warned and didn't listen. It was arrogance and stupidity that sank the Titanic – not the iceberg. They were told and they didn't listen.

She smiles at me. I'm not attacking you, she says. It's simply an observation.

And it's true, I say. Yes, I knew. I had been warned.

She listens to Verne's account, and the aftermath, the calmness since.

Sounds like a sea change, she says. She pauses. However, I do not want either of you to think that it was just the heart attack that brought about this change. You were well on your way to it before you went to Spain. So don't forget how you got there.

She joins her hands as if in silent applause and looks at us both. I glance at Verne. The two women are smiling.

Still, beside you

It takes over two long years for trust to take root again. Trust that the spots are fixed in their new pattern.

Then there is one more outbreak of temper, breaking of chairs, with one ricocheting off Verne. But at least I do not hit her – nor do I want to. I go back to Chris and he hypnotises me again, and we identify the trigger that did it.

Since then, whenever an argument – a big one, and we both know the signs – looms between Verne and me, we both walk away, often with a smile. A smile, almost, of collusion. As a result, Verne feels freer to defend herself in those moments of minor irritation that all couples experience. These days, whenever I criticise her unfairly, she replies in a level tone, but firmly, and sometimes she even uses choice phrases that would have raised the temperature in the past.

Why did you say those things? I ask her afterwards, with a half-smile.

Because I felt like saying them and I know now that it's safe. Sorry I said them, she says. And she smiles back at me.

No problem, I say, and I mean it.

How far we've come.

But I go back to Gill every six months. Just as a seismologist checks a dormant volcano or a doctor measures blood pressure, Gill and I check my reliability meter. Verne must be reassured along the route that we travel together that the volcanos are dormant, perhaps even dead. And so must I.

From the moment I first left Ireland I have been running. Moving on. And now I am not running any more. I am standing still. I am standing still on a mountain path in the Drakensberg mountains. The hotel is behind and below us in a hollow near the river. Even from here we can hear the water tumbling on the rocks. It has rained on the escarpment. We are on the path that goes up the valley. 'Tryme' buttress is above us on our left. Ahead is the towering mass of Cathedral Peak, and beyond that the kingdom of Lesotho.

Verne is resting. She is sitting on a rock beneath an old, fire-blackened Protea tree.

I look at her as I have so often done, and think to myself:

You, the woman in my life.

I look along the path winding upward and I sense your eyes are on me. You are silently asking, Am I holding you back? Do you want to go on, to leave me, like so often in the past?

And when in the past I have indeed wanted to go on, and you were tired, I was impatient – sometimes very impatient and angry, too, at something said. And some of those times words would lead to words. Horrible and hurtful. And if you defended yourself I might take your hair in my hand, not to stroke it as you deserved, but to force you to listen. And sometimes I took your shoulder, not in the passion of love as you deserved, but in the passion of anger. And sometimes, instead of making love – as we do so well – we put up the walls of anger and silence.

I should have stood still at your side like a companion, not forged ahead like a stranger.

Now you are sitting still, my love, and you are listening to the silence, the loud silence of the mountain, the silence of the eagle overhead, and to the stillness of the long autumn grasses.

I will not break our silence, our peace, again – for I have stopped running.

Epilogue

I have told you my story. Well, most of it. There are five other stories, lives that I have irrevocably shaped and influenced – those of our five children.

Five Odysseys

One day, when Tasha is fourteen, Nicky calls and asks if we will allow Tasha come to live with us. Tasha is a budding teenager, difficult, with her father's genes, and she wants to live with Angie, who is only eighteen months younger than she is. Nicky is concentrating on starting a new family with Charles, so it suits all of us. I am over the moon. Verne makes her so welcome that Angie thinks her Mom loves Tasha more.

Meanwhile, Graeme and Justin say that they want to go together to boarding school in Grahamstown. They do well, both on the playing fields and in the classrooms, and are good friends.

Roger, Angie and Tasha go to one of the first non-racial schools in the country. All five pass their matric exams – Roger with a distinction in maths, despite his dyslexia.

Because there is only a five-year gap between Tasha the eldest and Graeme the youngest, they all listen mostly to the same music, have the same romantic experiences, and get into the same kind of trouble – all in a synchronised way.

Then we start to export them, one by one. We take Tasha with us to Ireland, and she decides to stay with my parents. She lives with them until 1985, when they die. Angie falls in love with New York, where she obtains her Diploma in Art. Then she joins Tasha in Dublin and studies some more. Angie has her fair share of talent. The two girls hitch-hike around Europe and meet up with us in Spain. Cries of *¡Guapa!* from admiring Spanish youths follow them everywhere.

At some point during those years, we drop off Roger – all alone – on a German railway platform. His mother has tears in her eyes as she waves at her firstborn's head sticking out of a window of the disappearing train. He travels in the Middle East and works on a *moshav* in Israel. Then back to Germany and England, where he keeps himself going by working illegally.

We wave goodbye to Justin at Johannesburg airport, with a ticket to Texas in his hand. He travels to Mexico, wades into the Pacific at Acapulco beach, and steps out to find his clothes, passport and money gone. He is eighteen, and handles the next seventy-two hours admirably. Verne links him up with the Irish embassy for a new passport. He works his way across the US and up to Patrick and Eva in Canada, and then meets us in London. During this time, we drop Graeme off in Portugal. He obtains an international diploma in 'charming chicks' (as he puts it) around Europe. He's cool.

<hr/>

Back in Johannesburg one day, I hold up an airmail envelope.

Look at this letter, I say to Verne. It's a complaint from the European Commission in Brussels.

What about? she asks.

'Dear Sir and Madam,

We beg you most sincerely to cease abandoning children within the European Union. We have counted five so far.

Yours faithfully, etc.'

Are you serious? she laughs.

Each one of the five returned eventually, Tasha a few months pregnant. Ah, well. The next generation is upon us.

The marks of violence

This story will not be complete if it does not give voice to each of the children. This is what they have said to me:

Tasha 2000

It was the divorce that I hated. You were gone, and I resented you for that. But I was closer to you, too.

I remember in Ireland that Thomas hated Jem. I hated him too when I was living there. He was rude to your mother, always complaining, gruff and bitter. It was obvious, though, that he felt bad about himself.

He reminds me of you. You appear to have high-self esteem, Daddy, but you are vulnerable. You are afraid of not being good enough. You always got red-faced and angry when you thought that Verne wasn't listening or was arguing over some little thing, belittling you.

But I've discovered that I can be myself, not like you.

You say you've stopped – I hope you have. At least these days your outbursts are quieter. You told me that when Cúchulainn, the hero of Irish mythology, was in a rage, his one eye bulged out and one went back into his skull. He saw a red mist when he was in a fury. And the same energy or rage that he used against his enemies he could blindly turn against his own home and people. Was that you?

Justin 2001

I felt confused as an eight- and nine-year-old. For instance, Mum would say when anyone asked her about the scar on her forehead, My first husband pushed me down the stairs. And I didn't put this together with my knowledge of you. During holidays and whenever I met you. Because I was too young to remember Nigeria.

When you lived on Jan Smuts Avenue you were out of control, in a rage, with a bristling beard, and a red face like Thor in the thunderclouds. You so badly wanted to be absolved for some accusation. Once, Verne locked herself into the bathroom and was afraid to let me in. I thought of you as pathetic. I thought you were both pathetic. You were always insisting on answers. That was a big thing with you. And Verne giving the same answer, over and over. I wanted her to give a logical, reasonable answer and allow the argument to move on or go away.

As a result of all this I don't trust people. I always look for a hidden agenda. I feel that things can go wrong at any moment. When you and Verne are good together, you are wonderful. She loves the way your mind works, your ability to make her laugh. You tell her more than most men how much you appreciate her, how sexy she is, and how you appreciate what she does for you and the whole family.

She is good for you, Dad.

I have learnt to be invisible. I try to avoid displeasing anybody. And my life smells of mothballs. I've found it hard until now to stand still in one place.

Roger 2001

When there's a row, a violent one, your mind starts racing, the way a kid thinks, a million things at once. The shouting part of it is quite unnerving. Your voice, Bearnárd, gets high-pitched, scary. Being the eldest, I had a responsibility; but I was powerless, you being bigger. I could have done without all that. Even in a happy family it adds insecurity to your life, it leads to a lack of confidence. So I wouldn't try things. It spawns a whole load of unnecessary complications. I felt vulnerable.

And now? I'm a bit anti-social. And I'm dyslexic as well. But that's me, anyway. The violence had a big influence on my life. I should have a lot more confidence. Still, I'm amazed at the potential I believe I have inside me. I've a nervous problem as well, so all that stuff wasn't the ideal situation for me.

I remember on the Inca Trail in Peru, I was a bit scared. We were in the middle of nowhere. We should have been a team, united. I was trying to get you and Mom to make up because this was an epic, an epic journey. Being the eldest, I always went back to the source to see what set you off. At the age of thirteen, I knew that the person who did something wrong must apologise to the other. It's the right angle to come from, the only angle.

I wondered how it was that somebody could get as angry as you did. Ready to take off, irrational, no control whatever, unpredictable, and it didn't seem to have any end to it. It felt like it could go on forever. When you are rational, you are very rational. But when you got angry you put blinkers on. You may have been right to be angry, but when you were irrational you could not look at the bigger picture. Mom sometimes stoked the fires, which made me slightly angry – but that's her personality. With hindsight, there were times I should have punched you. But I didn't want to make an enemy of you. I still carry around a lot of anger. I think about things, but I don't do them.

Still, there were massive positives. We grew up a bit faster. We saw, felt a lot more, we asked more questions, analysed more, and experienced more. We extended our possibilities – and that means you don't become a dull person.

We spoke to Mom countless times about you splitting up. We wanted peace, wanted out of there. Then it seemed to get better. But if you've got a certain reputation, it's hard to disengage from that impression.

Angie 2001

Even after I'd left home, Mum used to call me, crying, to tell me about the latest row and maybe the violence. She asked me to go over to your house, and I always did. She would tell me all about it and I would comfort her.

But whenever Mom went back and it was all calm again, she never discussed it, would not talk about it, as if nothing had happened. But something *had* happened, something that I thought was terrible for me and for her. But she wouldn't talk; it was as if it had never happened.

I stopped leaning on Mom because she couldn't be there for me. She was a beaten woman. I couldn't lean on her because she was leaning on me.

Ma always used to say, Angie's fine. But I wasn't fine. My role was to be strong for my Mom. I felt that she needed me when there was a crisis. We would all say – Roger, Graeme and me – Leave him. Mom would say, But he pays, he keeps the roof over our heads. Then she would say, Right I'm leaving him. But then she'd go back to you and gave no explanation. That was the worst.

I'd ask, What's happening? There was no answer. It was as if to say, don't interfere, you have no right to ask. It was guilt. Guilt at not going through with her decision.

She hurt me the most. You couldn't hurt me, Bearnárd, because we didn't have a relationship.

My father was the first to let me down. As a kid, I adored him. But he let me down too.

Jason, my boyfriend, believed in me and changed my outlook. But at least you taught me to have a sense of humour, to look at the funny side of life, to look at a normal scene and find something funny in it. And South America was a fantastic experience. That was you showing us the world.

But there's no excuse for violence. That is the bottom line.

Often, I would think that you were in the right with Mom. But as soon as there was violence, *never*. Do you know what it is, B? It's putting the fear of God into somebody else in order to control him or her.

You know, the other day I was looking at some spoilt brats in the complex who were whining about something. And I thought about South America and our six days on the Inca Trail. I looked at these kids and thought, You need an Inca Trail.

Graeme 2002

I have the idea that drink, alcohol, had a lot to do with it. But I know it isn't only that. Going back, I can't remember what I actually saw or heard, or what Mom told me. In Rio we were outside the hotel room door, and we thought you were strangling her. I have a vivid memory of that. I remember lots of anger and lots of fear. I especially remember anger. It was mostly your anger. I remember Mom being very vocal and under the influence as well. Mom wasn't physical against you, but vocally aggressive. When you were both drinking, terrible things were said. The impact of that stays around a long time.

I recall Mom's fear. I thought it kept her in the relationship, not wanting to move on, her second marriage failing, and the effect of that on the three of us. It didn't give me a good understanding of relationships. I don't know what to look for exactly. I've always felt out of things.

The thing that impacted on all of us was that we avoid confrontation now. Confrontation sent us into a panic. So we hesitate.

There were good things too, though. The dinners at the Perfumed Garden, hiking in the mountains, camping in the forests, we were extraordinarily successful as a family unit. We were very different from other families we knew, and it's good to be different.

But always in the back of our minds, B, was the question, When's the next outburst going to be? It's funny. It's made me softer rather than harder. And I over-trust people, if anything. The whole scene with you and Mom made us more savvy, emotionally more mature, I think. At the age of thirty-six I understand that life is not all plain sailing.

People should talk about family violence. Keeping quiet is as bad as the violence itself. It's an equal evil.

And we should forgive each other. I have forgiven Mom. Mom could have married Mr Boring Right. But that's no life. I've always compared you guys with other couples, and I'm convinced that you have a better marriage, doing things together, prepared to work together, like you have. You have five kids, seven grandkids, friends; you travel, and you love each other. To my mind, it was all worthwhile. Today Mom is a different individual. You are both something else.

Glossary

aisling – vision, dream

banjaxed – exhausted

biltong – dried strips of meat

Black Sash – South African women's human rights organisation

bollix – from English bollocks, a load of b.– nonsense. You old b. (affectionate). You feckin' b. (aggressive). I'm bollixed – jaded

boreen – small country road

chair-o-planes – merry-go-round of seats hanging from chains

coddin' the young wans – joking with the young girls

coort – court

Coast, the – collective term for English colonies in West Africa

Connemara – mostly Irish-speaking area west of Galway City

codhladh sámh – sleep well

coloureds – South Africans of mixed blood

craic – fun, talk,

dash (West African slang) – bribe

Dáil – Lower House of Irish Parliament

drink taken – have been drinking heavily

eejit – idiot

feck, feckin' –a less offensive form of fuck, fucking

frenchie – french letter, condom

gombeen man – middle-man, one who charges interest

great gas – good fun

¡ Guapa! (Spanish) – goodlooking!

holliers – holidays

hoors – whores (fig.). Can be derogatory or affectionate, depending on the tone and context

het up – upset

hard chaw – a tough character

infarto (Spanish) – heart attack

Klippies (Afrikaans abbrev. for Klipdrift) – a South African Brandy

Kikuyu – a tough African variety of grass

laager (Afrikaans) – enclosure, corral

leaving certificate – matriculation

mano a mano (Spanish) – "hand-to-hand" contest between two bullfighters

mickey – penis

moue (French) – pout

Nuits St George – a red burgundy

naff (English) – inferior

¡ No me vaciles! (Spanish) – don't mess with me!

oul wan – old one, mother, woman

oidhche mhaith – goodnight

Orangeman – member of the Protestant Loyalist Orange Order

praties – potatoes

pinkeens – tiny fish

Peelers – policemen, after Sir Robert Peel, founder of the Metropolitan police force

plaza de toros – bullring

pondok (Afrikaans) – a cabin, small house

streeling – meandering along

stronso (Italian) – arsehole

Sasanach (Irish Gaelic) – an Englishman

Taigs – unflattering term for Catholics used by some Protestants in the North

Taoiseach – Prime Minister, literally a leader

yous – you (pl.) in Dublinese

your man – Irishism for the man in question or stranger that stands out in some manner

AbusersAnon

AbusersAnon was set up to fill a gap. As far as we
know, no organisation or service exists for male abusers in the
northern suburbs of Johannesburg, although several are
active in Soweto and Alexandra.

AbusersAnon aims to provide men with a support
group, consisting of men who have stopped and men who are
trying to stop physical, emotional, verbal and/or sexual abuse of
their partners. A psychologist may be recommended to assist
where appropriate.

For more information please visit www.abusersanon.com

Bearnárd O'Riain